Gerhard Jaritz, Ingrid Matschinegg (Eds.)

My Favourite Things

My Favourite Things

Object Preferences
in Medieval and Early Modern
Material Culture

edited by

Gerhard Jaritz and Ingrid Matschinegg

LIT

Cover Illustration:
Annunciation (detail), Master of Maria am Gestade,
panel of a winged altarpiece, 1460s.
Vienna, church of Maria am Gestade
Photo: Peter Böttcher, Institut für Realienkunde, University of Salzburg

The publication has been supported by

UNIVERSITÄT SALZBURG

Rektorat der Paris-Lodron-Universität Salzburg

LAND SALZBURG

Land Salzburg. Referat 2/04 Wissenschaft, Erwachsenenbildung, Bildungsförderung

Fachbereich Geschichte der Paris-Lodron-Universität Salzburg

Stiftungs- und Förderungsgesellschaft der Paris-Lodron-Universität Salzburg

Bibliographic information published by the Deutsche Nationalbibliothek
The Deutsche Nationalbibliothek lists this publication in the Deutsche Nationalbibliografie; detailed bibliographic data are available on the Internet at http://dnb.d-nb.de.

ISBN 978-3-643-90926-8 (pb)
ISBN 978-3-643-95926-3 (PDF)

A catalogue record for this book is available from the British Library.

Klosbachstr. 107
CH-8032 Zürich
Tel. +41 (0) 44-251 75 05
E-Mail: zuerich@lit-verlag.ch http://www.lit-verlag.ch

Distribution:
In the UK: Global Book Marketing, e-mail: mo@centralbooks.com
In North America: Independent Publishers Group, e-mail: orders@ipgbook.com
In Germany: LIT Verlag Fresnostr. 2, D-48159 Münster
Tel. +49 (0) 2 51-620 32 22, Fax +49 (0) 2 51-922 60 99, e-mail: vertrieb@lit-verlag.de
e-books are available at www.litwebshop.de

Table of Contents

List of Illustrations and Tables

Gerhard Jaritz – Ingrid Matschinegg

Things – Good, Better, Best

… dar nâch die fürsten giengen
in daz rîche palas,
dâ noch mê rîcheit inne was.
ein guldîn bette sie vanden,
daz oben unde unden
mit rîcheit was gezieret,
ze rehter mâze gevieret.
dar ûf lac ein bettegewant:
bezzerz nie kein man bevant.
ûf dem bette lac ein man
grôz, schœne und gar wol getân,
sîn hâr, sîn bart wîz als ein swan
gar tiure kleider het er an,
einen tiuren huot het er ouch.
sîn kost daz was wîrouch, …
(Ulrich von Etzenbach, *Alexander* c. 1270[1])

Middle High German literature is rich in the description of the speciality and extraordinary quality of material objects. The "best" and the "very best" can be found there, in particular, concerning dress and textiles in noble space, arms and armour, horses, but also with regard to food and drink or buildings. Sometimes it is the inimitable very best that no one in this world had ever seen before:[2]

- *daz aller beste gewant daz man iendert in der werlte vant* (Der Stricker, *Daniel von dem blühenden Tal*,1220/50),[3]

---

1 "Afterwards, the princes went into the rich palace, in which there was still more wealth. They found a golden bed, which was decorated with riches above and below, well constructed in correct measure. Bedclothes lay on it, of which nobody has ever found any better. A tall, handsome and well-built man lay on the bed, his hair and beard white as a swan. He wore really expensive clothes and also had an expensive hat. Incense was his food …;" Wendelin Toischer, ed., *Alexander von Ulrich von Echenbach*, Bibliothek des literarischen Vereins in Stuttgart 183 (Tübingen: Literarischer Verein in Stuttgart, 1888, repr. Hildesheim and New York: Olms, 1974), 60–61, lines 2264–78.

2 Concerning the phenomenon of "singular products" in today's economic sociology, see Lucien Karpic, *Valuing the Unique: The Economics of Singularities* (Princeton: Princeton University Press, 2010), in particular 10–20.

3 "the best dress ever to be found in the world;" Michael Resler, ed., *Der Stricker, Daniel von dem blühenden Tal*, Altdeutsche Textbibliothek 92, 3rd ed. (Berlin and Boston: De Gruyter, 2015), 246, lines 6519–20. Concerning dress, see also Gabriele Raudszus, *Die Zeichensprache der Kleidung: Unter-*

- *den besten harnasch den man vinden kann* (Der Pleier, *Meleranz*, 1240/70);[4]
- *ritterliche woffen cleit, die besten und die tursten, die nu under dem himel sint uff allem ertriche* (*Virginal*, 13th c.);[5]
- *si hânt diu allerbesten swert, diu über al die erden ie geslagen dorften werden* (Der Stricker, *Karl der Große*, 1220/50);[6]
- *das beste ros über allü lant* (*Eckenlied*, 13th c.);[7]
- *dô truoc man in ze trinken den allerbesten wîn, der in allen landen in fürsten hûse mac gesîn* (*Kudrun*, 1230/40);[8]
- *ein burc harte veste, diu schoenest und diu beste die si nie gesâhen* (Wirnt von Grafenberg, *Wigalois*, 1210/20);[9]
- and so on.

Such best objects could, however, also be used as material equivalent of a person's qualities (for instance, *kiusche was ir bestez kleit* – Hugo von Trimberg, *Der Renner*, c. 1300[10]) or in a moralising and didactic way showing their uselessness for one' life and symbolising vanity:

[...] von golde und von sîden
würken wir dier besten wât
die iemen in der werlte hât:
nû waz hilfet uns daz?

suchungen zur Symbolik des Gewandes in der deutschen Epik des Mittelalters, ORDO, Studien zur Literatur und Gesellschaft 1 (Hildesheim, Zurich, and New York: Olms, 1985), in particular 184–91.

4 "the best armour that one can find;" Markus Steffen, ed., *"Der Melerantz von Frankreich." Der Meleranz des Pleier: Nach der Karlsruher Handschrift. Edition – Untersuchungen – Stellenkommentar,* Texte des späten Mittelalters und der frühen Neuzeit (Berlin: Erich Schmidt, 2011) 63, line 2431.

5 "knightly armours, the best and most expensive that are now under the sky on all earth;" Elisabeth Lienert, Elisa Pontini, and Katrin Schumacher, eds., *Virginal. Goldemar*, Texte und Studien zur mittelhochdeutschen Heldenepik 10/1 (Berlin and Boston: De Gruyter, 2017), 416-17, stanza 949, lines 5–8.

6 "They had the very best swords which on all earth one ever could strike with;" Karl Bartsch, ed., *Karl der Grosse von dem Stricker*, Deutsche Neudrucke, Texte des Mittelalters (Berlin: De Gruyter, 1965), 76, lines 2846–48.

7 "the best horse of all lands;" Francis B. Brévart, ed., *Das Eckenlied: Sämtliche Fassungen*, part 1, Altdeutsche Textbibliothek 111 (Tübingen: Max Niemeyer, 1999), 18, stanza 34, line 2.

8 "He was served the very best wine to be found in any lands in the houses of princes"; Karl Stackmann, ed., *Kudrun, following the edition by Karl Bartsch*, Altdeutsche Textbibliothek 115 (Tübingen: Niemeyer, 2000), 71, stanza 336, lines 3–4.

9 "a strong and firm castle, the most beautiful and best that they had ever seen;" Johannes Marie Neele Kapteyn, ed., *Wigalois, der Ritter mit dem Rade von Wirnt von Gravenberc*, vol. 1, Rheinische Beiträge und Hülfsbücher zur germanischen Philologie und Volkskunde 9 (Bonn: F. Klopp, 1926), 31, lines 662–64.

10 "chastity was her best dress;" Gustav Ehrismann, ed., *Der Renner von Hugo von Trimberg*, vol. 1, Bibliothek des Litterarischen Vereins Stuttgart 247 (Tübingen: Literarischer Verein in Stuttgart, 1908, repr. Berlin: De Gruyter, 1970), 122, line 2956.

wirne leben niht deste baz
(Hartmann von Aue, *Iwein*, c. 1200).[11]

The very best objects did not only play a role as one's possession but were certainly also important to represent oneself to others – either used or worn when meeting them or as gifts to the latter, both to be seen as a relevant means of self-representation. Again, the literary sources offer a number of such cases as, for instance:

– "*[…] legt üwer beste kleider an,*
daz wir den vil werden man
schon empfauhen, daß ist min pett!"
Do klaidetten sich die an der stett
in das allerbest gewannt
daz yeman waz bekannt (Der Pleier, *Meleranz*, 1240/70).[12]
– *Dô sprach diu schoene Kriemhilt: "ir mîniu magedîn,*
die an dem antpfánge mit mir wellen sîn,
die suochen ûz den kisten diu aller besten kleit,
sô wirt uns von den gesten lob unt êré geseit" (*Nibelungenlied*, c. 1200).[13]
– *Ich gib iu silber unde golt*
Und mangen edeln stein
Und och die allerbesten wât,
Sô ez im land kein fürste hât (*Sigenot*, c. 1300).[14]

Such objects were not only part of the literary discourse, although they turn up there most explicitly. Similar rating of things with regard to their quality can, for instance, also be found in last wills, inventories, account books, normative sources, and so on, directly or indirectly. The Regensburg sumptuary law of 1485, for instance, tries to regulate and restrict the usage of obvious 'best objects,' not explic-

---

[11] "From gold and silk we produce the most splendid clothes of which one can think of. But, what does this help? We do not live better because of that." Georg F. von Benecke, Karl Lachmann, and Ludwig Wolff, eds., *Hartmann von Aue, Iwein: Text und Übersetzung*, 4th ed. (Berlin and New York: De Gruyter, 2001), 115, lines 6387–90.

[12] "'[…] put on your best clothes to welcome well the very honourable man, this is my request.' At once they put on the very best clothes that were known to anyone." Markus Steffen, "*Melerantz von Frankreich*," 190–91, lines 7431–36.

[13] "Beautiful Kriemhild said, 'My maidservants, who will be with me at the reception, take the very best clothes out of the chests, then we will receive praise and honour from the guests'." Helmut de Boor, ed., *Das Nibelungenlied*, following the edition of Karl Bartsch, 20th ed. (Wiesbaden: Brockhaus, 1972), 99, stanza 568, lines 1–4.

[14] "I give you silver and gold and some gems and also the very best clothes that no prince owns in this land." August Clemens Schoener, ed., *Der jüngere Sigenot, nach sämtlichen Handschriften und Drucken*, Germanische Bibliothek 3, Kritische Ausgaben altdeutscher Texte 6 (Heidelberg: C. Winter, 1928), 50–51, stanza 51, line 12–stanza 52, line 2.

itly qualified as such. They should only be worn at specific festive occasions of the community's self-representation:

> *Ueberhaupt warden anmit alle Arten von Geschmuck, Gestike oder gehefte Kleider verboten, und nur bei denen einer Ausnahme statt gegeben, die zu Zeiten unser Stadt Umgang, Umreiten oder sonst von der Stadt Ehre und Nutzens wegen ausgesandt, Fürsten, Frauen oder Hochzeiten entgegen reiten würden, oder sonst außerhalb der Stadt sind; die mögen gestikte oder gehefte Kleider tragen, doch ohne Perlen.*[15]

As a negative emphasis, worthless or bad objects could become the best available as, for instance, *brot und kalter brunne miest sin beste spise sin* (*Wolfdietrich*, c. 1250).[16]

Good, better and best objects also play a regular role in late medieval last wills. Close relatives, servants, and religious institutions are mostly the direct or indirect recipients of these high quality objects. Some examples out of source evidence from the collections of last wills made at Vienna from around 1400 may be offered. In a last will from 1420 a women gave her best blue coat to the three children out of her first marriage, the best rosary to her sister, and the best silver belt to the church of Saint Michael;[17] in 1414, a women bequeathed her better bathrobe to a servant of her brother;[18] in 1418, the wife of a Viennese burgher bequeathed her best silver belt and a silver rosary for the building activities at the church of Saint Michael;[19] in 1403, the parish priest of a Lower Austrian community gave his

---

[15] "Generally all kinds of jewellery, embroidered or stitched clothes are prohibited and only an exception allowed for those, who at the time of circulating or riding around the town or at other occasions are sent out on behalf of the honour and benefit of the city, ride towards princes, women, or weddings, or are otherwise out of the city; they are permitted to wear embroidered or stitched clothes, but without pearls." Carl Theodor Gemeiner, *Stadt Regensburgische Jahrbücher vom Jahre 1430 bis zum Jahre 1496, aus der Urquelle, den Königlichen Archiven und Registraturen zu Regensburg* (Regensburg: Montag und Weißische Buchhandlung, 1821; reprint Munich: Beck, 1971), 680, note 1390; Gerhard Jaritz, "Kleidung und Prestige-Konkurrenz. Unterschiedliche Identitäten in der städtischen Gesellschaft unter Normierungszwängen," in *Zwischen Sein und Schein. Kleidung und Identität in der städtischen Gesellschaft*, ed. Neithard Bulst and Robert Jütte, Saeculum 44 (Freiburg and Munich: Karl Alber, 1993), 22.

[16] "Bread and cold water had to be his best food." Walter Kofler, ed., *Ortnit und Wolfdietrich D: kritischer Text nach Ms. Carm 2 der Stadt- und Universitätsbibliothek Frankfurt am Main* (Stuttgart: S. Hirzel, 2001), 168, stanza 399.

[17] Last will of Gertraud, wife of Master Gerhard, 1420, July 30: *Item von erst schafft sy iren pesten plaben manntel iren drein kinden, die sy pey irem erern mann gehabt hat [...]. Item auch schafft sy iren pesten paternoster irer swester Elsen ze Ungarn [...]. Item auch hat sy geschafft ire peste silbergürtel hincz Sand Michel.* Gerhard Jaritz and Christian Neschwara, eds., *Die Wiener Stadtbücher 1395–1430*, vol. 5: *1418–1421*, Fontes Rerum Austriacarum III/10/5 (Vienna, Cologne, and Weimar: Böhlau, 2017), 379, n. 3033.

[18] Last will of Margareth, daughter of the Satler from Friesach, 1414, April 10: *den pessern padmantel.* Jaritz and Neschwara, eds., *Die Wiener Stadtbücher 1395–1430*, vol. 4: *1412–1417*, Fontes Rerum Austriacarum III/10/4 (Vienna, Cologne, and Weimar: Böhlau, 2009), 125, n. 2058.

[19] Last will of Catherine, wife of Ulrich Nagl, 1418, November 10: *Item sy hat geschafft ir peste silber gürtl gen Sand Michel zu dem paw und auch ein silbreine paternuster.* Jaritz and Neschwara, eds., *Die Wiener Stadtbücher*, vol. 5, 93, n. 2621.

best black horse to the judge of another Lower Austrian town;[20] in 1419, Ulrich Fleischhacker bequeathed an amount of his best last year's wine to buy a missal for the pilgrimage church of Saint Wolfgang in Upper Austria;[21] and in 1400 a schoolmaster mentioned three of his best books, without any details, to be given to a diacon.[22]

Sometimes, such kind of evaluating description of the quality of bequeathed objects could still become more detailed and differentiated when, for example, the second best bed with two cushions, two linens, one blanket and a head pillow was given to a poor maidservant.[23] The already mentioned last will of the wife of a Viennese burgher from November 1418 contains, among others, a bed with its belongings, "not the best and not the worst," and two golden rings, "not the best and not the lightest."[24]

A particular source for the reference to best objects can be found in the North German regulations concerning *Heergewäte*, actually the equipment of a warrior, and *Frauengerade*, specific female movables, that is, those parts of the inheritance that should be bequeathed to the closest male and female relatives respectively.[25] A particularly rich example comes from the town law codification of Lüneburg from 1401, but having connections to sources from about 1329:

> *Was zu Herwede und Frauenrade gehört: Dit is dat recht, und die dinge de da horet to dem herwede. Sin perd, sadel, kovertur, thom, syn beste harnsch, plate, muze, schild, swerd, syn exse, bil, glavye in dem hus. […] , syne besten kledere, syn beste gordel, syne bratzen vor dem hemmed, syne sulverne schale, syn bedde neghest dem besten, enen pol, en kussen, twen lakene neghest den besten, ene kolten neghest der besten, […] . Desse nascreven ding scal me nemen vor vrowenrade. Ere beste par kledere, eren besten duk, ere besten koghelen, ere beste hemmed, eyn par scho, ere beste bedde mit dem besten hovetpole, ere besten twe orkussen, ere beste par lakene, ere beste dekene, ere besten kisten, ere besten*

---

[20] Last will of Frederick, parish priest of Gars, 1403, September 14: *mein pestez swarczes pherd.* Jaritz and Neschwara, eds., *Die Wiener Stadtbücher 1395–1430*, vol. 3: *1406–1411*, Fontes Rerum Austriacarum III/10/3 (Vienna, Cologne, and Weimar: Böhlau, 2006), 103, n. 1338.

[21] Last will of Ulrich Fleischhacker, 1419, November 18. Jaritz and Neschwara, eds., *Die Wiener Stadtbücher*, vol. 5, 224, n. 2797.

[22] Last will of Konrad Weispacher, schoolmaster, 1400, January 31: *Item Jacobo Pistori, diacono, […] seiner pesten pücher drew.* Wilhelm Brauneder and Gerhard Jaritz, eds., *Die Wiener Stadtbücher 1395–1430*, vol. 1: *1395–1400*, Fontes Rerum Austriacarum III/10/1 (Vienna and Cologne: Böhlau, 1989), 327, n. 527.

[23] Last will of Ludwig Vischer, Vienna, 1419, Dezember 9: *Item das pett nach dem pesten schafft er ainer armen diern mit zwein leilachen, mit zwain kussen, mit ainer dekch und mit ainem haubtpolster.* Jaritz and Neschwara, eds., *Die Wiener Stadtbücher*, vol. 5, 239, n. 2826.

[24] See note 19*: Item darnach hat sy geschafft […] ain pett mit aller seiner zugehörung, nicht das pesst noch nicht das ergist, […] und zwen guldein ring, nicht die pesten und nicht die leichttisten.*

[25] Concerning *Heergewäte* and *Frauengerade,* see Werner Ogris and Heiko Steuer, "Frauengerade," in *Reallexikon der Germanischen Altertumskunde*, 2nd ed., vol. 9 (Berlin and New York: De Gruyter, 1995), 514–517; Ruth Schmid-Wiegand and Heiko Steuer, "Heergewäte," in *ibidem*, vol. 14 (Berlin and New York: De Gruyter, 1999), 114-15.

duklade, ere beste span, ere beste vingerne neghest den handtruwen, ere beste vestich, ere besten wumpel, ere beste tidebuk mit dem bokesbudele, ere beste banklaken, de besten ses stulkussene, enen disch, ere beste dischlaken, de besten handwelen, eren besten gropen, eren besten ketel, eren besten luchter, ere beste badelaken und en badebecken.[26]

* * *

The mentioned examples offer an overview of the importance that good, better and best objects of material culture, that is, favourite or even singular things had in the daily life of members of late medieval society. Such particular objects play a major role in recent studies on material culture too, also with regard to the Middle Ages and the early modern period.[27] Despite this wealth of existing research results, there is certainly still space for new issues. The question about favourite things is intended to advance the currently very productive discussion and to focus on what is special in the ties to things. The time-frame is determined by the Middle

---

[26] "What is part of the *Hergewäte* and the *Frauenrade*: This is the law and these are the things that are part of the *Hergewäte*. His horse, saddle, horserug, bridle, his best armour, breastplate, helmet, shields sword, battle axe, hatchet, lance in the house, [...] his best clothes, his best belts, his brooches for the shirt, his silver bowl, his bed next to the best, a pillow, a cushion, two bed sheets next to the best, one duvet next to the best, [...] . The following things one should take for Frauenrade: Her best clothes, her best cloth, her best coats, her best shirts, a pair of shoes, her best bed with the best head-bolster, her best two ear-cushions, her best pair of bed sheets, her best blanket, her best chest, her best cloth drawer, her best brooch, her best rings after the wedding ring, her best necklace, her best veil, her best Book of Hours with the girdle binding, her best bench cover, the best six cushions, a table, her best tablecloths, the best hand towels, her best tripod skillet, her best cauldron, her best candlestick, her best bath towels, and a bath trough." W. F. Volger, ed., *Urkundenbuch der Stadt Lüneburg*, vol. 3: *von 1387 bis 1402* (Lüneburg: Herold & Wahlstab, 1877), 435–36; a slightly different transcription in Wilhelm Theodor Kraut, *Das alte Stadtrecht von Lüneburg* (Göttingen: Verlag der Dieterichschen Buchhandlung, 1846), 20–21. See also Eckart Thurich, *Die Geschichte des Lüneburger Stadtrechts im Mittelalter* (Lüneburg: Museumsverein für das Fürstentum Lüneburg, 1960), 51–52; Susanne Mosler-Christoph, "Die materielle Kultur in den Lüneburger Testamenten 1323 bis 1500," phil. Diss. (Göttingen: Georg-August-University, 1998), passim (with wrong date of the source).

[27] See, for instance, Frank Trentman, *Empire of Things: How We Became a World of Consumers, from the Fifteenth Century to the Twenty-First* (Harmondsworth: Penguin, 2017); Tara Hamling and Catherine Richardson, eds., *Everyday Objects: Medieval and Early Modern Material Culture and Its Meanings* (London: Routledge, 2010); Elina Gertsman and Barbara Rosenwein, *The Middle Ages in 50 Objects* (Cambridge: Cambridge University Press, 2018); Jenny Adams and Nancy Mason Bradbury, eds., *Medieval Women and Their Objects* (Ann Arbor: University of Michigan Press, 2017); Pierre Bellemare and Veronique Le Guen, *Curieux objets, étranges histoires: 33 objets, 33 destins extraordinaires* (Paris: Flammarion, 2016); Claudia Theune and Stefan Eichert, eds., *Wert(e)wandel: Objekt und kulturelle Praxis in Mittelalter und Neuzeit*, Beiträge zur Mittelalterarchäologie in Österreich 31 (Vienna: Österreichische Gesellschaft für Mittelalterarchäologie, 2016); Caroline Walker Bynum, *Christian Materiality: An Essay on Religion in Late Medieval Europe* (Brooklyn: Zone Books, 2011).

Ages and the early modern period. At this point, we would like to thank all the participants who took part in a discussion on the topic of favourite things at the University of Salzburg in December 2014 and, in particular, those whose written contributions have made the publication of this volume possible.

The first two chapters address issues of current theory and the history of research into things. Keith Moxey begins by looking at the agency of things, investigating the question of the "material time" of things. The starting point for his reflections are natural objects that bear within them the traces of time but, when encountered, break up the concept of chronology. The collection of his favourite things includes such objects as petrified wood, shells, or corals. Moxey extends Bruno Latour's agency approach: agency is not targeted to situations.

Hans Peter Hahn approaches things via the question of their value and the criteria for their valuation. Things have no innate value, but they are valued in multifaceted and often conflicting decisions and practices. There is no doubt that socio-economic approaches are just as necessary as cultural ones, particularly for the question of the importance of things for cultural identity. Hahn's contribution presents the vital research on the question of the valuation of material goods carried out by ethnology and anthropology during the last century. He attaches particular importance to the temporal aspect: "When, at what historical moment is a particular material thing considered to be valuable?" The value of things is inseparably connected with appreciation, both on the subjective and individual level – as an established topic of psychological and psychoanalytical research – and in the historical and cultural dimension. If we are to achieve a more precise determination of the conditions under which certain objects, sacred and profane, can become favourite things, Hahn argues that the approaches described must be stronger interleaved and practical as well as theoretical approaches need to be integrated. There is no comprehensive theory on the appreciation of material objects.

Asa Simon Mittman uses his highly personal passion for original medieval objects as the starting point for his plea that objects should be experienced and understood with all our senses. Whether the ivory shrine of St Francis in Florence, the relics of the Holy Blood in Bruges or the *Beowulf* manuscript in London – as a professional art historian he seeks out the objects of his scholarly interest in collections of treasures, museums and libraries. He reflects on the veneration and incalculable power of the attraction of relics, not only for pilgrims from around the world but also for researchers who travel around the globe to make contact with such favourite things (even though these are now often available in digital form). Mittman does not see this as an act of religious or libidinous desire but instead suggests applying the sensual experience of objects entirely in line with the practical and theoretical approaches, in order to obtain new knowledge about the things. The stimuli for his personal encounters with the material objects that he explores derive from current thing theory.

"What is luxury?" – the popular interpretation includes things that, while not being based on any direct necessity, nevertheless have a particular individual status and are often of high material value. Gabriela Signori's chapter focuses on rings, in particular finger rings. Her attention centres on the workshop of the goldsmith Stefan Maignow from Konstanz on Lake Constance, whose account books from the last quarter of the fifteenth century she has edited. She begins by stating that the goldsmith's craft developed extremely well in such towns that could boast a bishopric in the late Middle Ages. In Konstanz alone, a town with a population of around 6,000, ten goldsmith workshops served the local and regional customers. Wealthy secular clerics were of particular importance as purchasers of goldsmiths' work. Signori first presents the social and family background of the master goldsmith Stefan Maignow. Using his account book, she draws up a consumer profile of purchasers who shared a predilection for finger rings, and refers to the gender-related aspects of favourite rings: "Gold and silver jewellery prove to be a primarily male and clerical medium of representation."

Just like jewellery, clothing also has a high potential for becoming a personal favourite thing. John Styles' chapter examines the production and life cycles of fabrics for clothing and household textiles in Europe from the fourteenth up to the eighteenth century. It is not only in our present age, in which we use the term "fast fashion" as we pursue the latest trends, that there has been a quick turnover in clothing. Styles shows how the European textile industry switched to yearly cycles and, within them, to seasonal products, predominantly in the garments sector. The changes concerned practically everything, the materials, patterns, colours and accessories. "The main trend was a move towards fabrics that were lighter, more colourful, more highly patterned." During the course of the sixteenth century, Italy's influential silk production lost terrain, to be replaced by Lyon as the new textile centre in Europe. He examines why fabrics from there, in particular, were so popular and Lyon's innovations so successful. In this context, from the seventeenth century onwards, the influence of periodicals dealing in detail with the latest fashion trends reached special influence. The periodic natures of the print media and of the short-lived fashion cycles were closely linked.

Ottó Gecser examines the perception of the taste of hot spices and the long-term change in taste preferences in Europe during the transition from the Middle Ages to the modern period. His marker object is pepper. To what extent did the import of comparatively cheap chili pepper from America "depose" the high prestige pepper from Asia as a luxury spice? When chili first came to Europe, the ground had been well prepared, since mediaeval cooking, at least the one of the social elites, was still very much favourable to spices. Gecser analyses the consumption of spices on the basis of cookbooks and household accounts, and reveals geographically differing patterns in the quantity and variety of the use of spices. A comparison between England, France, Spain, Italy, Germany, and the Scandinavian countries shows clear differences in preferences for. The chili plant was introduced to Europe in the sixteenth century, it flourished well and was planted widely, with the result that chili pepper soon became an affordable product. Gecser examines whether there were trickle-down or bottom-up processes involved but sees no clear patterns. In central and northern Europe, the taste of this new "fake pepper" was less successful than in Spain and Italy, where "it was regarded as genuinely better than a regular pepper".

In the last chapter, Janine Maegraith examines gift-giving practices and the particular importance of food gifts in an early modern small-town society. Her detailed analysis is based on the memoirs of Michel Stüeler from Graupen/Krupka in north western Bohemia, where he worked as a tanner and held various public offices. In his records, kept between 1629 and 1649, he noted very precisely whom he honoured with food gifts and from whom he and his family received gifts of food. Maegraith uses this to reconstruct a complex network of relationships within the communal world of Bohemia in the second half of the seventeenth century, a time when the population suffered under the military operations of the Thirty-Years War. Food gifts were an almost daily activity in the provision of food. In the gift-giving society, described by Stüeler, food gifts, with their short durability, were subject to a different logic than long-lived gifts; but durability was created through the practice of repetition. The gifts in Stüeler's records were affordable, but still of particular importance, specifically for the recipient.

All the contributions in this volume concentrate on the perception of medieval and early modern material culture, in particular exceptional objects that can be seen as favourite things. The chapters lead from theoretical issues to specific groups of objects, their exclusivity and function as social markers. The analyses touch religious as well as secular space and offer new results with regard to the relation of humans and the material world, and its development.

KEITH MOXEY

Material Time

> The name of the game is not to extend subjectivity to things, to treat humans like objects, to take machines for social actors, but *to avoid using* the subject-object distinction *at all* in order to talk about the folding of humans and non-humans.[1]

Fig. 1: Things. Photo: Keith Moxey

Recent theorizations of the "agency" of objects ask us to rethink how we come to grips with the temporality of things (fig. 1). Chronology's function as a distancing or objectifying device has been compromised by the competing claims of different historical narratives. By contrast, anachrony, chronology's binary opposite

[1] Bruno Latour, *Pandora's Hope: Essays on the Reality of Science Studies* (Cambridge, MA: Harvard University Press, 1999), 193–94.

and shadowy twin, has energized much recent thinking about our "favourite things." Where chronology orders the past according to an effective temporal framework, anachrony enables an understanding of the interruption or breaking of time inherent in the phenomenological encounter with objects. Things refuse to observe chronological protocols because of their immediate appeal to the viewer. To which of these forms of time are we to pay attention? Do we insist on objectivity, thus refusing objects the status of "thing," that is, objects with which we have an intimate relation – or do we respect their ubiquitous presence by appreciating that they have the potential to stand outside the orderly march of time? What happens if we approach things as if they were neither subjects nor objects but that they belong in a continuum between these poles? What if the distinction "human/non-human" is arbitrary, in other words, and that objects have many of the characteristics of subjects and vice-versa? Time, that invisible but omnipresent dimension of this enduring struggle might be the ground on which they meet?

Why things now? The familiar world of the humanities has lately been rendered strange by the animation of what have been traditionally considered the inert objects of its concerns. In an extraordinary exchange of roles, subjects seem to have become objects and vice-versa. Rather than frame the discussion of my "favourite things" in terms of period or place, I want to use them to reflect on the temporal nature of the encounter. What happens when we transform objects into "things" – let alone "favourite things"? What is it about our relation to them that defies objectification?

Natural objects appeal to me the most (fig. 2). In bringing to mind nature rather than culture, I don't mean to step outside of time. Far from it. The nature/culture distinction is, in fact, my target. The objects I intend to mention matter to me precisely because of their capacity both to illustrate and contain time. Rather than belonging to no particular temporality, it is their age that makes them fascinating. Knowing little or nothing about geology, I have nevertheless always been enchanted by the rocky record of ages past. On many hikes I continue pick up these remnants of geological events transpiring millions of years ago into which I have no possible insight. Time, that most indiscernible yet persistent aspect of our everyday lives, appears suspended and sedimented in rocks. Rocks bear not only the traces of time's passage, the form, substance, and texture that indicate its relentless presence, but also – being objects in which time has become concrete – they actively exude time as well. Possessing both representational *and* ontological status they simultaneously illustrate and embody their own temporality.

Natural forces of breathtaking intensity and violence have left their traces in the marvelously varied shapes and colours that constitute the stratigraphic record. The rocks that surround us are a record of volcanic, sedimentary, or metamorphic events. Are they the result of convulsive energy bursting from the earth's mysterious interior, or the gentle action of ocean currents and the lives and deaths of countless sea creatures laid down on the placid beds of warm seas, or evidence of the unimaginable pressures of continental drift, of the upsurge and down draft of entire geological formations, continents, that bend and twist existing rocks into fantastic new shapes and substances? What stories do the rocks convey, prompting the very narratives we spin about them?

Fig. 2: Natural objects from the sea. Photo: Keith Moxey

What enables the vital matter of the universe to transform itself into this sublime variety? Can evolutionary theory really account for these improbable and unlikely shapes? Surely, no teleology could possibly be served by these protean transformations. Far from intimating a divine plan, the heterogeneity and chaotic multiplicity of these forms embodies the presence of a more ancient force, one that long anticipates the arrival of humans a mere 200,000 years ago. The shape of this formidable energy makes itself evident in material forms. Time is material and materials are temporal. The life processes governing the kaleidoscopic variations of animals, sea creatures, even plants are different from those that rule the rocks. Where does the distinction between animate and inanimate lie? Their intricate structures and patterns defy understanding. Aware that they confront us with questions that cannot be answered lies no doubt at the heart of their allure.

Here is a piece of petrified wood from the Petrified Forest in California that sits on my mantle (fig. 3). About 3,4 million years ago a volcanic explosion buried a giant redwood (sequoia) forest with volcanic ash. Originally preserved because a lack of oxygen prevented its aerobic decomposition, over the course of hundreds of thousands of years water seeped through the ash, replacing the organic material of the trees cell by cell with crystalized minerals. Quartz, calcite, pyrite, iron carbonate and calcium phosphate now fill the pores of the wood's tissues. Elements such as manganese, iron, and copper stain the petrified wood in a variety of colours. When contaminants are added, quartz crystals take on yellow, red, or other bright hues.

Fig. 3: Petrified wood. Photo: Keith Moxey

The object bespeaks the temporal process to which it has been subjected. Some of the trees destroyed by the volcano were 2,000 years old when they fell, but their own time is then inscribed by the time of the water that slowly substituted minerals for their original organic material. Can we distinguish the temporal process of petrifaction from the object itself? My object is too intricately rendered, too finely crafted, to be reduced to the status of a scientific phenomenon or an aspect of an unconscious "natural" world. Holding it in my hand, I remotely sense the intensity of the temporalities that formed it, the violence of the volcano, the death of the forest, the mountain of ash, the seepage of water, the crystallization of quartz, and the colour of dissolving iron oxide. The moment of the "now" confronts another moment 3.4 million years ago, two horizons that chronology dictates are inconceivably distant, but which nevertheless meld in my hand. Time becomes so recognizably familiar, yet so impossibly opaque.

Let's look at something entirely different. This smooth object is actually not a rock at all but glacial till (fig. 4), compacted material deposited directly by the ice as it once moved downhill. It is composed of sand and rock eroded from the mountains through which the glacier long ago flowed and deposited on the side walls of the valley through which it passed. This piece comes from the Perito Moreno glacier in the Argentine Patagonia which, like all glaciers, is fast receding because of global warming. When I came across what looked like fossilized mud on the exposed rock along which the glacier had previously travelled, I was mystified. The forces that had shaped this unexceptional looking thing are intriguing to consider. The weight of the ice had not just crushed the rock in its path but fused it into something that resembled concrete. The time of snow, snow into ice, ice into ice-sheet, ice-sheet into ice-river, the tearing and grinding of rock, and finally the time of its retreat, all these forms of time are embodied in this thing.

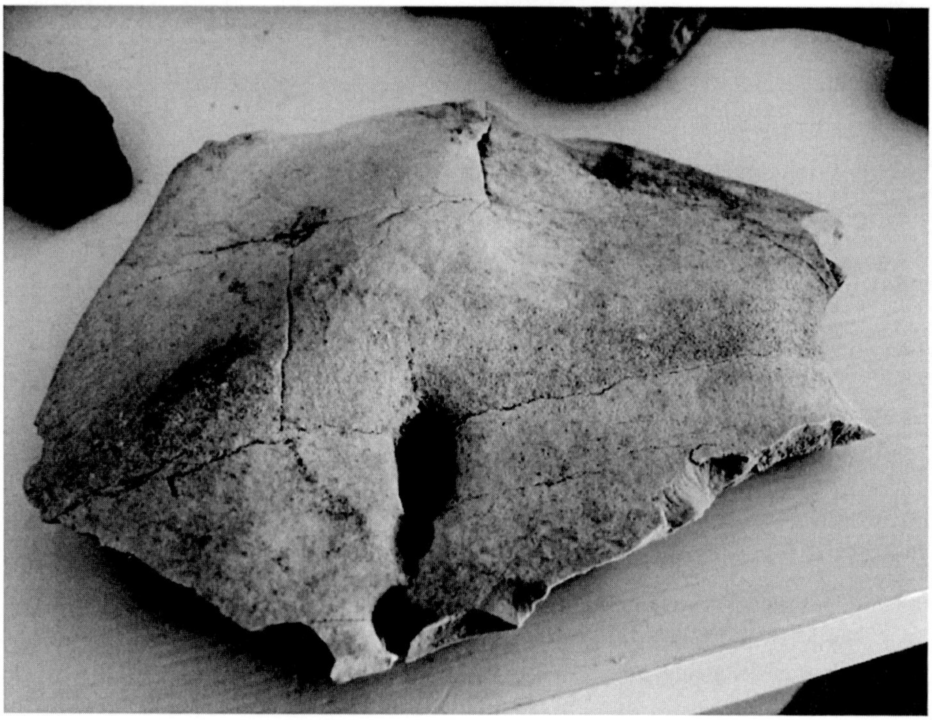

Fig. 4: Glacial till. Photo: Keith Moxey

Among the many shells in my collection, there are also some examples of coral (fig. 5). This branch coral from Lizard Island in the Great Barrier Reef, for example, is formed from the tiny calcium carbonate deposits left by thousands of coral polyps over hundreds of years. Coral fossils date from the Devonian period, 600 million years ago, so they are one of the most ancient forms of life on earth. These simple creatures have a symbiotic relation to the single-cell algae that live within them. Receiving protection from the stony skeleton of the polyp and food from its digestive process, these zooxanthellae provide their host with food in return. Where the algae obtain carbon dioxide and water from the polyp's cellular respiration, the coral polyp receives sugars, fats and oxygen from the algae's photosynthesis. Something about the simplicity, juxtaposed with the massive scale on which this process takes place, dramatizes the passage of time. It is perhaps no accident that Charles Darwin drew the shape of branching coral to visualize his theory of evolution (fig. 6).[2]

Fig. 5: Branch coral. Photo: Keith Moxey

Substituting the image of branches of coral for the more traditional image of a tree in which the development of living forms is conceived as teleological in nature, he argues that life proceeds in many directions at once. Time, that is, serves no purpose and has no function. It flows through matter in the same way as the polyp's respiration is exchanged for the algae's photosynthesis. Opportunistic and protean in its energy, time like life, is both as accessible and unknowable as is this small piece of coral.

[2] Horst Bredekamp, *Darwins Korallen: Die frühen Evolutionsdiagramme und die Tradition der Naturgeschichte* (Berlin: Wagenbach, 2005), 11.

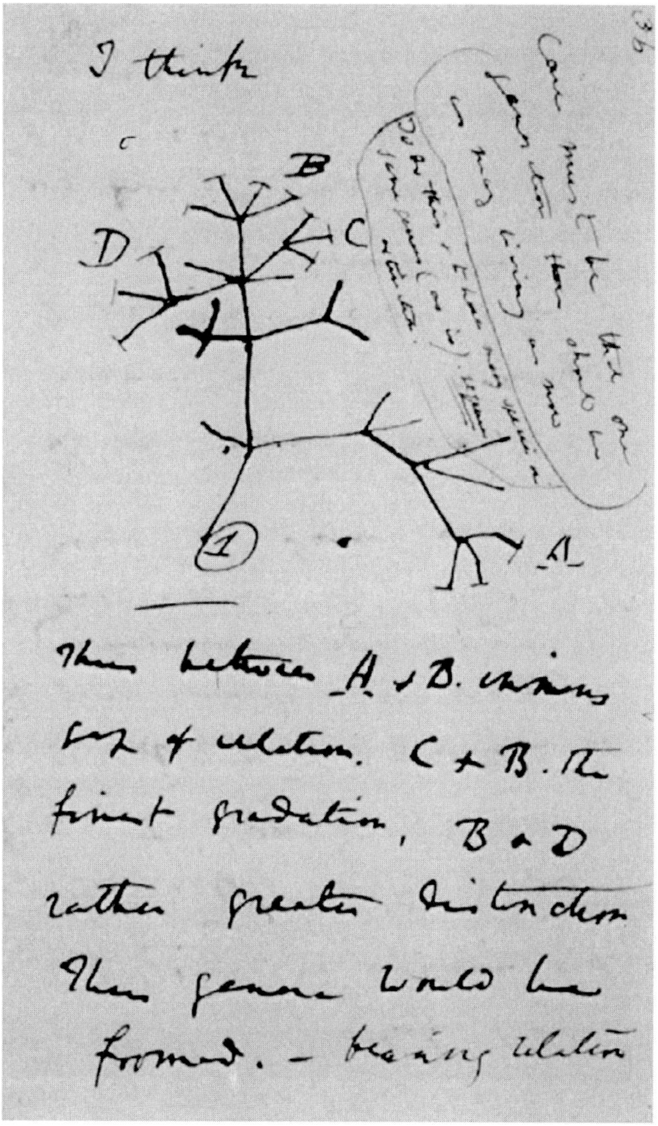

Fig. 6: Charles Darwin, Branching coral. Pen drawing in his notebook B: Transmutation of species (1837–1838), http://darwin-online.org.uk/content/frameset?pageseq=38&itemID=CUL-DAR121.-&viewtype=image (accessed August 2018)

It is time, perhaps, that contributes to the current fascination with thing theory, especially today to the notion of "favourite things"? The new found interest in the "agency" of objects coincides with a perplexity about time. If the limitations of chronology have become all too obvious, if its intimate attachment to the forces of colonialism and capital mark its contingency, then anachrony, the continual encounter of different times in ways that cannot be systematically ordered, offers us a potentially more interesting form of temporality. Far from denying the power of the past, anachrony acknowledges it. Rather than attempt to calibrate the past according to a single standard, one that betrays the interests of its designers, anachrony enables different temporal horizons to encounter each other haphazardly. History thus severs its impossible aspirations to science and metamorphoses into a form of poetry.

The nature/culture distinction has always been emphasized and enforced by time. Many of the world's great religions argue that in contrast to natural time that, they allege, has no beginning and no end, human time is motivated and that it is teleological in nature. This conviction, secularized but perpetuated by Hegel's philosophy of history at the beginning of the nineteenth century and exported across the globe in the age of empire, still dominates historical thinking. As Foucault predicted, the concept of "man," together with the subject/object distinction that depends upon an ideal consciousness capable of knowing both the world and itself, has disappeared.[3] Scholars across a number of disciplines now argue that the natural world, from which we have carefully excluded ourselves, is actually as conscious and animated as are we.

According to the philosopher of science, Bruno Latour, the time has come to abandon the myth of humanist subjectivity that empowered the subject/object and the nature/culture binaries. His notion of the "collective" serves as a way to acknowledge that humans do not act upon an inert non-human universe, but that they are in turn acted upon by it.[4] The subject/object distinction becomes a heuristic device that necessarily misconstrues the hybrid unity that binds those poles together. Even if it is, as he argues, only language that creates the distinction in the first place, can we actually avoid making it?[5] Can we avoid distinguishing between subjects and objects when attempting to come to terms with the natural world that surrounds us?

Latour's position finds adherents and critics across the spectrum of those engaged in material studies. Less radical than Latour, for example, are the positions of Lorraine Daston, from the philosophy of science, Arjun Appadurai and Alfred Gell, from anthropology, and W.J.T. Mitchell, from literary and visual theory. According to Daston, "…reality is a matter of degree, and […] phenomena […] may become more or less intensely real, depending on how densely they are woven into scientific thought and practice."[6] This definition of objects is remarkably close to

[3] Michel Foucault, *The Order of Things: An Archaeology of Knowledge*, trans. from the French (London: Routledge, 1970).

[4] Latour, *Pandora's Hope;* idem, *Politics of Nature: How to Bring the Sciences into Democracy* (Cambridge, MA: Harvard University Press, 2004).

[5] Latour, *The Pasteurization of France* (Cambridge, MA: Harvard University Press, 1988), 155: "Are words forces? Are they capable of fighting, revolting, betraying, playing, or killing? Yes, indeed, like all materials, they may resist or give way. It is materials that divide us, not what we do with them."

[6] Lorraine Daston, "The Coming into Being of Scientific Objects," in *Biographies of Subjective Objects* ed. Lorraine Daston (Chicago: University of Chicago Press, 2000), 1–18, 1.

that of Latour, as it argues against the existence of "facts" in favor of "matters of concern,"[7] meaning that the world of objects only becomes "real" when humans pay attention to it. On the other hand, rather than dissolve the subject/object divide, Arthur Gell argues that humans invest objects with a "secondary agency" that reflects their own,[8] while Arjun Appadurai and W.J.T. Mitchell ask us to approach them "as if" they had lives of their own, even if they actually do not.[9] None of these authors is an animist, however, and therefore the actual "life" of objects is never in question. Rather, they understand objects as an integral aspect of the human experience and ascribe them a status that might be described as a shadowy "subjectivity."

Daniel Miller, another anthropologist and materials studies theorist, offers an attractive model with which to understand the continuing fascination of objects in a situation where their relation to humanity is acknowledged as hybrid. Following Hegel, he bases his account of subject formation on the principle of projection, arguing that our encounter with objects is analogous to our encounter with other human beings. Meeting another human, or another "thing," is a process in which the subject projects its own ideas on to the "other" in order to understand what it encounters. These ever more perceptive projections are then absorbed back into the subject by means of sublation or introjection so that the subject is itself transformed. There is, therefore, no absolute distinction between subject and object but a spectrum of subjectivities and objectivities that they share. The end result of this interaction is the formation of self-awareness or self-consciousness, in which the subject becomes aware of the circumstances that have led to its constitution.

The hybridity of the relation between humans and the world that surrounds them, argued so persuasively by Latour, reflects the protean nature of temporality as it fractures and splinters into materiality. We are surrounded by different forms of time, of which only some can be recognized in our "favourite things." Time flows through us at uneven speeds and varied tempos. Shaped by psychological, cultural and social, not to mention gendered and ethnic considerations, its nature both shapes and is shaped by our individuality. Posing radical challenges to the chronological time of human convention, the time of objects is anachronic. Unlike chronology, its representational "other," the time of the object belongs to its ontology. Material time has the potential to make chronological time stand still. The collision of epistemology and ontology is the instant when the object becomes part

---

[7] Latour, "Why Has Critique Run Out of Steam? From Matters of Fact to Matters of Concern," in *Things*, ed. Bill Brown (Chicago: University of Chicago Press, 2004), 151–73, 157.

[8] Alfred Gell, *Art and Agency* (Oxford: Oxford University Press, 1998).

[9] Arjun Appadurai, *The Social Life of Things: Commodities in Cultural Perspective* (New York: Cambridge University Press, 1986); W.J.T. Mitchell, *What Do Pictures Want? The Lives and Loves of Images* (Chicago: University of Chicago Press, 2005).

of the experience of an individual person. It is the moment when it becomes what Heidegger would have called a "thing."[10]

We may discern in this narrative analogies with and implications for, our fascination with objects. What we meet when we encounter things – perhaps especially in our favourite things – is among other "things," time. The "otherness" of the object's time dramatizes our own tenuous and uncertain location within it. As George Kubler reminds us the present remains as unknown as the interval between the flashes of a lighthouse.[11] Rather than impose our time over the time of other humans or objects, the meeting of temporalities encourages an appreciation of their mysteries. We are caught up in the same mysterious process to which everything else in the world is subject, including our "favourite things." The time of volcanoes, ash, and minerals, of polyps and algae, of glaciers and rock, appears before us, intimating the inexorable forces that created petrified wood, branch coral, and glacial till as those that course through and determine the shape of our own lives.

The Enlightenment still casts its long shadow across the sciences and humanities, but the utopian project of rendering humans and the world they inhabit transparent to one another is increasingly acknowledged to be a dream that cannot be realized. Attention is now directed towards those parts of experience that resist codification and comprehension and to the ways in which they engage our perception, if not our understanding. A crucial dimension of the unknown that invades our consciousness while simultaneously hiding its identity is nothing other than time – the time of the object, *material time.*

---

[10] Martin Heidegger, *What Is a Thing?* (Lecture 1935–36), trans. W. B. Barton and Vera Deutsch (Chicago: Henry Regnery and Co, 1967).

[11] Geoge Kubler, *The Shape of Time: Remarks on the History of Time* (New Haven: Yale University Press, 1962).

Hans Peter Hahn

The Values of Things, Pragmatically, Symbolically and Emotionally

Some Remarks on Object Appreciation

Introduction

Quite frequently, things of particular value are at the focus of society's public awareness. People pay attention to what is valued, and care is taken of things perceived as being of high value. Respect for valuables and care for the material heritage are among the fundamental norms of modern societies. The connection between things of value and the social order of society cannot be overstated. This context includes the most basic economic considerations, such as the handling of money, but also the recent history of the museums, which are regarded as places for the preservation of invaluable treasures. Negotiations about the correct valuation of certain things – whether these might be monuments or personal valuables – are regularly linked with a reconfirmation of identity in a society.[1]

The purpose of this paper is to question some of the implications of the said assumptions about how the value of material things is established in the social sphere. It will be shown that there are very different paths along which ideas about the value of things are acknowledged. It is not only that there is a wide range of modes of value allocation and value generation, but there are also conflicts over value concepts. What a particular person in any society considers as something valuable is a worthless object or even something disturbing for others. Who can decide what the real value of a thing is?

In the following, a supplementary argument will be presented, which will lead to a further differentiation of the concept of "value of things". In addition to (1) the diversity of the value forms and (2) the negotiable character of such assignments of value, a third aspect, the temporal embedding of value propositions, will be discussed. When, at what historical moment is a particular material thing considered to be valuable? The answer to this question cannot be a general one, and requires careful case studies. Quite often, value and esteem increase within short periods of time, thus giving relevance and recognition to the

---

[1] Hans P. Hahn, "Notizen zur Umwertung der Werte. Perspektiven auf ökonomische Konzepte im interdisziplinären Diskurs," in *Kultur der Ökonomie. Zur Materialität und Performanz des Wirtschaftlichen*, ed. Inga Klein and Sonja Windmüller (Bielefeld: transcript, 2014), 17–36.

objects in question. But there are also processes of the loss of value. The so-called "tulip mania" in the Netherlands of the seventeenth century is an outstanding example of such dynamics.[2]

In the light of these three initial arguments, the value of a thing is obviously not an issue that would be adequately covered by the description of any immanent property of an object. As a matter of fact, contexts and forceful actors decide whether a thing is of worth or not. The idea of value as an object-immanent feature has also been rejected by classical concepts from anthropology. Based on ethnographic studies, these concepts explain how values are generated through negotiation and knowledge, that is, through context and not through the material properties.

Probably the most important anthropological author on the topic of the 'value of things' is Nancy Munn, who carried out ethnographic field research in the southern Pacific. She investigated the valuation of a number of specific material possessions of a local chief on a Pacific island.[3] Her most important findings relate to the importance of connecting a thing as such and the related stories. The consideration of any object, according to her study, refers primarily to the past. The general recognition of the value of such an object arises from the fact that the past is linked to the object presently in the possession of the chief.[4] A valuable object in this sense may have played a role in certain events or distinguished itself by a famous prior owner. Following Munn's important insights, the link between value and memory has been confirmed in numerous studies.[5]

There are, for example, so-called 'biographical objects', which play a prominent role as reminiscent of certain events in the life of the person or a close relative and therefore have a special value.[6] Another example of the many applications of the work of Munn concerns the notion of the 'inalienable object'. Based on Munn's research, Annette Weiner has described how certain objects are given the character of inalienable objects. In this framework, characterizing something as an object that may not be given away or sold is considered as a form of appraisal.[7]

---

[2] Zbigniew Herbert, *Der Tulpen bitterer Duft* (Frankfurt/Main: Suhrkamp, 1993).

[3] Nancy Munn, "The Transformation of Subjects into Objects in Walbiri and Pitjantjatjara Myth," in *Australian Aboriginal Anthropology: Modern Studies in the Social Anthropology of the Australian Aborigines,* ed. Ronald M. Bernd (Nedlands: University of Western Australia Press for the Australian Institute of Aboriginal Studies, 1971), 141–63.

[4] Nancy Munn, *The Fame of Gawa. A Symbolic Study of Value Transformation in a Massim (Papua New Guinea) Society* (Cambridge: Cambridge University Press, 1986).

[5] Robert J. Foster, "Commodities, Brands, Love and Kula. Comparative Notes on Value Creation. In Honor of Nancy Munn," *Anthropological Theory* 8 (1) (2008): 9–25; Daniel Miller, "The Uses of Value," *Geoforum* 39 (2008): 122–32.

[6] Janet Hoskins, *Biographical Objects. How Things Tell the Stories of People's Lives* (London: Routledge, 1998).

[7] Annette B. Weiner, "Why Cloth? Wealth, Gender and Power in Oceania," in *Cloth and Human Experience*, ed. Annette B. Weiner and Jane Schneider (Washington D.C.: Smithsonian Series in Ethnographic Inquiry, 1989), 33–72. (German translation: Annette B. Weiner, "Stoffe: Reichtum,

The second classical approach to the value of things has an important advocate, Mary Douglas. She investigated certain forms of money in Central Africa, and – based on her own research – she was able to show the limits of the ostensible equivalence of money and commodity. According to Douglas, the idea of money as a universal equivalent is in contradiction with current practices in this society.[8] As she found out, among the Lela in Central Congo, the exchange is always welcome for the receiver of Raphia cloth; but, giving away one of these highly valued items in order to acquire whatever goods one might get, is disapproved of. Raphia cloth is, on the one hand, money in the sense of a universal unit of measure for the value of many other things. On the other hand, the equivalence function is only theoretical. In practice, the reputation and value-storing function of Raphia cloth is so dominant that a socially renowned owner will scarcely ever give it away for everyday goods. For the owner and his family, money is an 'iron reserve' which is only brought to the market in extreme situations.

Referring to these research findings, Douglas postulates the inequality of all valuable material items.[9] Everything, even money, has a value, but there are no balanced value relations. The value that receives the highest recognition is a question of power in political and social contexts. Thus, the introduction of coin money in the Congo led to a significant devaluation of the Raphia money. Shortly after the introduction of the colonial currency, many owners of Raphia money agreed to exchange their pieces of cloth for French colonial francs. According to Douglas there is a general rule: The acceptance of a claim about the value of an object is always the result of a symbolic process, which also signifies the recognition of political power. Douglas' concept of the social embedding of value ascriptions was then documented within a short time by several other ethnographic studies.[10] More recently, the concept of the social definition of value has also been confirmed by economic studies dealing with the role of money in consumer societies.[11]

In social and cultural anthropology, the interest in the question of why certain things are valued but not others, recently attracted quite a lot of interest. One of

---

Geschlecht und Macht in Ozeanien," in *Frauenmacht ohne Herrschaft*, ed. Ilse Lenz and Ute Luig (Frankfurt/Main: Fischer, 1995), 330–74; Annette B. Weiner, *Inalienable Possessions: The Paradox of Keeping-while-giving* (Berkeley: University of California Press, 1992).

[8] Mary Douglas, "Raffia Cloth Distribution in the Lele Economy," *Africa: Journal of the International African Institute* 28/2 (1958): 109–22; Mary Douglas, *"Primitive Rationing: A Study in Controlled Exchange,"* in *Themes in Economic Anthropology*, ed. Raymond Firth (London: Tavistock, 1967), 119–46.

[9] Douglas, "Primitive Rationing."

[10] Trude S. Epstein, *Capitalism, Primitive and Modern: Some Aspects of Tolai Economic Growth* (Canberra: Australian National University Press, 1968); Maurice Godelier, "'Monnaie de Sel' et circulation des marchandises chez les Baruya de Nouvelle-Guinée," *Cahiers Vilfredo Pareto* 21 (1970): 121–47; Jean Poirier, *Monnaie et para-monnaie dans les sociétés non-industrielles*, Revue européenne des sciences sociales. Cahiers Vilfredo Pareto 21 (Geneva: Librairie Droz, 1970).

[11] David Graeber, *Toward an Anthropological Theory of Value: The False Coin of our Own Dreams* (Basingstoke: Palgrave Macmillan, 2001).

the sensitive issues is that case studies like those mentioned above link economic questions with those of cultural specificity. In this way, concepts about universal laws of value, lumping all societies together, collide with observations on local cultural features. For example, Marcel Mauss' general theory of the gift,[12] which suggests the exclusion of exact value calculations, is in sharp contrast with the descriptions of the potlatch practiced on the American west coast. In the context of potlatch, the value of things plays a role as a tool for destroying the prestige of the recipient.[13] More recently, this juxtaposition of universal value theories and concepts of the specific cultural embedding of value turned up in the controversial reception of David Graeber's universal history of *Debt: the First 5000 Years.*[14]

What is "Appreciation"?
I. Personal and Subjective

Thus, the two prominent anthropological positions on the concept of the value of things have been briefly presented. These concepts match seamlessly the positions of other disciplines, which also highlight the negotiation character and the impossibility of establishing equivalence relations of material values. The arguments of Nancy Munn and Mary Douglas, as presented here, concern the question of social recognition, that is, the social and cultural sphere. Other theories, such as psychology, are based on similar assumptions, but focus much more on the level of the individual. Especially in the field of individual evaluation, the psychoanalyst Tillman Habermas should be mentioned in first place. His book *Beloved Things* describes the different configurations leading to the particular appreciation of material objects.[15] Congruent with the anthropological theories, Habermas points to the current or past embedding of a thing, which makes it something of known value.

The famous question about the five objects that you would take with you if your apartment or the house you are living in is about to burn down, might reveal what your personal and favourite, even your intimate things are.[16] This may be a teddy bear, or a diary, or a personal collection of photos, or precious jewellery, or even a gift that you received many years ago from a special person. All these things are first and utmost emotional items. This can be stated as a general outcome from

---

12 Marcel Mauss, *Gift: Forms and Functions of Exchange in Archaic Societies* (Glencoe: Free Press, 1954) [originally published in 1925].

13 Homer G. Barnett, "The Nature of the Potlatch," *American Anthropologist* 40/3 (1938): 349–58.

14 David Graeber, *Debt: The First Five Thousand Years* (New York: Melville, 2011).

15 Tilmann Habermas, *Geliebte Objekte. Symbole und Instrumente der Identitätsbildung* (Frankfurt/Main: Suhrkamp, 1999).

16 Foster Huntington, *The Burning House: What Would You Take?* (New York: ItBooks, 2012); John J. Watson, Steven Lysonski, Tamara Gillan, and Leslie Raymore, "Cultural Values and Important Possessions: A Cross-Cultural Analysis," *Journal of Business Research* 55 (2002): 923–31.

psychological approaches: "Value of things" almost always has to do with emotions.[17]

The ability to create a close and permanent attachment toward material objects is a structural process that develops very early in the life of a child. Long time ago, the fundamental role of material items in the creation of emotional links to the social environment was described by Donald Winnicott with the concept of the 'transitional object'.[18] This concept refers to the fact that hardly anything can be more important for the cognitive development of a child than the ability to acknowledge the constancy of the material environment through time. By providing psychological comfort, transitional objects facilitate the shift towards relative independence. It is of some importance to transfer the original framework of this concept, that is, individual development, to the sphere of the social that serves as a proxy for access to material items. This may happen via gift giving or shopping or even such mundane activities like 'provisioning.'[19]

The core statement of this theory assumes the ability to value material objects. This ability is important at an early stage of the development of the individual, it precedes the acquisition of language. Obviously, the identification of favourite things is something more deeply inscribed in the human mind than language. The second aspect to be learned from Winnicott is that valuing things is something positive. It helps people create self-confidence, and thereby also their social embedding. One can also put this the other way round: without favourite things, without transitional objects no one would be what he currently is.

However, relationships to objects are never just a question of the individual, but rather something permanently negotiated in the sphere of the social. The identification of valuable objects is something contested and sometimes disapproved by the community. Examples of highly disputed "values of things" concern objects that might be called 'memorable items' or 'souvenirs.'[20] Do such items represent

---

[17] Eric J. Arnould, Caroline F. Curasi, and Linda L. Price, "Inalienable Wealth in North American Households," in *Values and Valuables: From the Sacred to the Symbolic*, ed. Cynthia A. Werner and Duran Bell (Walnut Creek: Altamira, 2004), 210–30; Russell W. Belk, Melanie Wallendorf, and John F. Sherry, "The Sacred and the Profane in Consumer Behavior: Theodicy on the Odyssey," *Journal of Consumer Research* 16 (1989): 1–38; Melanie Wallendorf and Eric J. Arnould, "'My Favorite Things:' A Cross Cultural Inquiry into Object Attachment, Possessiveness, and Social Linkage," *Journal of Consumer Research* 14 (1988): 531–47.

[18] Donald W. Winnicott, "Transitional Objects and Transitional Phenomena: A Study of the First Not-Me Possession," *International Journal of Psycho-Analysis* 34 (1953): 89–97.

[19] Daniel Miller, "The Social Life of External Objects," *British Journal of Psychotherapy* 14/4 (1998): 483–92; Ian Woodward, "Towards an Object-Relations Theory of Consumerism: The Aesthetics of Desire and the Unfolding Materiality of Social Life," *Journal of Consumer Culture* 11/3 (2011): 366–84.

[20] Jon Goss, "Souvenir: Conceptualizing the Object(s) of Tourist Consumption," in *A Companion to Tourism*, ed. Alan A. Lew, C. Michael Hall, and Alan M. Williams (London: Blackwell, 2004), 327–35; Günter Oesterle, "Souvenir und Andenken," in *Der Souvenir. Erinnerung in Dingen von der Reliquie zum Andenken*, ed. Ulrich Schneider (Cologne: Wienand, 2006), 16–45.

individual memories or are they rather linked to a shared experience? Taking together psychology and the role of memorable objects, it is possible to identify a universal rule that applies to the individual as well as to social groups, peoples and nations, namely: In all societies, there is a capacity to elevate singular objects with regard to their outstanding value from the multitude of things that surround us.

This capacity of elevating or discrimination includes the "singularization" of the object – in Igor Kopytoff's words – but also the relation to particular features of these objects that are accepted characteristics for the particular appreciation.[21] Referring to the example of valuable jewellery, one can find similar objects with different stories. Such stories may involve a family heritage or the crown jewels of the Queen of the United Kingdom.[22] No one will contest the idea that the value of such objects has to do as much with the form and material as with the context. As this example shows, it is quite clear that Nancy Munn's approach to object appreciation is not so different from the more psychological approaches referred to in the last section. In both cases, the embedding gives reason for the appreciation of an object.

What is "Appreciation"?
II. Historical and Cultural

Souvenirs and historical moments remind members of later societies about a past nation, its strengths and power. Similar motives contribute to the appreciation of a museum's collection.[23] Medieval times were a particular moment when relics were among the most favourite things. At that time, appreciation was not so much directed towards the highly elaborate reliquaries but rather towards inconspicuous substances stored inside. This might be a piece of wood (said to originate from the wooden cross of Jesus) or a piece of bone that had been stolen from the tomb of a saint. As a rule, it is neither the materiality as such nor the aesthetic of the object, but rather the associated story.[24]

---

[21] Singularization has been described more extensively by Kopytoff in the context of his idea about object biographies, see Igor Kopytoff, "The Cultural Biography of Things," in *The Social Life of Things. Commodities in Cultural Perspective*, ed. Arjun Appadurai (Cambridge: Cambridge University Press, 1986), 64–91.

[22] As a matter of fact, Malinowski himself already compared the crown jewels with the valuable items of the Kula exchange system in the southern Pacific; see Bronislaw Malinowski, *Argonauts of the Western Pacific: An Account of Native Enterprise and Adventure in the Archipelagoes of Melanesian New Guinea* (London: Routledge, 1922).

[23] Hans P. Hahn, "Sammlungen – besondere Orte von Dingen," in *Massendinghaltung in der Archäologie. Der material turn und die Ur- und Frühgeschichte*, ed. Kerstin P. Hofmann, Thomas Meier, Doreen Mölders, and Stefan Schreiber (Leiden: Sidestone, 2016), 23–42.

[24] Alexandra Walsham, "Introduction: Relics and Remains," *Past and Present* 5 (2010): 9–36.

In a similar manner, the valuation of an African fetish in its original context depends on the related stories and ascribed powers.[25] When these artful wooden sculptures are presented nowadays in a museum, they have lost their original appreciation since long time before. The material object in the museum is displayed primarily for aesthetic considerations; therefore the value of this object has little to do with the original valuation.[26] Understanding the original appreciation requires a closer look, not at the wooden sculpture as such but rather at the magical substance that had been stored within it. The magical substance is hidden in the interior. In spite of its invisibility, it has power over the wellbeing or illness of people at the place of origin. Not the sculpture, but the hidden substance constitutes the true reason for the fetish's original valuation.

During the Renaissance and the Baroque, the chambers of curiosity and the so-called "Wunderkammern" emerged and became fashionable. Scholars claim that these assemblages are the precursors of modern museums.[27] However, others insist on the functional differences.[28] In principle, a "Wunderkammer" served the spiritual relief of Christian believers. Kings and dukes and other dignitaries were convinced that the presence of these rare objects could help them in moments of depression and despair to regain self-confidence, self-consciousness and a spiritual balance.[29]

Another, much more recent place for the public appreciation of things is the department store, emerging in the second half of the nineteenth century. These places constituted artful environments for valuing material items as commodities. Probably the most famous description of the goods on display, the architecture and the manners of the sales staff comes from Émile Zola in his famous novel "The Ladies' Paradise"[30] Entering the glass and steel department stores, observing, experiencing and finally shopping have become practices of appreciation that are

---

[25] John Picton, "Treasures of Heaven. Relics and their Consequences. An Africanist's View," *Material Religion: The Journal of Objects, Art and Belief* 8/2 (2012): 250–53; William Pietz, "The Problem of the Fetish I.," RES: Anthropology and Aesthetics 9 (1985): 5–17.

[26] Stefan Eisenhofer, "Fetisch," in *Handbuch Materielle Kultur. Bedeutungen, Konzepte, Disziplinen*, ed. Stefanie Samida, Manfred K. H. Eggert, and Hans P. Hahn (Stuttgart: Metzler, 2014), 206–10; Johannes Fabian, "On Recognizing Things. The "Ethnic Artefact" and the "Ethnographic Object"," *L'Homme. Revue française d'anthropologie* 170 (2004): 47– 69.

[27] Gabriele Beßler, "Die Welt in der Kammer," in *Wunderkammern: Weltmodelle von der Renaissance bis zur Kunst der Gegenwart*, ed. Gabriele Beßler (Berlin: Reimer, 2012), 89–103; Bénédicte Savoy, "Zum Öffentlichkeitscharakter deutscher Museen im 18. Jahrhundert," in *Tempel der Kunst. Die Geburt des öffentlichen Museums in Deutschland 1701–1815*, ed. Bénédicte Savoy (Mainz: von Zabern, 2006), 9–26; Hildegard Vieregg, *Museumswissenschaften. Eine Einführung* (München: Fink, 2006).

[28] Eilean Hooper-Greenhill, *Museums and the Shaping of Knowledge* (London: Routledge, 1992).

[29] Ilse Jahn, "Sammlungen – Aneignung und Verfügbarkeit," in *Macrocosmos in Microcosmos: Die Welt in der Stube. Zur Geschichte des Sammelns 1450 bis 1800*, Berliner Schriften zur Museumskunde, ed. Andreas Grote (Opladen: Leske+Budrich, 1994), 475–500; Stefan Laube, *Von der Reliquie zum Ding. Heiliger Ort – Wunderkammer – Museum* (Berlin: Akademie Verlag, 2011).

[30] Original version : Émile Zola, *Au Bonheur des Dames* (Paris: Georges Charpentier, 1883).

still part of the modern consumer's worldview. Even in the twenty-first century, the mall (now substituting the department store) is a place of miracles and the enchantment of commodities, thereby seducing the consumer to buy.[31]

These examples make it possible to reconstruct a historical development. The first stage is represented by relics and fetishes, which represent the idea that the presence of an object can alter the status of the observer, be it via benediction or via black magic. The second level is constituted by the "Wunderkammer". Material objects in the "Wunderkammer" are highly appreciated but they are not conceptualized as having a physical impact on the people in their presence. The third period is exemplified by the department store. Obviously, the commodities in these shops generate positive emotions like happiness, but these emotions simply serve to motivate acquisition and ownership.

Taking these three historical practices of valuation together, it is possible to identify a historical development: These practices define a narrowing down or a reduction of the impact of the material on the observer or owner. It is a reduction with regard to the culturally acknowledged intimacy and imagined moral impact that things might have on people. Relics and fetishes actively changed the people in their presence, whereas the "Wunderkammer" collections – although being of high value – only have an influence on mental well-being. Finally, the narrowest relation between man and object is established through consumerism, limiting the human-object-entanglement to positive emotions towards things. The consumer is attracted, he likes the available commodities and consequently acquires. Although publicity promises that the consumer will be happy if only he manages to own any of these commodities, it is obvious to everyone that he should not believe what is promised in adverts. The world of commodities implicitly assumes that the consumer has a basic rationality in approaching the goods offered to him and will buy according to a "rational" decision, whatever rationality in this case might mean. The three historical practices mentioned here – (1) the fetishes' physical impact on the individual, (2) the mental edification through collections of curiosities, and (3) emotional messages from goods, which should not prevent rational choice – may be considered as points of a linear development: the focus on how appreciation is explained becomes narrower and narrower, and the value of things is increasingly conditioned by rationality.

There might be one exception to this rule, an apparently important one. This is the case of the mobile phone. This object generates emotional attachment, but it is much more than this. Many owners of such devices discover its value only when the phone gets lost. The loss of the item reveals its importance for the social network, and if it is not possible to retrieve the data, part of the social network might

[31] Denis J. Brion, "The Shopping Mall," in *Law and Semiotics*, vol. 1, ed. Roberta Kevelson (New York: Plenum, 1987), 65–108; Gerhard Keim, *Magic Moments. Ethnographische Gänge in die Konsumwelt* (Frankfurt/Main: Campus, 1999).

be threatened.[32] Perhaps mobile phones are the relics of our times. The ethnographic documents[33] as well as the manufacturer's advice to synchronize the mobile phone data indicate that this is a question of a very particular appreciation of objects.

What is "Appreciation"?
III. Approaches that Combine Past and Present

The last two sections presented a wide range of individual and social concepts of appreciation, including historical and contemporary perspectives. Considering the diversity of these approaches and the difference between them and the presented classical theories at the beginning of this chapter, the following section focuses on some approaches that combine historical and contemporaneous perspectives both at the level of the individual and the social level.

In order to understand pathways toward appreciation from the past and in the present, Hartmut Böhme's theory of object fetishism is quite useful.[34] According to this theory, the sometimes irrational dealings with everyday objects are remains of the older fetishistic practices. Whereas the rationalist attitude dominates in modern societies, traces of pre-modern thinking still exist in the relations to the material world. The irrational appeal of specific things is an articulation of object relations that normally should not exist in the rational discourses of today.[35] Taking this particular relationship seriously enables Böhme to draw a quite different image of modern societies. This approach combines pre-modern and modern object relations, and also claims that there is a hidden continuity. Human-object relations appear to be universal, independent of time horizon and culture. Although Böhme does not refer to Nancy Munn or Mary Douglas, it is possible to consider his theory as a confirmation of the universal capacity of people to develop object attachment. However, the role of the term "fetishism" in Böhme's approach appears somewhat ambivalent. This term is heavily charged with a dubious assumption

---

32 Hannah Bethke and Jan Grossarth, "Bild von dir machen. Das Smartphone bringt unser Leben zum Leuchten," *Frankfurter Allgemeine Zeitung*, nr. 34 vom 10. 2. 2016, 9.

33 There are ethnographic studies that impressively document the despair and the crisis of identity at the moment when a mobile phone is lost. Cf. Daniel Miller, "The Unpredictable Mobile Phone," *BT Technology Journal* 24/3 (2006): 41–48. Ori Schwarz, "Good Young Nostalgia. Camera Phones and Technologies of Self among Israeli Youths," *Journal of Consumer Culture* 9/3 (2009): 348–76.

34 Hartmut Böhme, *Fetischismus und Kultur. Eine andere Theorie der Moderne* (Reinbek bei Hamburg: Rowohlt, 2006).

35 Böhme exemplifies his theory by fashion clothing and luxury cars, see Hartmut Böhme, "Das Strahlen fetischistischer Dinge im Konsum: Autos und Mode," in *Gegenwart des Fetischs. Dingkonjunktur und Fetischbegriff*, ed. Christine Blättler and Falko Schmieder (Vienna: Turia & Kant, 2014), 31–52.

about those cultures that were once said to produce fetishes, and still carries the connotation of a construction of alterity.[36]

Taken together, the examples used in this chapter show a wide range of things, including individual memory objects, including jewellery but also monuments and commodities in department stores. What is the shared feature of this extremely broad range of things? Juxtaposing these examples of values of things makes once again clear that there is no common material property defining this valuation. There is no immanent common property that might serve as a definition of the status of any material object as a favourite thing.

The challenge of diversity becomes even clearer when considering gold as one of the most widely acknowledged "valuated materials". One might expect that the reference to this expensive and rare material provides evidence for a universal understanding. However, the ethnographic comparison of cultures worldwide shows that the question about the contexts of this precious metal is more complex. On a global scale, the use of gold is unevenly distributed.[37] One obvious aspect is the question of gender: Sometimes gold is just for women, in many other cases it is more a male attribute. In some societies, it is widespread – most families own at least a few gold items – in many other societies gold is so very much associated with power that most families do not own any gold at all. Possessing gold objects may be the symbol of socially defined groups, with others within the same society not having any gold.[38]

These observations make it possible to be more specific regarding the answer to the question about shared features. Appreciation and valuation of things are obviously not 'properties' of the thing as such, but rather modes of people's dealings with the object and the practices associated. Thus, on a more general level it is possible to assume that value of things is not something attached to the object itself. It is rather generated through the way people approach the object. It may refer to the place where the object is stored, or the frequency of usage.

The identification of practices that indicate the valuation of the object is one of the most challenging tasks for historians, sociologists and anthropologists, but it is also highly meritorious. Only if we know which objects were favoured, and why this was so, can we constitute the foundations of the past or other people's life-worlds. On this basis, it is possible to state a firm link between appreciated objects and specific practices, which might be labelled rituals or everyday activities.

---

[36] William Pietz, "The Problem of the Fetish, II." *RES: Anthropology and Aesthetics* 13 (1986): 23–45; idem, "William Pietz, The Problem of the Fetish, IIIa. Bosman's Guinea and the Enlightenment Theory," *RES: Anthropology and Aesthetics* 16 (1988): 105–24.

[37] Hans P. Hahn, "Die Sprache des Glanzes: Wert und Werte als Kontext von Gold," in *Metalle der Macht – Frühes Gold und Silber*, Konferenz des Mitteldeutschen Archäologentages Oktober 2013, ed. Harald Meller, Roberto Risch, and Ernst Pernicka (Halle/Saale: Landesmuseum für Vorgeschichte, 2014), 21–31.

[38] Nikila Mehrotra, "The Cultural Value of Gold," in *The Eastern Anthropologist* 51/4 (1998): 333–49.

Referring to practices means relating the question about value of things to the so-called practice theory developed by Pierre Bourdieu.[39] One of his earliest case-studies deals with the Berber house in the Algerian mountains.[40] In his research, Bourdieu describes different objects in the house and indicates what is the appropriate place of valuable things or rather of mediocre things. He thereby links places with practices and subsequently establishes a hierarchy of valuation.

Looking at "practices in space" makes it possible to develop a grid of spatial movements, which stay at a distance or get closer. According to Bourdieu, "practices in space" establish or articulate the valuation of the material objects included within the space in question.[41] Again, gender is a key argument, as the Berber house is divided into male and female spheres. The place of the most valuable objects is linked to the male space, whereas the place for the more common objects is associated with the women.

The house is much more than just the spatial arrangement of objects with different contexts. Simultaneously it is the expression of overlapping but independent structural layers. These structures refer to day and night, to man and woman, to clean and dirty and to high and low. Therefore, it is not misleading to place this theory in the larger framework of a structuralist perspective on material culture.[42] The main achievement of this text is to show how structures constitute themselves: this happens via routines, through everyday practical actions that do not have any particular meaning as such. The results of such repetitive actions is a structure inscribed in the society, and the placing of the things on a higher or lower level of appreciation.[43]

In Bourdieu's most important insight is the close correlation of agency and values or social order. His ethnographic study provides a very good basis for explaining why some things are appreciated and others considered with dismay. Like in a transparent crystal or in prism, different levels of meanings are reflected through objects, crossing each other in the different way things are handled. Elfie Miklautz coined the term "crystallized sense" for material culture, a quite appropriate metaphor in this context.[44]

---

[39] Pierre Bourdieu, *Esquisse d'une théorie de la pratique, précédé de trois études d'ethnologie kabyle* (Geneva: Librairie Droz, 1972).

[40] Pierre Bourdieu, "The Berber House or the World Reversed," *Social Sciences Information* 9/2 (1970): 152–70.

[41] Daphne Spain, *Gendered Spaces* (Chapel Hill: University of North Carolina Press, 1992).

[42] Bourdieu published this text in an edited volume commemorating the sixtieth birthday of Claude Lévi-Strauss. For the affinity between Bourdieu and Lévi-Strauss see Pierre Bourdieu and Pierre Lamaison, "De la règle aux stratégies: entretien avec P. Bourdieu," in *Terrain. Revue d'ethnologie de l'Europe* 4 (1985): 93–100.

[43] Thomas F. Gieryn, "What Buildings Do," *Theory and Society* 31 (2002): 35–74.

[44] Elfie Miklautz, *Kristallisierter Sinn. Ein Beitrag zur soziologischen Theorie des Artefakts*, Technik- und Wissenschaftsforschung 27 (Munich: Profil, 1996).

Bourdieu's volume on social differentiation in the French middle class society, entitled *Distinction: A Social Critique of the Judgment of Taste*, deals with a broad range of things which are not connected through a specific material feature but rather by the practices of people evaluating them as distinctive features for their social milieu.[45] The message of the practice theory is the following: Material culture is an expression of a particular order and the social identity of a group. This has to do with particular objects, but also with the capacity to show the appropriate usage.

The advantages of practice theory are apparent, and it has achieved the status of one of the major approaches to the social meanings of material culture.[46] However, there are also limitations to this theory when considering the historical perspective on material culture. One considerable shortcoming of practice theory is its focus on the synchronic perspective on meanings. The readjustment of values as a historical process can hardly be seen through the lenses of this theory. Practice theory is blind with regard to temporal change;[47] it overestimates the explanatory power of current practices, and neglects change.[48] To put this criticism in a positive form, it is possible to highlight the particular strength of historical approaches to document the time depth of material culture.

Relics have already been mentioned as a particular category of 'favourite things'. Relics are also a good example of appreciation changing as a result of the emergence of new practices. Relics quickly lost their value during the sixteenth century, but precisely in this time horizon some specialized traders bought entire collections of relics, then travelled to Bavaria or Italy – areas still under Catholic dominance – and sold these objects at a profit.[49] Sacred objects had become commodities only in order to be desacralized in the material environment of the new owner.

Conclusion

Historical information about changes in valuations are quite important for an appropriate understanding of 'favourite things'. As has been shown in the previous

---

[45] Pierre Bourdieu, *Distinction: A Social Critique of the Judgment of Taste* (Cambridge, MA: Harvard University Press, 1984).

[46] Theodore R. Schatzki, "Practice Minded Orders," in *The Practice Turn in Contemporary Theory,* ed. Theodore R. Schatzki, Karen Knorr-Cetina, and Eike von Savigny (London: Routledge, 2001), 50 –63 .

[47] Nigel Thrift, "Strange Country: Meaning, Use and Style in Non-Representational Theories," in *Spatial Formations*, ed. Nigel Thrift (London: Sage, 1996), 1–50.

[48] David G. Stern, "The Practical Turn," in *The Blackwell Guide to the Philosophy of the Social Sciences*, ed. Stephen P. Turner and Paul A. Roth (Malden: Blackwell, 2003), 185–206. Bourdieu's concept neglects the question of how the appreciation for new items emerges and how some things get into oblivion within a short stretch of time; Christine Resch, *Schöner Wohnen: Zur Kritik von Bourdieus "feinen Unterschieden"* (Münster: Westfälisches Dampfboot, 2012).

[49] Patrick Geary, "Sacred Commodities: The Circulation of Medieval Relics," in *The Social Life of Things. Commodities in Cultural Perspective*, ed. Arjun Appadurai (Cambridge: Cambridge University Press, 1986), 169–94.

section, practice theory is one of the most widely adopted tools to describe valuations at any particular moment. However, as has been explained, there are limitations when it comes to the analysis of historical shifts. Probably this is the most important aspect of understanding the appreciation of material things: to explain how appreciation increases, but also how valued things fall into oblivion.

There is no better way to understand the emergence of valuation than through a historical perspective. The importance of material culture in the wider realm of the humanities is linked to the material objects' capacity to reveal stories not only about the rise and decline of objects themselves but also about groups of objects and people as their owners and users.

One last example might make this point even clearer. One of the most impressive cases of the dynamics of changing valuations has to do with drinking water. Water as a substance has an incredibly broad range of different valuations.[50] Extreme contexts are quite revealing in this respect, like the holy water of Lourdes (as a healing power), but also the floods in Bangladesh and Pakistan (as a threatening element). Although it is evident that surface water can create diseases, the distinction between water that carries illness and tap water has been less clear than one might think. Many people simply do not trust the communal water provider and consider tap water as not ideal for their health.

Nowadays water in plastic bottles has achieved the status of purity and health. The astonishing high appreciation of commodities provided by the bottled water industry is far from being rational. Why do so many people appreciate the commodified, advertised and promoted form so much more than tap water? There is an obvious parallel to mediaeval times. At that time water for washing hands was served to honorable guests in so-called aquamaniles. Were these precious sculptures not as irrational as our plastic bottles today?

The many examples given in this chapter make clear how difficult it is to find a general theory of the appreciation of things. But most examples point to a particular aspect, which is the historical change in valuation. These changes have occurred again and again throughout time, and it is important not to assume the stability of an object's value but rather the process of an increasing or decreasing valuation. This is a challenge for ethnographers as well as for historians. But it is a rewarding task, for an understanding firstly of the value of things as such, and, secondly of the change of favourite objects through time. If it becomes possible, thirdly, to give some probable reasons why favourite objects change, then the level of a fairly advanced analysis has been reached.

---

[50] Hans P. Hahn, "Water as Substance and Meaning: Anthropological Perspectives," in *People at the Well. Kinds, Usages and Meanings of Water in a Global Perspective*, ed. Hans P. Hahn, Karlheinz Cless, and Jens Soentgen (Frankfurt/Main: Campus, 2012), 23–43.

ASA SIMON MITTMAN

Touching the Past/Being Touched by the Past

Desire for Contact

I want to touch the Middle Ages. I want to hold all of the works of art in all the museums. I want to turn the pages, not by touching a screen or mouse in the British Library's *Turning The Pages*™ app, but by touching vellum in the British Library's reading room. I want to open and close the wings on altarpieces, to feel ivories warm in my hand, to drink from the Mérode Cup while achieving checkmate with the Lewis Chessmen. I have even been tempted, like John, to *eat the occasional book* (fig. 1). Lead paints (and laws) make this a bad idea. Some of this is impossible; some is not. With a bit of planning and funding and effort, I can get myself to the British Library, where the generous librarians allow me access to wonders. With the right letters of introduction and negotiations, I can gain access to other collections, other treasures, other experiences, but I will never drink from a medieval cup, I suspect. I am deeply fortunate to have the sorts of access I have, and I try not to push my luck, so that such privileges may continue and expand.

Fig. 1: Saint John Eats the Book Received from the Angel, Getty Apocalypse. Los Angeles, The J. Paul Getty Museum, MS Ludwig III 1, fol. 15v. England (probably London), ca. 1255–1260. Digital image courtesy of the Getty's Open Content Program

Michael Camille, though so dedicated to the "image" that the term opens the title of his most prominent work,[1] nonetheless remained committed to haptic experiences. He argued against the dominance of the "linguistic model," writing in 1996:

> We cannot treat works from the past [...] as things only to be read in our heads. Our images are not just about networks but about textures. They are not read on screen but felt on flesh, and pushed out of matter even to the level of pain.[2]

Openness about scholarly lusts for physical contact has become more frequently expressed in the two decades since. Angela Bennett provides a particularly open, even naked example of such desires in her "Touched for the Very First Time: Losing My Manuscript Virginity." She invokes Barthes' *The Pleasure of the Text* in writing that:

> I had [...] expected to encounter a Barthesian erotic body of bliss within the page, one that would adumbrate the shape of the creators as I thumbed through the pages of the codices. Instead, what I encountered was a multiplicity of bodies reaching out through the pages. Seeking a lover, I stumbled upon and into an orgy.[3]

Though it was avoided for generations of medieval studies, sexualization of contact with manuscripts is easy, owing to their fleshly pages, pungent scents, and their fetish-bindings of leather and clasps and chains. Owing to all the wonderfully sexual imagery in the margins of Gothic manuscripts, all the penises and penetrations, which after a while become a bit overwhelming in their flowering profusion (fig. 2). – Owing to tremulous, fevered poems written on the pages of these volumes and animating medieval objects, such as the riddles of the Exeter Book. Riddle 33/91, for example, tells us:

Min heafod is homere geþuren,
searopila wund, sworfen feole.
Oft ic begine þæt me ongean sticað,
þonne ic hnitan sceal, hringum gyrded
hearde wið heardum, hindan þyrel
forð ascufan þæt frean mines
mod ꝥ freoþað middelnihtum.
Hwilum ic under bæc bregde nebbe,

[1] Michael Camille, *Image on the Edge: The Margins of Medieval Art* (Cambridge, MA: Harvard University Press, 1992).

[2] Michael Camille, "Rethinking the Canon: Prophets, Canons, and Promising Monsters," *Art Bulletin*, 78:2 (1996), 200–01.

[3] Angela R. Bennett (as Angela R. Bennett Segler), "Touched for the Very First Time: Losing My Manuscript Virginity," in *Transparent Things: A Cabinet*, ed. Maggie M. Williams and Karen Eileen Overbey (Brooklyn: Punctum Books, 2013), 43.

hyrde þæs hordes, þonne min hlaford wile
lafe þicgan, þara þe he of life het
wælcræfte awrecan willum sinum.[4]

My head is beaten with a hammer,
wounded with sharp tools, scoured by a file.
Often, I gape wide at what stabs against me,
when I, girded with rings, must strike,
hard against hard, pierced from behind,
must shove forth what protects my lord's
heart-joy, at midnight.
Sometimes I drag with a beak under my back
when, guardian of the horde, my lord wishes
to take the relics of those he had ordered
driven from life by slaughter-craft for his own purpose.[5]

Fig. 2: Nun Picking Fruit of the Penis Tree, Guillaume de Lorris and Jean de Meun, *Le Roman de la Rose.* Paris, Bibliothèque nationale de France, MS Français 25526, f. 106v (detail), France, fourteenth century. Image in the public domain

[4] Paull F. Baum, *Anglo-Saxon Riddles of the Exeter Book* (Durham: Duke University Press, 1963), riddle 33/91, available online at *Anglo-Saxon Riddles of the Exeter Book* (September 2016), accessed September 2018 <https://en.wikisource.org/ wiki/Anglo-Saxon_Riddles_of_the_Exeter_Book>.

[5] My thanks to Susan M. Kim for her advice on the translation of this riddle.

What *is* the object speaking here? It is not, ultimately, clear, but it is still pretty *hot.* As Sarah Higley argues, the text of some of the riddles may well be intentionally unclear, making the pious monk struggle and sweat over exactly what prurient meaning is concealed in the vague grammar of the poem.[6] The Onion riddle is a clear joke, and tricks my students into sexual readings of innocent objects, just as surely as it did Anglo-Saxon monks:

Ic eom wunderlicu wiht   wifum on hyhte
burgsittendra   nymþe bonan anum
staþol min is steapheah   stonde ic on bedde
neoþan ruh nathwær   neþeð hwilum
ful cyrtenu   ceorles dohtor
modwlonc meowle   þæt heo on mec gripeð
ræseð mec on reodne   reafað min heafod
fegeð mec on fæsten   feleþ sona
mines gemotes   seþe mec nearwað
wif wundēn locc   wæt bið þæt.[7]

I'm a wonderful thing, a joy to women,
useful to neighbours. I scathe no
city-dweller except only my destroyer.
My position is tall and lofty over the bed;
Down below, I'm hairy in unknown places. Sometimes dares
a fully beautiful churl's daughter,
a proud damsel, to grip me.
She rushes me to redness, plunders my head,
connects with me firmly, soon feels
my meeting, seeks to squeeze me,
a woman with braided locks. Wet is that eye.

I love it. The riddle is a beautiful exercise in Anglo-Saxon alliteration and linguistic play – *staþol min is steapheah   stonde ic on bedde* – full of clever misdirection and clear intent to fool by playing to base interests. This is a moment of human contact across a millennium. My students may have quite a lot of trouble connecting with medieval mystical practices or abstruse theological debates, but they, like so many humans before them, still titter at sex jokes. But while I agree that there is sexual content all over manuscripts and other medieval objects – oh, the pilgrimage badg-

[6] Sarah L. Higley, "The Wanton Hand: Reading and Reaching into Grammars and Bodies in Old English Riddle 12," in *Naked Before God: Uncovering the Body in Anglo-Saxon England*, ed. Benjamin C. Withers and Jonathan Wilcox (Morgantown: West Virginia University Press, 2003), 29–59, here esp. 57.

[7] Baum, *Anglo-Saxon Riddles,* 74/25.

es! – and I love the provocative writing of Camille and Segler, the act of sex is, I think, too easy an answer, to rough a metaphor, to describe *my* desire to hold manuscripts, anyway. The experience of handing thousand-year-old books is exciting, no question, but not *arousing*. It is, at least for me, nothing at all like sex. How else, then, can we move to describe the experience?

The other obvious metaphor for the experience of traveling long distances to spend meaningful time with resonant objects comes from *within* the period we study, the Middle Ages. It is autochthonous, authentically medieval in a way that post-Freudian readings of manuscript use cannot really be. *Id est:* Our desire for the objects of our attention is like that of medieval pilgrims for the relics they traipsed across the world not only to see, but to touch, taste, imbibe, to be anointed with, to strap to their ailing bodies, to sleep next to, or even with (linking back to Camille and Bennett).

But this is also too easy, too facile a comparison. Surely, our goals are not theirs. As Peter Brown writes, the earliest Christians sought contact with "men – raw individuals who believed that they were the agents of vast forces," but that this soon gave way to an interest in things.[8] As he writes, these objects

> lasted while mere men came and passed away. The new devotion was an upsurge of loyalty to holy *things*, while the enthusiasm of previous centuries had concentrated on holy *men*. In Rome and in Gaul, the relic and the martyr's grave totally ousted the living holy man in the popular imagination.[9]

Brown italicized "things" and "men" to highlight the shift he was tracking in early pilgrimage practices, but the key commonality linking these nouns is the adjective that proceeds both: "holy." Christian pilgrimage began with travel to the so-called "Holy Land," and this was the main destination until the Umayyad conquest of the

[8] Peter Brown, *The World of Late Antiquity: AD 150–750* (London: Thames and Hudson, 1971, repr. 1974), 52. Emphasis is original. The following two paragraphs are rooted in research I conducted with Elina Gertsman, which resulted in the following essay: Mittman and Gertsman, "Rocks of Jerusalem: Bringing the Holy Land Home," in *Natural Materials of the Holy Land and the Visual Translation of Place, 500–1500*, ed. Renana Bartal, Neta Bodner, and Bianca Kühnel (New York: Routledge, 2017), 140–71.

[9] Brown, *The World of Late Antiquity*, 182. Emphasis is original. For more on Christian pilgrimage to holy men, see Jaś Elsner and Ian Rutherford, "Introduction," in *Pilgrimage in Graeco-Roman and Early Christian Antiquity: Seeing the Gods*, ed. Elsner and Rutherford (Oxford: Oxford University Press, 2006), 26, and Georgia Frank, *The Memory of Eyes: Pilgrims to Living Saints in Christian Late Antiquity* (Berkeley: University of California Press, 2000). For more on the shift toward pilgrimage to holy things, see Elsner and Rutherford, "Introduction," 29, and Hippolyte Delehaye, *Les origines du culte des martyrs* (Brussels: Société des Bollandistes, 1912), 60–119; Delehaye, *Sanctus: Essai sur le culte des saints dans l'antiquité* (Brussels: Société des Bollandistes, 1927), 196–207; and Delehaye, "Loca Sanctorum," *Analecta Bollandiana* 48 (1930): 5–64.

region in 638.[10] We often talk about these pilgrims as proto-tourists, and cite texts like *The Canterbury Tales* and *The Book of John Mandeville* as evidence of medieval pleasure-travel. For example, Jeffrey Jerome Cohen describes travel to Jerusalem as "this pilgrimage that all serious medieval tourists eventually take."[11] But is this the right metaphor?

Early in its history, as the practice of pilgrimage became more common, the importance of travel to the "Holy Land" diminished. As Jaś Elsner and Joan-Pau Rubiés write:

> By the end of the fourth century, the entire landscape of the Roman empire would be dotted with martyria, shrines and churches marking the specific spots where important saints had lived, the places where their bodies finally came to rest, and the location of significant artefacts associated with them, such as the True Cross.[12]

The cities in the "Holy Land" were replaced by portable objects distributed throughout Europe.[13] Gregory of Tours, as Peter Brown notes, described how "relics were everywhere, scattered throughout the entire Christian world. In every region, there were specks of dust unlike all other specks of dust, fragments of bone unlike other fragments, tombs unlike other tombs."[14] Similarly, the medieval objects we now travel to find are scattered from their original locations. Yes, the Hereford Map, probably produced around 1305 for and perhaps in Hereford,[15] is still in the Cathedral, where I have seen it several times. The Franks Casket, a complex eight-century carved English box, is still in England, or rather, *again* in England after a sojourn of unknown length in Auzon, France, where it was discovered in the nineteenth century.[16] Since we do not know where in England it was made, we do not know how far from its point of origin its current resting place, the British Museum, is. However, one panel from the English Franks Casket has been de-

---

[10] Derek Krueger, "The Religion of Relics in Late Antiquity and Byzantium," in *Treasures of Heaven: Saints, Relics, and Devotion in Medieval Europe*, ed. Martina Bagnoli, Holger A. Klein, C. Griffith Mann, and James Robinson (Baltimore: The Walters Art Museum, 2010), 11.

[11] Jeffrey Jerome Cohen, "Pilgrimages, Travel Writing, and the Medieval Exotic," *The Oxford Handbook of Medieval Literature in English*, ed. Elaine Treharne and Greg Walker, with William Green (Oxford: Oxford University Press, 2010), 613.

[12] Jaś Elsner and Joan-Pau Rubiés, "Introduction," in *Voyages and Visions: Towards a Cultural History of Travel*, ed. iidem (London: Reaktion Books, 1999), 17–18.

[13] Brouria Bitton-Ashkelony, *Encountering the Sacred: The Debate on Christian Pilgrimage in Late Antiquity, Transformation of the Classical Heritage* (Berkeley: University of California Press, 2005), 200.

[14] Peter Brown, *The Rise of Western Christendom: Triumph and Diversity, A.D. 200–1000*, revised edition (Chichester: John Wiley and Sons, 2013), 164.

[15] Thomas de Wesselow, "Locating the Hereford Mappamundi," *Imago Mundi* 65/2 (June 2013): 180–206, 184, concludes that "a variety of evidence proves that the map triptych was made sometime around 1300." Marcia Kupfer, *Art and Optics in the Hereford Map* (New Haven: Yale University Press, 2016), 1, also places it "c. 1300."

[16] Arthur S. Napier, *The Franks Casket* (Oxford: H. Hart, Printer to the University, 1900), 3.

tached since the time of its sale "presumably in the first half of the [nineteenth] century" to "a Professor Mathieu of Clermont Ferrand, in Auvergne, who in vain offered a reward for the missing end, which had quite disappeared."[17] In order to see this "missing end," missing no longer, we must – "must" – head to Florence, as it is now housed in the Museo Nazionale del Bargello (fig. 3). Things do not generally stay where they were made over the span of several hundred years and more. Even buildings sometimes wander. I can visit the twelfth-century chapter house of the Cistercian monastery of Santa Maria de Ovila, built in Trillo, Guadalajara, Spain, just by driving ten miles up the road from Chico, California to the Abbey of New Clairvaux in the tiny town of Vina. Their Spanish-style wines are a nice compliment to the strangely displaced architecture, intended as one of William Randolph Hearst's medievalist fantasies, but abandoned in the Depression. It might have become an indoor swimming pool for Hearst's mother, but instead has become reincorporated into a monastery.[18]

Fig. 3: Right panel, Franks Casket. Florence, Museo Nazionale del Bargello. England, eighth century. Photo: Asa Simon Mittman

These are my travels, but what do they have in common with those of medieval pilgrims? There are objects at the core of both, but this is a thin thread of connectivity. What were they after, all of these pilgrims traveling to these relics, be they in Bethlehem or Bristol, Cavalry or Canterbury? Some sought travel and pleasure, of course, but a great many sought healing, contact with the *divine*, and experiences that were otherworldly. From the earliest pilgrims, such as Paula, an early Christian disciple of Saint Jerome, to Margery Kempe in the fifteenth century, pilgrims claim to have not only visited places in the present, but to have witnessed events in the past, as if there and *then*. At Bethlehem, Paula claimed

[17] Napier, *Franks Casket*, 3.

[18] "Abbey of New Clairvaux: The long, arduous journey of the stones of the Abbey of New Clairvaux," *Atlas Obscura* (no date) <http://www.atlasobscura.com/places/abbey-of-new-clairvaux> (accessed October 2018).

> that she could behold with the eyes of faith the infant Lord wrapped in swaddling clothes and crying in the manger, the wise men worshipping Him, the star shining overhead, the virgin mother, the attentive foster-father, the shepherds coming by night to see the word that had come to pass.[19]

Similarly, Margery Kempe said that "*sche saw Seynt Anne gret wyth chylde*," that she

> *wept and sobbyd so plentyuowsly as thow sche had seyn owyr Lord wyth hir bodyly ey sufferyng hys Passyon at that tyme. Befor hir in hyr sowle sche saw hym veryly be contemplacyon, and that cawsyd hir to have compassyon. And whan thei cam up onto the Mownt of Calvarye … in the cite of hir sowle sche saw veryly and freschly how owyr Lord was crucifyed. Beforn hir face sche herd and saw in hir gostly sygth the mornyng of owyr Lady, of Sen John and Mary Mawdelyn, and of many other that lovyd owyr Lord.*[20]

These medieval pilgrims *see* the divine events of salvation history unfolding before their eyes, because of their proximity to the sites and objects connected therewith. I, on the other hand, do not seek divine visions, healing, or other otherworldly phenomena. I seek knowledge, understanding, contact with the *human*, and experiences *terrestrial* rather than extra-terrestrial. And while I enjoy the sexualized vocabulary of fleshly contact with manuscripts, I reject sloppy pseudo-mystical terminology to describe the experience of contacting medieval works of art. They are fascinating, charged objects, which build up their potential over the centuries, but they are *human* artifacts, not meteors that fell from heaven.

I have been on a few pseudo-pilgrimages, long treks to bring me into physical proximity to relics and "relics," to bits of human bone and blood relinquished by saints, and to bits of animal bone and skin relinquished by or ripped from beasts before being wrought by human hands, and then cast into deep history, enduring the same vicissitudes of chance that have taken so many of their similars and simulacra from us. As Dario Gamboni, reminds us regarding *all* artefacts, "it is their normal fate to disappear."[21] This is particularly true of early medieval work. Anglo-Saxonists have dwelled on this sorrowful fact at length, so much so that comments on loss are something of a trope with which surveys on the period tend to begin.[22] C. R. Dodwell provides a list of many forces that destroy art, medieval and modern: grave robbers, fire, reconstruction of churches, reclaiming of precious metals

[19] Jerome, *Letters* 108.10, translated by W. H. Fremantle et al., *Nicene and Post-Nicene Fathers,* second series, vol. 6 (Buffalo: Christian Literature Publishing Co., 1893).

[20] Lynn Staley, ed., *The Book of Margery Kempe* (Kalamazoo: Medieval Institute Publications, 1996), lines 406, 1568–77, available online at *The Book of Margery Kempe* (no date) http://d.lib.rochester.edu/teams/publication/staley-the-book-of-margery-kempe (accessed October 2018).

[21] Dario Gamboni, *The Destruction of Art: Iconoclasm and Vandalism since the French Revolution* (New Haven: Yale University Press, 1997), 25.

[22] See Asa Simon Mittman and Susan M. Kim, *Inconceivable Beasts: The* Wonders of the East *in the* Beowulf *Manuscript* (Tempe: ACMRS, 2013), 229–31.

and gems, tithings, raiders, and on.[23] Some losses were rooted in altruism and self-preservation, as when St. Æthelwold and others "all sold off treasures to pay for food for themselves and others during various famines."[24] These losses are profoundly distorting. Leslie Webster notes "the very obvious fact that what survives today represents but a tiny fraction of the rich art treasures that once filled the halls and courts, churches and monasteries."[25] These poor rates of survival "give a totally inadequate picture of the splendours and grandeur" of some Anglo-Saxon arts, most particularly gold work, textiles, and wall painting.[26] In a sense, then, all works from the period are precious relics, odd, chance survivals that dodged the many forces that claimed the majority of contemporary creations. Each object that slipped through – by dint of centuries of protective care, or by complete accident – is a wonder, a marvel, a treasure, a time capsule, a time machine.

Fig. 4: Reliquary bust of Saint Balbina. New York, The Metropolitan Museum of Art, South Netherlandish, possibly Brussels, Belgium, ca. 1520–30. Digital image courtesy of Open Access for Scholarly Content, New York, The Metropolitan Museum of Art, www.metmuseum.org

[23] C. R. Dodwell, "Art Survivals and Written Sources," in *Anglo-Saxon Art: A New Perspective* (Ithaca: Cornell University Press, 1982), 1–23.

[24] Dodwell, "Art Survivals," 12.

[25] Leslie Webster, *Anglo-Saxon Art* (Ithaca: Cornell University Press, 2012), 9. It is worth mention that David Wilson argued against this trend, particularly referencing Dodwell. Wilson argues that there are enough survivals for "a true sequence of Anglo-Saxon art [that] can, despite all the losses, be built up on the evidence of what survives."

[26] Dodwell, "Art Survivals," 12.

I have laid my hands on a few purported *actual* relics: The skull of St. Balbina, a virgin martyr, enshrined in an ornate, naturalistic reliquary bust in Belgium, c. 1520, and now housed in The Cloisters Museum in New York City (fig. 4); the blood of Christ, or, at least, a rock crystal vial containing his blood (fig. 5); or a glass cylinder surrounding the rock crystal containing his blood; or someone's blood; or something's; or something. These contacts were perhaps disrespectful, since I did not approach them with anything like devotion. I have seen people genuflect before them. I have seen them cry. But I did not, would not. Rather, I unintentionally played into the medieval trope of the doubting Jew who mocks the power of relics and the credulousness of those who seek them out, until the moment in the tale where I should be miraculously affected, but at each contact, I am neither punished nor healed. My experience runs counter, for example, to the familiar apocryphal story of a Jewish attack on [Mary's] funeral procession

> […] a Jewish leader assaults Mary's bier […] but his hands become stuck so that he cannot remove them, his arms palsy and wither, he feels agonizing pain, and every Jew in the mob that accompanies him is immediately struck blind.[27]

Fig. 5: Relic of the Holy Blood, Basilica of the Holy Blood, Bruges, Belgium, 1388. Photo: Ayack. Image courtesy of Creative Commons Attribution-Share Alike 3.0 Unported

Numerous images of this narrative survive, such as a bas-de-page in the fourteenth-century Taymouth Hours (London, British Library, MS Yates Thompson 13, folio 133v) (fig. 6). Here, the Jew – small, stunted, in full profile to show off his bulbous nose – is suspended from the purple cloth draped over Mary's bier. She is hidden from view, but the power of her relics is witnessed by the pain suffered by

[27] Adrienne Williams Boyarin, *Miracles of the Virgin in Medieval England: Law and Jewishness in Marian Legends* (Cambridge: D. S. Brewer, 2010), 85.

the Jewish man who seems barely noticed by the apostles who hold her, and therefore him, aloft.

The *Golden Legend* contains a pointed version of this tale, centered on a figure known only as "the prince of the priests," who assaults the Virgin Mary's funeral bier:

> *Tunc ad arma concurrunt et sc mutuo hortabantur dicentes: venite, omnes discipulos occidamus ac corpus illud, quod seductorem illum portavit, ignibus comburamus. Princeps autem sacerdotum hoc videns obstupuit et ira repletus ait: ecce tabernaculum illius, qui nos et genus nostrum conturbavit, qualem gloriam nunc accipit. Et hoc dicens inanus ad lectum misit volens illud evertere et ad terrain deducere. Tunc manus cjus subito ambae aruerunt et lectulo adhaeserunt, ita ut ad lectulum, manibus penderet et nimio cruciatu vexatus lamentabiliter ejularet, reliquus autem populus ab angelis, qui crant in nubibus, caecitate percussus est.*[28]

Fig. 6: Bas-de-page scene of the Funeral Procession for the Virgin, Taymouth Hours. London, British Library Yates Thompson MS 13 f. 133v, England (London?), 1325–1350. Image courtesy of Creative Commons Public Domain Mark 1.0

---

[28] Jacobi de Voragine, *Legenda Aurea, Vulgo Historia Lombardica Dicta*, ed. Johann Georg Theodor Grässe (Leipzig: Libraria Arnoldiana, 1850), 508.

> Then all ran to arms, and urged one another, saying: 'Come, let's kill all the disciples, and with fire burn the body that bore the deceiver.' Astonished and filled with wrath, the prince of the priests, seeing this, was struck with wonder at the sight, and filled with rage, and he said: 'Behold the tabernacle of that one, who has thrown us and our people into confusion, and what glory it now receives!' Saying this, he reached out to the bed, saying he wanted to overthrow it and bring it to the ground. Suddenly, his hands withered, and both adhered to the bed, so that he hung from it by the hands, and, under great torture, wailed and lamented. The rest of the people were struck with blindness by the angels who were in the clouds.

Following the trope of the Jewish witness, he will eventually repent and convert and be healed. Of course. Unlike this fictional medieval Jewish figure, I bring no animosity to the relics I have touched; unlike the many medieval Christians – fictional and historical – who touched relics, I bring them no devotion. None of the medieval narratives remotely approximate my experience with them. My vision remains as impaired as ever, my neck as stiff, my teeth as brittle, but my hands also remain, at least for now, as free.

I have also traveled long distances to touch so-called "relics" of the Middle Ages, art objects that come down to us from the period. The Great Google tells me that it is over five thousand miles from Chico, California, where I live, to London, England, where I conduct much of my research: The Old English Illustrated Hexateuch (London, British Library, Cotton MS Claudius B.iv); the *Beowulf* Manuscript (British Library, Cotton MS Vitellius A.xv); maps by Matthew Paris (British Library, Royal MS 14 C.vii), and so on; more recently, the astonishing Franks Casket, down the road in the British Museum. My contact with Christian bodily relics amused me. My contact with some of these icons of medieval art history has made me tremble and sweat. I had trouble breathing when a curator at the British Library handed me the *Beowulf* Manuscript. Why? I did not experience anything like this when I touched facsimiles of it, or when I looked at images on-screen, or even when I stared through the Plexiglas vitrine, smudging its surface as I banged my forehead in my attempt to get *closer*. I am neither medieval pilgrim nor modern tourist. When I travel to the British Library or Parker Library, much as I generally enjoy the experience, I am a professional practicing my craft. The tax write-off is not a scam; this *is* my job.

Contact

So: several pages in, and I have covered what contact with medieval objects is *not*: Not sex; not religion. What is our experience with these objects, then? How else could we describe this? Many have turned to phenomenology, since as James Elkins notes, it "is not only the best available account of sense-transcriptions, it is effectively the only one."[29] But, Elkins continues, Maurice Merleau-Ponty, the foundational figure in the field, "does not provide the vocabulary to describe individual artworks," and so "talk about materiality in art history and theory is effectively detached from the sources on which it depends."[30] Others have employed the hard sciences to see what they can yield. For example, how rough *is* a piece of parchment? As Angela Bennett writes, "I want to know if we can *quantify* the different *feels* of the various textures on parchment surfaces."[31] Bombard the surface with laser beams and measure the backscatter, and one can quantify just how rough that parchment is, but this is, in a sense, less information than we get rubbing our fingers over the surface. It *is* good to be able to say more than "pretty smooth," and "kinda rough," and such data might allow us to answer questions of provenance and production, but the data does not get at the *human* experience. Using a microscope and spectrograph photon detector, and feeding the input through data collection software is an indirect method to experience the texture of vellum. This produces black and white images that do not look anything like the surfaces of manuscripts (fig. 7). They are abstractions.

Fig. 7: Algorithmically reconstructed surface imaging produced with Princeton instruments IsoPlane Spectrograph, corrected for astigmatism. Image courtesy of Angela Bennett and Jason P. McClure

[29] James Elkins, "On Some Limits of Materiality in Art History," *31: Das Magazin des Instituts für Theorie* 12 (2008): 25–30. Slightly edited and hosted on *Academia* (December 24, 2008): https: //www.academia.edu/168260/On_Some_Limits_of_Materiality_in_Art_History (accessed October 2018).

[30] Elkins, "On Some Limits of Materiality in Art History," 3, 7.

[31] Angela R. Bennett, "Making Parchment: Material Data and Agential Cuts," in *A Material Piers Living in a Digital World* (June 21, 2014) <https://materialpiers.wordpress.com/2014/06/21/ making-parchment-material-data-and-agential-cuts/> (accessed October 2018).

Similarly, Catherine Karkov and I are in the process of organizing a team of humanists and scientists to re-examine the Franks Casket. It has not had much careful scientific analysis since a Professor E. Ray Lankester "took a small fragment of the casket bone with him for microscopical examination," with the help of a Dr. Ridewood and Prof. Charles Stewart, who compared the fragment to samples of bone from the Museum of the Royal College of Surgeons.[32] They did this in time to receive mention in a footnote in Arthur Napier's publication on the Casket from 1900. We are now, 118 years later, hoping to raise funds to have the Casket tested using the latest in proteomics by York's *ZooArchaeology by Mass Spectrometry* team. We might soon know more about the bone than Lankester, who was "*certain* that the bone of the casket is the bone of a whale, but [I] cannot say of what species or what size."[33] If collagen survives in the bone fragments, we may learn the species of whale (a beached sperm whale is the current thinking, which is, of course, the best possible answer), and possibly if all the panels actually come from a single whale, as the runic text on the front of the casket suggests (reading "hronæsban," whalebone), or if they are from multiple whales, if, like Bennett's manuscript, we have "a multiplicity of bodies reaching out" to us as we reach out to it. I am hoping that this knowledge will impact my experience of the object, and I will only know if and how it will do so once the scientific research has been funded and conducted.

Thing Theory and Object Oriented Ontology are now giving art historians a new set of terms that seem to be proving powerful. These approaches encourage longer, slower looking and more focused analysis of the materials out of which objects are wrought. Medieval artisans were cognizant of the practical strengths and limitations of different materials, and medieval writers attributed quasi-magical properties to many. Being attentive to the specifics of the materials is therefore not anachronistic, even if it tends now to be more firmly rooted in Bruno Latour, Jane Bennett, Ian Bogost, and Bill Brown than in medieval lapidaries and Aldhelm's *Ænigmata*.[34] One of the strengths of Thing Theory is that it takes seriously the activity and agency of objects without recourse to mysticism or magic. Objects do have their own activities and affect changes on their human interactants.

---

[32] Napier, *Franks Casket,* 6, n. 1.

[33] Napier, *Franks Casket,* 6, n. 1.

[34] For a discussion of the dynamics of medieval and postmodern approaches to medieval art, see Benjamin C. Tilghman, "On the Enigmatic Nature of Things in Anglo-Saxon Art," *Different Visions: A Journal of New Perspectives on Medieval Art* 4 (January 2014): 1–43. See also Bruno Latour, *Reassembling the Social: An Introduction to Actor-Network-Theory* (Oxford: Oxford University Press, 2005); Jane Bennett, *Vibrant Matter: A Political Ecology of Things* (Durham: Duke University Press, 2010); Ian Bogost, *Alien Phenomenology, or, What It's Like to Be a Thing* (Minneapolis: University of Minnesota Press, 2012); Bill Brown, "Thing Theory," *Critical Inquiry* 28:1 (2001): 1–22; and *The Social Life of Things: Commodities in Cultural Perspective*, ed. Arjun Appadurai (Cambridge: Cambridge University Press, 1986).

Objects slowly (or quickly) transform on their own, without our help. They rust and tarnish and rot and crumble, they fade and fray. These all might seem to be degradations, but only if we insist on stasis. The beach erodes, as we see it, but that sand is merely moving somewhere less convenient for tourists, home owners, and piping plovers. Its new location is likely no less amenable to the quartz, basalt, and mica, coral and shell fragments, and other bits of debris that comprise it, nor to other organisms living where it comes to rest.

Art, too, like all objects, changes over time, and has differing impacts on us as it does so. Even gold, precious precisely because of its resistance to change over time, *does* alter over the course of centuries. The Crowland Psalter (Oxford, Bodleian Library, MS Douce 296) is famous for its calendar crammed full of Anglo-Saxon saints – Augustine of Canterbury, Æðeldreda, Cuthbert, Dunstan, Guthlac, and others all make an appearance.[35] Its illuminations contain gold that surely has impurities. It has become coarse, flaky, almost bubbly. Turning the pages causes the gold to spark and catch fire (fig. 8). It is variegated and beautiful, striking in a way that better preserved gold accents rarely are. The gold is flaking off in places, but rich and warm in tone, even reddish. A note on the flyleaf claims that the gold is tarnished. Of course, *pure* gold does not tarnish, but truly pure gold is a rarity, and thankfully so, as it is mixings and minglings and blendings that make for much of the interest in the world. I suspect others would also find beauty in this curious form of decay; the Anglo-Saxons by and for whom this manuscript was made prized a particular variety of beauty described by the Old English *fah*, "meaning hostile or guilty but also beautiful or decorated in variegated colouring [...] both beautiful and deadly."[36]

This is, in principle, always at the root of the beauty of gold, which refuses to be a single colour or shade but instead must always reflect and refract the colours and lights around it. It is most effective not only in person, but also in motion, as I gently turn the stiff vellum of this folio that holds its form like a sheet of cardboard, but for the flex about an inch from the gutter, where it buckles. Turning the folio reveals a wide variety of tones within the gold – reds, silvery sections, straight golds. First, the left bow of the "O" catches the light, which courses along its double-curves. Then the warrior's helmet and shield ignite, and then, along with the right bow of the letter, each golden dot on the dragon's back scintillates in se-

[35] Oxford, Bodleian Library, MS Douce 296. Elżbieta Temple, *A Survey of Manuscripts Illuminated in the British Isles: Anglo-Saxon Manuscripts 900–1600* (London: Harvey Miller, 1976), 96, no. 79, dates this manuscript to the second quarter of the eleventh century, possibly from Crowland. Helmut Gneuss, *Handlist of Anglo-Saxon Manuscripts: A List of Manuscripts and Manuscript Fragments Written or Owned in England up to 1100* (Tempe: Arizona Center for Medieval and Renaissance Studies, 2001), 98, no. 617, agrees.

[36] Catherine E. Karkov, *Text and Picture in Anglo-Saxon England: Narrative Strategies in the Junius 11 Manuscript* (Cambridge: Cambridge University Press, 2001), 75–76. For more on Anglo-Saxon goldwork and *fah*, see Asa Simon Mittman and Patricia MacCormack, "Rebuilding the Fabulated Bodies of the Hoard-Warriors," *postmedieval* 7:3 (2016): 356–68.

quence. Then, my attention is snapped back to the text as the light jumps to the text of the opening verse of this psalm: "Quid gloriaris in militia: qui potens es iniquitate?" ["Who are you, who finds glory in wickedness, whose power is in iniquity?"].

Fig. 8: Warrior and Dragon, Crowland Psalter. Oxford, Bodleian Library, MS Douce 296, England, 1025–1036. Photo: Asa Simon Mittman

Who is this little dragon-fighter? Elżbieta Temple has tentatively identified the man as St. Michael, but this is untenable.[37] He is too human in his little peaked helmet and stockinged legs, too vulnerable without any armour (unless his technicolor tunic is meant to represent mail) and, of course, he is rather wingless for the mightiest of the archangels. But more importantly, he is too dynamic, too active to be a miraculous defeater of evil. He strikes me as entirely human, as human as I am while holding this book. On the recto of this folio, an impressive, massive figure of Christ effortlessly tramples a small lion and dragon. Turning the leaf over, we find a much smaller man and a larger dragon. While our erstwhile hero battles the obvious danger below him, another beast lurks, unobserved, leering at him from above. Christ stands with both feet firmly planted on the beasts; the little warrior carefully avoids stepping on the fearsome dragon. The text of Psalm 90 does not read "Christus conculcabit" ["Christ will trample"], but rather, "conculcabis leonem et draconem," that is, "*you* will trample underfoot the lion and the dragon." Read in sequence, as they are placed in the manuscript, these two images yield new meaning. The first image shows us the divine power of Christ to overcome all dangers. The second exhorts us to face our own dragons, even though we are but small and weak in comparison with Christ. In this manner, we are exhorted to join

[37] Temple, *Anglo-Saxon Manuscripts*, 96.

Christ in the battle, to stand by "Crist ðu goda hyrde" ["Christ, you good shepherd"] as Wiglaf stands by Beowulf, the *folces hyrde* ["shepherd of the people"], when he faces the dragon by which he is ultimately overcome.[38]

If he is not Saint Michael, just who is this little warrior, steadfastly facing down the dragon? Is he a figure out of Anglo-Saxon history or myth? Is this the great, unique, unidentified image of Beowulf, himself? He is well-armed, with a round shield and a long sword, as well as an elaborate, wonderfully stylized mail coat. His oversized sword might recall Beowulf's "sweord . . . gomele lafe, ecgum unslaw," ["sword . . . the ancient, sharp-edged relic"].[39] His armour might also recall the *brunfagne helm* ["burnished helmet"] and *hringde byrnan* ["mailcoat fourmed of rings"] worn by Wiglaf when he rushes to his lord's side and joins the battle against the "hringbogan heorte gefysed sæcce to seceanne," ["the coiled serpent, its heart incited to seek battle"].[40] And yet, just as he seems too modest in scale and in confidence to be Michael, so too, he can hardly be the bragging warrior Beowulf. Might the warrior be a rare early depiction of the saintly dragon slayer, Saint George? This seems unlikely, as George – at least in later images – is usual depicted on horseback, haloed, defeating the dragon with a long spear.[41] Or could this little warrior even be Saint Guthlac, the eighth-century founder of the monastery at Croyland, where this manuscript was likely produced?[42] A warrior and marauder early in his life, Guthlac experienced a divine calling and sought a monastic life. He first joined the monastery of Hrypadum but after two years "þa ongan wilnian westenes" ["at that time he began to wish to enter the desert."][43] The "desert" he desired was a most remote island in the "rugan fennas . . . þe man hateð Cruwland," ["wild fens that men call Crowland"].[44] Once there, *Godes cempa* ["the soldier of God"] began to fortify himself for the struggles ahead:[45]

---

[38] R. Morris, ed., *The Blickling Homilies*, EETS, vol. 73 (London: Oxford University Press, 1967), 191, and R. D. Fulk, Robert Bjork, and John Niles, eds., *Klaeber's Beowulf*, 4th ed. (Toronto: University of Toronto Press, 2008), line 2644. For the full account of the battle with the dragon, see lines 2529–723. J. R. Clark Hall, *A Concise Anglo-Saxon Dictionary* (Toronto: University of Toronto Press, 1996) cites *hyrde* as a variand of *hierde*, which he defines as shepherd and herdsman, and then as guardian, keeper and pastor. Joseph Bosworth and T. Northcote Toller, *An Anglo-Saxon Dictionary, Based on the Manuscript Collections of the Late Joseph Bosworth* (Oxford: The Clarendon press, 1882) treat *hyrde* as a variant of *hirde*, translated as herd, shepherd, pastor, and so on. These terms were used for both military and religious leaders.

[39] *Beowulf*, lines 2562–64.

[40] *Beowulf*, lines 2615 and 2561–62.

[41] Surprisingly, Saint George does not seem to have been a popular subject for illustration in the Anglo-Saxon period. There are no entries for him in Thomas Ohlgren, *Insular and Anglo-Saxon Illuminated Manuscripts: An Iconographic Catalogue, c. A.D. 625 to 1100* (New York: Garland Publishing, 1986). This is, no doubt, a topic worth some consideration.

[42] Temple, *Anglo-Saxon Manuscripts*, 96.

[43] Felix, *The Anglo-Saxon Version of the Life of Saint Guthlac, Hermit of Crowland*, ed. and trans. Charles Wycliffe Goodwin (London: John Russell Smith, 1848), 18.

[44] Ibid., 20 and 22.

[45] Ibid., 24.

> *Ða sona wið þam scotungum þara werigra gasta þæt he hine mid gastlicum wæpnum gescylde, he nam þone scykd þæs Halgan Gastes geleafan; and hyne on þære byrnan gegearowode þæs heofonlican hihtes; and he him dyde heolm on heafod clænera geþanca; and mid þam strælum þæs halgan sealmsanges a singallice wið þam awerigedum gastum sceotidoe and campode.*[46]
>
> Then, immediately against those missiles of those cursed spirits, that he might shield himself with spiritual weapons, he took up faith in the Holy Ghost as a shield; and he equipped himself with the armour of heavenly exultation; and he took as his helmet on his head chaste thoughts; and with the arrows of holy psalm-singing, he fought always continually against the attacks of accursed spirits.

The Croyland warrior, with his shield and helmet, reminds the reader that the surest weapon with which to assail the accursed spirits of the devil is the Psalter, the very text he helps to form. The layout of this folio reinforces my reading of the man as a stand-in for the *Godes cempa*. This initial actually accompanies Psalm 51, which begins:

> *Quid gloriaris in malitia qui potens es in iniquitate? Tota die iniustitiam cogitavit lingua tua sicut novacula acuta fecisti dolum.*
>
> Who are you, who finds glory in wickedness, whose power is in iniquity? All day, thinking about injustice, you have done treachery with your tongue, sharp as a whetted razor.

This text snakes its way around the initial, which divides a few words from one another. However, the initial also cuts one word in two: *iniquitate*. The dragon's body is inserted within the Latin word for iniquity, for sin. This small helmed, armed warrior is not only battling for his life. He is also battling for his soul, striving to conquer the dragon of sin. And, sitting in my hand, I am personally exhorted to do the same. The workings of this image are intimate, and rely on turning the page by hand, being guided by the light's movement over the pitted, variegated surface of the gold, and connecting with the small warrior on a personal and individual level.

This is what I am after each time I hop a plane to Europe, as I did to reach Salzburg, Austria, for the meeting on which this volume is based. I am angling for an experience, to learn the things I cannot know any way other than through physical proximity and contact, to *know* the works – not in a biblical or spiritual sense – but in the personal sense, so that when I see them again, years later, trapped behind Plexiglas, I'll be able to say, "I *know* you!" When I write applications to see those most select of objects, the ones that require special application and long negotiation – *Beowulf*, the Franks Casket, and so on – I list all of the tiny details I

[46] Ibid., 24.

know I need to consult: the sequence of production, revealed in the layering of inks and paints; the nature of stray dots on illuminations, as they appear in reproductions; the subtle differences in colours from folio to folio; and so on. All of these are absolutely true. The first draft of the letter Susan Kim and I wrote to the British Library to request access to the *Beowulf* Manuscript was nearly as long as the first draft of this essay, and quite precise; ultimately, though, what we needed was to know what we did not know, to experience what we could not in any reproduction, to learn in the most fundamental and unsurpassable way, through personal contact. And yes, we came away having answered most of our detailed questions, for instance: "What is the dark crescent directly above the figure's right hand?"; "Is there any demarcation of a boundary at the top of what would be a skirt/kilt, or not?"; "Are the genitals highlighted with any colouration?"; "Is the darker tone a ground beneath the colour?" (Answers: a bit of debris; no; no; and no.) (fig. 9). But more importantly, we left the library with our understanding of the manuscript fundamentally transformed in ways that we could never have anticipated. The *Beowulf* Manuscript is, I was rather shocked to discover, *beautiful*, grand, powerful, and impressive, all in ways I had misunderstood, and in ways that all then-published scholarship on the manuscript (largely based on poor reproductions) had profoundly underestimated. The manuscript is a wholly different sort of thing than we had all been saying it was, and it was holding it that taught me this.

My favourite of medieval texts is located in this very manuscript – the odd, laconic Anglo-Saxon *Wonders of the East*. This peculiar text fights against my desire for contact with the Middle Ages and its surviving representatives. A few of the wonders (barely) contained by the text and images defy even *narrative* contact. On the second folio of the *Beowulf* Manuscript's version of the *Wonders*, we confront the Burning Hens (see fig. 9). This is a text containing giant, fire-breathing, anthropophagic, dog-headed people and hundred-and-fifty-foot dragons, so a pair of chickens seems pretty innocuous at first glance:

> *Sum stow is mon fereð to þære readan sæ seo is haten lentibelsinea þæm beoð henna acenned onlice þonne þe mid us beoð reades heowes . gif hi hwylc man niman wile oþþe him o æthrineð* þonne forbærnað hy sona eal his lic[.] *þ[æ]t syndon ungefrægelicu liblac.*[47]

> There is a certain place, as one travels towards the Red Sea, which is called Lentibelsinea, where hens like our own red hens are born. If any person wishes to take hold of them or ever touches them, *they at once burn up all of his body*. Those are inconceivable witchcrafts.[48]

[47] Mittman and, *Inconceivable Beasts,* 41, emphasis added.

[48] Ibid., 58, emphasis added.

Fig. 9: Burning Hens; Inconceivable Beasts, *The Wonders of the East,* The *Beowulf* Manuscript. London, British Library, Cotton MS Vitellius A.xv, f. 2r [99r]. Image courtesy of Creative Commons Public Domain Mark 1.0

The Burning Hens are said to live at an impossible remove from their Anglo-Saxon audience, at the far end of the inhabitable world, but even were they around the corner, contact would be impossible, or, at any rate, fatal, and so knowledge transmitted by that contact could never be acted upon.

This short passage is something of a metonym for the basic ontological enterprise: try to know what something is, reach out for it, achieve the most fleeting of contact, and be changed beyond recognition, perhaps even be obliterated by this experience. In the closely related passage from the *Wonders* that follows the Burning Hens, the two-headed, eight-footed "inconceivable beasts" press the incendiary nature of the contact between humans and wonders further:

> *Eac þonne þær beoð wildeor acenned. Þa deor þonne hy mannes stefne gehyrað þonne eoð hy feor þa deor habbað eahta fet. wælcyrian eagan . twa heafdu gif him hwylc mon onfon wille þonne hiera lichoman þæt hy onælað þæt syndon þa ungefrælicu deor.*[49]

> Wild beasts are also born there. When they hear the voice of a person, the beasts flee far. Those beasts have eight feet and the eyes of Valkyries and two heads. If any person wishes to seize them, they set fire to their bodies. They are inconceivable beasts.[50]

The pronouns are slippery, so it is not clear who is burned up. *Whose* bodies? It might be those who wish (*why?*) to seize them, or the beasts themselves (is the conjoined creature already plural, or is the text claiming that there are multiple such beings?). Perhaps it is both. Human and wonder, the text implies, cannot come into contact without producing radical, even deadly, transformations.

I hope I survive all my meetings with medieval objects. What I want as I reach out to touch them is somewhat inconceivable, something akin to the impossible. I can cross vast spaces with relative ease. I traveled some 5,782 miles as the crow flies to get from Chico to Salzburg, which is more than twice the distance Matthew Paris contemplated on his list maps that chart the journey from London to Jerusalem as a series of "journee" increments – that is, the distance that can be traveled in one day. His theoretical journey half-way across the world of which he knew would take at least 46 days.[51] Mine took about 20 hours, door to door. Tiring, yes, but hardly epic. But the journey I might like to make is as impossible as the Anglo-Saxon's voyage to Lentibelsinea, by the Red Sea. My desire is not some tacky Michael Crichton fantasy of academic time travel.[52] For all I know, that will be possible sooner than later, and would almost surely be a horrifying experience. What I want to feel, as I reach out to a medieval work, is not merely the past, but all the intervening moments between the time of the object's genesis and my precisely present moment. Sitting in the stifling, airless back office of the Bargello, holding the detached panel of the Franks Casket, what I wanted was to experience everything from the whale's life, to its beaching on the shore, to the box's moment of manufacture, to its presentation as the gift it likely was, to its long use, reuse, abuse, breaking up for sale, reassembly, presentation, preservation, conservation, curation, and on, right up to the moment that the curator handed it over in a surprisingly casual manner for Susan Kim and my utter ravishment.

In the margins of a manuscript are the traces of the animal from which the folio was made, the parchment maker, scribe, illuminator, binder, patron, readers, book dealers, collectors, librarians, and scholars. And, somehow, absurdly, *me*. This

[49] Mittman and Kim, *Inconceivable Beasts*, 41–42.

[50] Mittman and Kim, *Inconceivable Beasts*, 58–59.

[51] Suzanne Lewis, *The Art of Matthew Paris in the Chronica Majora* (Berkeley: University of California Press, 1987), 342.

[52] Michael Crichton, *Timeline* (New York: Knopf, 1999).

is the "multiplicity of bodies reaching out" that Bennett encountered in her manuscript. The touch I seek is not singular but multiple, not divine but historical, not rooted in "quod autem *relictus* erat," that which was left *behind*, but rather, that which has moved *forward*, that which has survived and endured and which transmits all of its history, in fragmented and fracturing ways, as it reaches out to touch me back.

Gabriela Signori

Ringomania:

Ring Production and Consumption in Late Medieval Konstanz

In *Luxury and Capitalism*, Werner Sombart (1863–1941) put forth the provocative thesis that until the dawn of the modern consumerist society, luxury was the motor of the national economy.[1] For Sombart, luxury pertained to "any expenditure that goes beyond the necessary."[2] Following this idea, one has to know what is necessary in the respective case. A difficult question which is thankfully superfluous when, as in the following, rings, or finger rings, are concerned.[3] Neither nowadays, nor in the Middle Ages were rings items of necessity. It is also unlikely that the production of luxurious items attained an importance akin to the eighteenth century.[4] After all, a workshop is not a manufactory. Nonetheless, the sheer number of late mediaeval goldsmiths' workshops is impressive. They can be found not only in major cities like London, Paris, or Florence,[5] but even in small episcopal cities like Konstanz, which – including children – had a population of a mere 6,000

---

[1] Werner Sombart, *Luxus und Kapitalismus* (Munich and Leipzig: Duncker & Humblot, 1913), since 1967 *Liebe, Luxus und Kapitalismus: Über die Entstehung der modernen Welt aus dem Geist der Verschwendung* (Berlin: Wagenbach, 1967).

[2] Sombart, *Luxus und Kapitalismus*, 71. See Christopher J. Berry, *The Idea of Luxury. A Conceptual and Historical Investigation* (Cambridge: Cambridge University Press, 1994), 3–42.

[3] Heinz Battke, *Die Ringsammlung des Berliner Schlossmuseums. Zugleich eine Kunst- und Kulturgeschichte des Ringes. Mit 134 Abbildungen auf 16 Lichtdrucktafeln* (Berlin: Preiss, 1938); Heinz Battke, *Geschichte des Ringes in Beschreibung und Bildern dargestellt durch die Sammlung Battke mit 205 Abbildungen* (Baden-Baden: Woldemar Klein, 1953); Fritz Falk, *Edelsteinschliff und Fassungsformen im späten Mittelalter und im 16. Jahrhundert. Studien zur Geschichte der Edelsteine und des Schmuckes* (Ulm: Kempter, 1975); John Cherry, "Medieval Rings, 1100–1500," in *Rings Through the Ages*, ed. Anne Ward, John Cherry, Charlotte Gere, and Barbara Cartlidge (New York: Rizzoli, 1981), 51–87; Ronald W. Lightbown, *Medieval European Jewellery with a Catalogue of the Collection in the Victoria & Albert Museum* (London: Victoria & Albert Museum, 1992); Bernhard Prokisch and Thomas Kühtreiber, eds., *Der Schatzfund von Fuchsenhof. The Fuchsenhof Hoard. Poklad Fuchsenhof*, Studien zur Kulturgeschichte von Oberösterreich 15 (Linz and Weitra: Bibliothek der Provinz, 2004).

[4] Maxine Berg, *The Age of Manufactures. Industry, Innovation and Work in Britain 1700–1820* (London: Blackwell, 1985).

[5] Over two-hundred masters worked in London alone by the end of the 15th century. See Stephanie R. Hovland, "Apprenticeship in the Records of the Goldsmiths' Company of London, 1444–1500," *Medieval Prosopography. History and Collective Biography* 22 (2001): 89–114. As early as the end of the 13th century, there were over two-hundred masters in Paris. See Henry Havard, *Histoire de l'orfèvrerie française* (Paris: Ancienne Maison Quantin, 1896), 290.

at the end of the fifteenth century.[6] At times, ten goldsmiths were simultaneously active (table 1),[7] as many as today, when the population has swelled to more than ten times the amount (approximately 80,000 inhabitants).

1. Hermann Brack	1481–88; 1493
2. Bernhard Dietrich	1482–87; 1494; 1497
3. Sigmund Gaishuser	no date
4. Stoffel Goldschmied	no date
5. Hans Schwarz (guild master)	1482; 1486
6. Konrad Schwarz	1482
7. Hans Stos	1479; 1481–84; 1486–87; 1489–92; 1504; 1506
8. Konrad Stos	1493
9. Thomas Unger	no date
* Jakob Erlin	1509
** Hans Rösch (journeyman from Landshut)	1482
*** Ulrich Rad (Feldkirch)	1479; 1488
*** Gabriel Wägrich (Radolfzell)	1479; 1482–83

Table 1: Konstanz goldsmiths working or trading with Stephan Maignow (1479–1501) or settling accounts with his widow (1501–1509)

The situation is similar in Aachen, Augsburg, Cologne, Mainz, Regensburg, Salzburg, Trier or Vienna, all episcopal cities with a significant amount of wealthy secular clerics.[8]

My focus in the following will be on Konstanz, where the currently only known account book of a late medieval goldsmith can be found: the account book of the

6 Bernhard Kirchgässner, *Das Steuerwesen der Reichsstadt Konstanz 1418–1460*, Konstanzer Geschichts- und Rechtsquellen 10 (Konstanz: Thorbecke, 1960), 26.

7 Hans Rott, *Quellen und Forschungen zur südwestdeutschen und schweizerischen Kunstgeschichte im XV. und XVI. Jahrhundert,* vol. I: *Bodenseegebiet/Quellen* (Stuttgart: Strecker & Schroeder, 1933), 118–20.

8 See August Weiss, "Das Handwerk der Goldschmiede in Augsburg bis zum Jahre 1681," Diss. (Zurich, 1897); Hugo Loersch and Marc Rosenberg, "Die Aachener Goldschmiede, ihre Arbeiten und ihre Merkzeichen bis zum 18. Jahrhundert," *Zeitschrift des Aachener Geschichtsvereins* 15 (1893): 63–96; Norbert Lieb, *Jörg Seld. Goldschmied und Bürger von Augsburg. Ein Meisterleben im Abend des Mittelalters* (Munich: Schnell & Steiner, 1947); Sigrid Boesken, *Die Mainzer Goldschmiedezunft. Ihre Meister und deren Werke vom Ende des 15. bis zum ausgehenden 18. Jahrhundert* (Mainz: Stadtbibliothek, 1971); Birgit Wiedl, "Das Goldschmiedehandwerk in der Stadt Salzburg im Spätmittelalter und in der Frühen Neuzeit," *Mitteilungen der Gesellschaft für Salzburger Landeskunde* 135 (1995): 497–604; Peter Germann-Bauer, "Wir Werchgenossen Goltsmid tzu Regenspurg – Goldschmiede und andere metallverarbeitende Handwerke im mittelalterlichen Regensburg," in *Regensburg im Mittelalter,* ed. Martin Angerer, Beiträge zur Stadtgeschichte vom frühen Mittelalter bis zum Beginn der Neuzeit 1 (Regensburg: Universitätsverlag, 1998), 453–68; Anne-Marie Zander, "Die Trierer Goldschmiede vom späten Mittelalter bis zum Beginn des 19. Jahrhunderts," *Trierer Zeitschrift* 62 (1999): 247–313; Carolin Wirtz, "Kulturelle Beziehungen zwischen Köln und Venedig im 15. und 16. Jahrhundert am Beispiel von Goldschmieden," *Geschichte in Köln* 49 (2002): 63–83.

goldsmith Stefan Maignow (d. 1501).[9] Only rarely did Maignow's customers pay in cash; instead, they almost invariably remunerated in installments. This explains the necessity to have an account book. But the account book is not only illuminating with regard to the typical payment modalities of the day; it also allows us to create a customer profile of a late medieval goldsmith.[10] My contribution is split into the following two parts: First, I will introduce the account book and the goldsmith to whom we are obliged for this in many ways unique information. In the second part, I will consider select regular customers, who had in common a penchant for finger rings of the most diverse craftsmanship.

As is the case with most late medieval account books, that of the Konstanz goldsmith Stefan Maignow is a hybrid document. In the last part, the account book is complemented by numerous receipts, payrolls, interest registers, and notes on family history.[11] It consists of an unpaginated register of twenty-three folios ordered by first names, and a business part, consisting of 144, to a greater or lesser extent full, pages of text with entries from 1477 to 1501.[12] In addition, there are scattered supplements from the years 1501 to 1520, exclusively settlements in the name of Stefan Maignow's widow Walpurga, as well as originally loose slips of paper that were glued to the last, blank pages of the volume when it was restored in 2008.[13] These supplements reveal that Walpurga did not continue to conduct her late husband's business after his passing, and merely collected the outstanding sums and settled her own bills. There was no son who might have taken over his father's reins. Of the couple's five children, only his four daughters survived their father.[14] Hans Ulrich, son of Stefan's brother Gorius Maignow (d. 1484), passed away in 1490, two years before the birth of Stefan Maignow's eldest daughter

---

[9] Stadtarchiv Konstanz D I Band 207 = *Das Geschäftsbuch des Konstanzer Goldschmiedes Steffan Maignow*, ed. Gabriela Signori and Marc Müntz, Konstanzer Geschichts- und Rechtsquellen 42 (Ostfildern: Thorbecke, 2012).

[10] Gabriela Signori, "Die Wirtschaftspraktiken eines spätmittelalterlichen Goldschmieds: Stefan Maignow und sein Geschäftsbuch (1477–1501)," *Vierteljahrschrift für Sozial- und Wirtschaftsgeschichte* 99 (2012): 281–99.

[11] On these notes, see Birgit Studt, "Introduction," in *Haus- und Familienbücher in der städtischen Gesellschaft des Spätmittelalters und der Frühen Neuzeit*, ed. Birgit Studt, Städteforschung A/69 (Cologne, Weimar, and Vienna: Böhlau, 2007), ix–xx.

[12] The same division into a register and a business part can be found in the account book of Ulrich Meltinger; see Matthias Steinbrink, *Ulrich Meltinger. Ein Basler Kaufmann am Ende des 15. Jahrhunderts,* Vierteljahrschrift für Sozial- und Wirtschaftsgeschichte, Beihefte 197 (Stuttgart: F. Steiner, 2007), 51–63, as well as in the somewhat younger debt register of the Basel merchant Ludwig Kilchmann, see: *Das Schuldbuch des Basler Kaufmanns Ludwig Kilchmann (gest. 1518)*, ed. Gabriela Signori, Vierteljahrschrift für Sozial- und Wirtschaftsgeschichte, Beihefte 231 (Stuttgart: Steiner, 2014), 29.

[13] *Steffan Maignow*, ed. Signori and Müntz, 93 /fol. 106^r: 1508–1510 and 1512–1513.

[14] *Steffan Maignow*, ed. Signori and Müntz, 108/fol. 139^r.

Elisabeth.[15] And so, with Walpurga's demise, the name "Maignow" forever vanished from the city's fiscal and corporative memory (table 2).

Mathis Maignow, goldsmith & ?

Gorius († 1484) & ?

Hans-Ulrich († 1490) & ?

Stefan († 1501)
& Walpurga Berchtold († 1520),
butcher's daughter from the
neighbourhood

Elisabeth Ursula Dorothea Appolonia
son died before baptism

Table 2: The descendants of Mathis Maignow

His whole life long, Stefan Maignow lived and worked in his father's house, who like both his sons was a goldsmith.[16] The house, called "The Blue Hat," was near the cathedral precinct on the street which the Konstanz tax scribe referred to as being above the fish market.[17] Stefan and his brother Gorius worked together in the first years.[18] In 1470, their joint assets were taxed with a value of 800 Heller pounds, roughly the amount they were bequeathed by their father.[19] Shortly afterwards, the brothers worked independently.[20]

Stefan Maignow's first proper commission dates back to December 1, 1477, the feast of Saint Eligius – a symbolic date, as Eligius was considered the patron saint of goldsmiths across most of Europe (fig. 1 and 2).[21] Only three years later, he had amassed a fortune of 1,500 Heller pounds. In 1490, this had risen to 2,700 Heller pounds, in 1500, a year before Stefan's death, 3,800 Heller pounds. Finally, in 1510, his widow Walpurga had a considerable fortune of 4,524 Heller pounds to her name, which she maintained over the next years.[22] In the course of his twenty-year-long "career" as a goldsmith, Stefan Maignow had become exceptionally wealthy. None of the other goldsmiths in Konstanz at the time was as successful

15 *Steffan Maignow*, ed. Signori and Müntz, 109/fol. 140r.

16 Stefan's father Mathis Maignow is mentioned in the edited tax books since 1425 (*Die Steuerbücher der Stadt Konstanz*, ed. Peter Rüster, Konstanzer Geschichts- und Rechtsquellen 3 (Konstanz: Thorbecke, 1958), vol. 1: *1418–1460*, 47, no. 1268, 79, no. 1235, 113, no. 1270, 143, no. 1169, and 176, no. 1241.

17 *Steffan Maignow*, ed. Signori and Müntz, 108/fol. 138v. See Markus Bauer, *Der Münsterbezirk von Konstanz*, Konstanzer Geschichts- und Rechtsquellen 35 (Sigmaringen: Thorbecke, 1995).

18 *Steuerbücher der Stadt Konstanz*, ed. Rüster, vol. 1, 214, no. 1083.

19 *Die Steuerbücher der Stadt Konstanz*, ed. Peter Rüster, vol. 2: *1470–1530*, Konstanzer Geschichts- und Rechtsquellen 9 (Konstanz: Thorbecke, 1963), 18, no. 989.

20 *Steuerbücher der Stadt Konstanz*, ed. Rüster, vol. 2, 48, nos. 963 and 964.

21 Karin von Etzdorf, "Der heilige Eligius und die Typen seiner Darstellung als Patron der Goldschmiede und Schmiede," Diss. (Munich, 1956). Marion Remnos, "Der heilige Eligius," *Das Münster am Hellweg* 41 (1988): 12–17.

22 *Steuerbücher der Stadt Konstanz*, ed. Rüster, vol. 2, 78, 107, 147.

nor as wealthy. This allowed him to hold political offices towards the end of his life. Repeatedly, he served as guild master between 1495 and 1499 in the "im Thurgau" corporation, the guild of goldsmiths, painters, glass painters, sculptors, and joiners.[23]

Fig. 1: Petrus Christus, A goldsmith, possibly Saint Eligius, in his workshop, oil on oak, 1449. New York, Metropolitan Museum of Art, Robert Lehman Collection, accession number: 1975.1.110

Stefan Maignow's success is largely due to his business practice: He almost exclusively manufactured mass merchandise, instead of liturgical art objects that are time consuming to produce and on which the producers only rarely relied. Other goldsmiths were responsible for such products in Konstanz, namely Bernhard Dietrich, Hans Stos, and Hans Schwarz.[24] Locally, Maignow traded gold and silver on a large scale, as manifested, among other things, in the detailed balance accounts with his colleagues Hermann Brack (1481–1487), Bernhard Dietrich (1482–1487), Sigmund Gaishuser (no dates), Hans Stos (1481–1492), and Hans Schwarz

[23] Konrad Beyerle, *Die Konstanzer Ratslisten des Mittelalters* (Heidelberg: C. Winter, 1898), 189 and 191.

[24] Hans Rott, *Quellen und Forschungen zur südwestdeutschen und schweizerischen Kunstgeschichte im XV. und XVI. Jahrhundert*, vol. 1: *Bodenseegebiet / Text* (Stuttgart: Strecker & Schroeder, 1933), 121–22; *Gold: Schatzkunst zwischen Bodensee und Chur*, ed. Tobias G. Natter (Ostfildern: Hatje Cantz, 2008), 22–33.

(1482; 1486) (table 1).[25] He invested at least part of his wealth in Konstanz's real-estate market, as seen in the interest registers he added to the last pages of the account book.[26] What he did with the remaining money, we do not know.

Fig. 2: Niklaus Manuel (Deutsch), panel of a Saint Anne altarpiece: Saint Eligius in his workshop, mixed technique on spruce, 1515. Kunstmuseum Bern, Burgergemeinde Bern

In line with Werner Sombart, Stefan Maignow's regular and wholesale customers were mainly gentry and landed gentry from the region, above all the Konstanz family of Muntprat as well as the Lords of Landenberg and Randegg, noble houses closely related by marriage to the local gentry of Konstanz.[27] Nobles preferably

[25] The numbers refer to the years in which Stefan Maignow traded with the aforementioned goldsmiths: *Steffan Maignow*, ed. Signori and Müntz, 20–24, 28–31, 36, 49–53/fols 13^{r}–15^{r}, 20^{r}–21^{r}, 27^{r}, 52^{r}–53^{v}.

[26] *Steffan Maignow*, ed. Signori and Müntz, 98/fol. 120^{r}.

[27] *Steffan Maignow*, ed. Signori and Müntz, Landenberg fols 4^{r}, 5^{r}, 7^{v}, 8^{r}, 10^{r}, 23^{v}, 24, 24^{v}, 36^{r}, 42^{v}–44^{r}, 55^{r}, 55^{v}, 88^{r}, 95^{r}, 101^{r}, 102^{r}, 107^{r}, Randegg fols 18^{v}–19^{v}, 20^{v}, 44^{r}, $57a^{v}$, 58^{r}–61^{r}, 62^{r}, 93^{r}–94^{r}, 122^{v}–123^{r}, 124^{r}, 125^{r}, 128^{v}–129^{v}, 142^{r}. On the lords of Landenberg see Julius Studer, *Die Edeln von Landenberg. Geschichte eines Adelsgeschlechts der Ostschweiz* (Zurich: Schulthess, 1904); Emil Stauber, *Geschichte der Herrschaften und der Gemeinde Mammern* (Frauenfeld: Huber, 1934); Christoph Heiermann, *Die Gesellschaft 'zur Katz' in Konstanz. Ein Beitrag zur Geschichte der Geschlechtergesellschaften in Spätmittelalter und früher Neuzeit*, Konstanzer Geschichts- und Rechtsquellen 37 (Stuttgart: Thorbecke 1999), 112–14; on the lords of Randegg see Johann Jakob Rüeger, *Chronik der Stadt und Landschaft Schaffhausen*, vol. II (Schaffhausen: Schoch 1892), 902–15; *Oberbadisches Geschlechterbuch*, ed. Julius Kindler von Knobloch, vol. III (Heidelberg, 1919), 328–29; on the Muntprats see Aloys Schulte, *Ge-*

purchased together with kinship, although this was true more for the payment[28] than for the commissions themselves, as seen among other things in the settlements Kaspar of Randegg entered by his own hand in Maignow's account book in 1486 for himself and his brother Balthasar.[29] This phenomenon can also be observed in other contexts:[30]

> I, Kaspar of Randegg, settled the accounts of myself and my brother Balthasar with Master Stefan Maignow on Monday after St. George's Day [April 24] in the year 1486, and after all calculations, we still owe him eleven Gulden.[31]

In 1496, Kaspar also balanced the accounts of his cousin Burkhard of Randegg,[32] on whose behalf his brother, canon Johannes of Randegg, had already been active in 1484 and 1486.[33] Johannes in turn issued further bills for his cousin Heinrich of Randegg in 1490 and 1492.[34] Burkhard, Heinrich, and Johannes of Randegg were by far the goldsmith's best customers.

Most of the landed gentry who were regular customers with the goldsmith belonged to the socially exclusive "Fish and Falcon" order of chivalry, as evidenced by the countless fish and falcons in gold and silver commissioned with Maignow.[35] The insignia of the society – fish and falcons connected with a sword that was

---

schichte der Großen Ravensburger Handelsgesellschaft (1380–1530), Deutsche Handelsakten des Mittelalters und der Neuzeit 1 (Stuttgart and Berlin: Deutsche Verlagsanstalt, 1923), vol. 1, 189–93; Heiermann, *Die Gesellschaft „zur Katz" in Konstanz*, 252–56.

28 Usually people ordered *en bloque* in the close family circles (siblings, parents and sons or couples), not in broader kin relations.

29 Kaspar (d. 1497) and Balthasar (d. 1494) were sons of Hans of Randegg, see *Oberbadisches Geschlechterbuch*, ed. Julius Kindler von Knobloch, vol. III, 329 (plate III).

30 *Ludwig Kilchmann*, ed. Gabriela Signori, 19.

31 *Steffan Maignow*, ed. Signori and Müntz, 86/fol. 93^r: *Jch, Caspar von Randegg, han gerechnot mit maister Stephan Maynow vff gůttintag nach sant Jergen tag jm lxxxvj jar von min vnd mins brůder Baltasars wegen, vnd blibent jm nach aller rechnung schuldig xj gulden.* See p. 87/fol. 94^r.

32 Burkhard (d. 1499) was the son of Rudolf of Randegg, see *Oberbadisches Geschlechterbuch*, ed. Julius Kindler von Knobloch, p. 328 (plate II), married with Fides, the daughter of Junker Konrad Muntprat. Maignow called Burkhard a junker, he called himself a knight (*Steffan Maignow*, ed. Signori and Müntz, 66/fol. 62^r).

33 *Steffan Maignow*, ed. Signori and Müntz, 62/fol. 59^v, 63/fol. 60^r, 64/fol. 60^v. On the cathedral canon Johannes of Randegg (d. 1513), son of Rudolf of Randegg, cathedral canon of Konstanz, see Jürg Abbühl, "Die Konstanzer Domherren von 1487–1526," Diss. (Zurich, 1987), 162.

34 *Steffan Maignow*, eds. Signori and Müntz, 99/fol. 122^v, 100/fol. 124^r. On Heinrich of Randegg (d. 1506) from Staufen, son of the eponymous father, see *Oberbadisches Geschlechterbuch*, ed. Julius Kindler von Knobloch, 329 (plate II).

35 *Steffan Maignow*, ed. Signori and Müntz, 9/fol. 1^r, 14/fol. 5^r, 17/fol. 8^r, 32f./fol. 23^v, 33/fol. 24^r, 42/fol. 43^r, 50/fol. 52^r, 57/fol. 57^v, 58/fol. 58^r, 60/fol. 58^v, 61/fol. 59^r, 86/fol. 93^r, 88/fol. 95^v, 90/fol. 96^r. See Holger Kruse, Werner Paravicini, and Andreas Ranft, eds., *Ritterorden und Adelsgesellschaften im spätmittelalterlichen Deutschland. Ein systematisches Verzeichnis*, Kieler Werkstücke 1 (Frankfurt am Main et al.: Lang, 1991), 218–21 (list of members, ibid., 427–28); Norbert Honegger, "Die Turniergesellschaft vom Fisch und Falken," *Hegau* 34 (1977): 59–68.

crossed with a sceptre (fig. 3) – were difficult to maintain, a point reflected in the numerous times Maignow had to repair them, among others for Melchior of Landenberg.[36] Although all members of the "Fish and Falcon" society also belonged to the powerful but not exclusive order of the "St. George Shield," only Heinrich of Randegg – not a junker but a knight – ordered signs that designated him a member of that order, in addition to sundry fish and falcons.[37]

The noble*men* were very fond of supplying gold and silver jewellery as befitted their social status. From toothpicks to finger rings with gems, to extremely heavy chains of silver and gold,[38] the men's predilection was shared by their wives, but not with the same (literally) weighty proportions. The noble gentlemen also readily bundled their purchases of finger rings: seven rings for 25 Gulden for Count Ulrich of Monfort, three rings for the same price for Kaspar of Landenberg, five rings for 20 Gulden for Balthasar of Landenberg, five for 33 Gulden for Jakob Nagel of Tettnang, etc.[39] Junker Gallus Muntprat had to dig deepest into his pockets when he bought three rings for 58 Gulden.[40] With a fortune of 13,000 Heller pounds, he could afford it.[41] The account book clearly attests to the fact that in Konstanz and surroundings, jewellery was predominantly but not exclusively a man's preserve.[42]

---

36 *Steffan Maignow*, ed. Signori and Müntz, 32/fol. 23^{v}, 35/fol. 24^{v}. On Melchior of Landenberg, son of Hugo of Landenberg and Adelheid of Enzberg, see Studer, *Die Edeln von Landenberg*, plate V.

37 *Steffan Maignow*, ed. Signori and Müntz, 59/fol. 58^{r}. See Herbert Obenaus, *Recht und Verfassung der Gesellschaften mit St. Jörgenschild in Schwaben. Untersuchungen über Adel, Einung, Schiedsgericht und Fehde im 15. Jahrhundert*, Veröffentlichungen des Max-Planck-Instituts für Geschichte 7 (Göttingen: Vandenhoeck & Ruprecht, 1961), 15, 98, 130, 146, 187, 192, 219.

38 On toothpicks, see Werner Maleczek, "Sachkultur am Hofe Herzog Sigismunds von Tirol," in *Adelige Sachkultur des Spätmittelalters*, Österreichische Akademie der Wissenschaften, Sitzungsberichte phil.-hist. Klasse 400 = Veröffentlichungen des Instituts für mittelalterliche Realienkunde Österreichs 5 (Vienna: Verlag der Österreichischen Akademie der Wissenschaften, 1982), 159.

39 *Steffan Maignow*, ed. Signori and Müntz, 43/fol. 43^{v}, 54/fol. 55^{r}, 78/fol. 84^{r}, 90/fol. 98^{r}.

40 *Steffan Maignow*, ed. Signori and Müntz, 71/fol. 66^{r}. See Heiermann, *Die Gesellschaft „zur Katz" in Konstanz*, 253, no. 199.

41 *Steuerbücher der Stadt Konstanz*, ed. Rüster, vol. 2, 71, no. 591.

42 Research finds other results, which suggest a late Middle Age clothing order and rules of luxury, among others see Hermann Kantorowicz, "De ornatu mulierum. A Consilium of Antonius de Rosellis with an Introduction of Fifteenth-Century Sumptuary Legislation [1933]," in *Rechtshistorische Schriften*, ed. Helmut Coing and Gerhard Immel, Freiburger Rechts- und Staatswissenschaftliche Abhandlungen 30 (Karlsruhe: C. F. Müller, 1970), 341–76; Veronika Baur, *Kleiderordnungen in Bayern vom 14. bis zum 19. Jahrhundert*, Miscellanea bavarica monacensia 62 (Munich: Wölfle, 1975), 39–46; Lightbown, *Medieval European Jewellery*, 79–89; Jane Bridgeman, "Pagare le pompe: Why Quattrocento Sumptuary Laws did not work," in *Women in Italian Renaissance, Culture and Society*, ed. Letizia Panizza (Oxford: European Humanities Research Centre, 2000), 209–26.

Fig. 3: Bernhard Strigel, Hans Caspar von Landenberg, tempera on wood, 1508/09. Karlsruhe, Staatliche Kunsthalle

The orders of noblewomen were usually recorded in the entries of their husbands, in most cases without even naming them.[43] The noblewomen only emerged as independent business partners of the goldsmith when they were widowed, as for example Adelheid of Landenberg, "my Lady" Brisacherin, and her sister, "my Lady" Bessererin of Ravensburg, Barterin of Kattenhorn, and "my Lady" Bruchlin.[44] Adelheid of Landenberg, by birth of Enzberg,[45] mother of Junker Hans, Kaspar, Melchior, and Balthasar of Landenberg, ordered two rings on April 5, 1479 – one with a ruby, the other with a turquoise:

---

[43] On Count Alwig VII. of Sulz (d. 1493), the court judge to Rottweil, see *Beiträge zur Geschichte der Landgrafschaft Klettgau – Grafen von Sulz – Gemeinde Jestetten*, ed. Kurt Hodapp, 2 vols. (Waldshut-Tiengen: [s. n.], 2008), B: *Die Landgrafschaft Klettgau, ihre Inhaber und deren Beziehungen zu Jestetten 1408–1687,* 11.

[44] *Steffan Maignow*, ed. Signori and Müntz, 13/fol. 4^r, 16/fol. 7^r, 30/fol. 20^v, 32/fol. 23^r, 67/fol. 62^v, 67/fol. 63^r.

[45] On Adelheid of Enzberg, see Studer, *Die Edeln von Landenberg*, plate V. On personal naming of noble women see Joseph Morsel, "Personal naming and representation of feminine identity in Franconia in the later Middle Ages," in *Personal Names Studies of Medieval Europe. Social Identity and Familial Structures*, ed. G. T. Beech, M. Bourin, and P. Chareille (Kalamazoo: Western Michigan University, 2002), 157–79.

> I also gave my Lady of Landenberg, by birth of Enzberg, a ring with a ruby for eight Gulden, a small ring with a turquoise, which costs one Gulden, and gave it to her on Monday in the Holy Week of the year 1479 [April 5, 1479].[46]

Maignow's account book normally does not reveal more on the making of the finger rings. Shortly thereafter, Maignow lent Adelheid of Landenberg six Gulden and also sold her a musk-ball,[47] a toothpick, eight rubies, and six pairs of gilded buttons.[48] A sum of more than twenty Gulden thus accrued. Further purchases would follow in the years 1482, 1483, and 1485.[49]

Similarly, the widowed Ursula Munprat, called "Brisacherin," ordered several rings with gems from Maignow in November 1481, in addition to gold necklaces, gold crosses, and an Agnus Dei.[50] Individual pieces of jewellery were as expensive as Adelheid of Landenberg's complete order. Half of Ursula's order consisted of rings with various gems (garnets, balas-rubies, diamonds, and rubies) for a price of one-and-a-half to four Gulden. Some of her entries included several orders from her son. At the time, he was living together with his mother in his father's house, situated in the quarter called "Tümpfel."[51]

> My Lady Brisacherin owes me four Gulden and three Ort for a ring with a ruby; 2 ½ Gulden for a ring with a garnet; 2 ½ Gulden for a ring with a garnet; 5 ½ Shilling dinar for twelve pairs of small rings; five Gulden less half an Ort for a small gold necklace; twelve Shilling dinar for an Agnus Dei pendant; further, Junker Karl owes eighteen Shilling dinar for a small collar ring;[52] I also gave my Lady two gold crosses and a ring with a ruby and diamonds, which cost 21 Gulden together; Further, Junker Karl owes me one pound and seven Shilling dinar for a pipe; 4 ½ Shilling dinar for two pins on a thread; With trust, I lent a ring with a balas-ruby and another ring together

46 *Steffan Maignow*, ed. Signori and Müntz, 13/fol. 4^{r}: *Jtem jch hab gebben miner frowen von Landenberg, geborn von Enczberg, ain ring mit aim robin vm viiij gulden, j ringel mit aim turgusly, kost j gulden, gab jch ir am mentag jn der applas wochen jm lxxix. Mer hab jch gelichen miner frowen vj gulden jn gold. Mer hab jch geben miner frowen ain bisemoͤpfel, kost ij gulden, ain zenstorer, kost iiiij ß d. <Mer han jch glichen miner frowen iij gulden; mer ij gulden.> Mer sol mier min frow j gulden vmm viiij robin. Mer han jch gemacht miner frowen vj par knoͤpf fergult, wegen v quinty etwas mer, kosten j lb d.* The pointed brackets mean "crossed out".

47 Metal balls filled with musk and usually hung on a paternoster, see Ruth-Elisabeth Mohrmann, "Zwischen Amulett und Talisman. Bisamäpfel als Standesabzeichen?" in *Symbole des Alltags – Alltag der Symbole. Festschrift für Harry Kühnel zum 65. Geburtstag*, ed. Gertrud Blaschitz et al. (Graz: Akademische Druck- und Verlagsanstalt, 1992), 497–516.

48 See note 46.

49 *Steffan Maignow*, ed. Signori and Müntz, 14/fol. 4^{r}.

50 Ursula Muntprat, the wife of Marquard Brisacher (d. 1461), see Schulte, *Geschichte der Großen Ravensburger Handelsgesellschaft* I, 154; Heiermann, *Gesellschaft „zur Katz" in Konstanz*, 228, no. 52.

51 *Steuerbücher der Stadt Konstanz*, ed. Rüster, vol. 2: *1470–1530*, 47, no. 857. Mother and son taxed joint movables of 8,412 Pounds Heller.

52 Rings which hold neck scarves (*goller*).

> worth two Gulden and 1 ½ Ort.[53] For these rings I requested two Gulden as salary; a ring with a ruby and a diamond, which costs four Gulden; a chain, which costs 22 Gulden bar 1 ½ Ort; a ring with a ruby and diamonds, costs four Gulden; and I also gave my Lady a cross, which costs eight Gulden; and eight pins, which cost four Shilling dinar.[54]

In 1482, further purchases of rings followed, including an emerald ring and a ring with an amethyst worth six and two Gulden respectively, as well as a musk-ball and five pairs of small rings for a few Shillings.[55]

The by far most prominent customers of the Konstanz goldsmith were the Bishop of Konstanz, Otto of Sonnenberg (d. 1491),[56] Hugo of Landenberg (d. 1530), the future Bishop of Konstanz who at the time was still a provost of the Church of St. Mary in Erfurt,[57] the Dean of the cathedral chapter, Heinrich of Hewen (d. 1505), who would later become the Bishop of Chur.[58] Bishop Otto of Sonnenberg commissioned a seal ring, two gems sealed in gold – a cornelian and a jacinth – six Agnus Dei, four hearts, a gold chain, a cross with jacinths, and four

[53] See *Steffan Maignow*, ed. Signori and Müntz, 59/fol. 58v. This refers to the *annulus fidei*, the proposal ring, see *Schatzfund vom Fuchsenhof*, ed. Prokisch and Kühtreiber, 763. The wedding ring is termed *machelring*, 85/fol. 90v.

[54] *Steffan Maignow*, ed. Signori and Müntz, 67/fol. 63r: *Jtem min frow Brisacharin sol mier iiij gulden iij ort vmm j ring mit aim robin; mer iij gulden vm j ring mit aim granaten; mer iij gulden vmm ain ring mit aim granaten; mer vj ß d vm xij par ringly; mer v gulden minder j ort vmm j guldis kettly; mer xij ß d vm j angnusdey; mer sol juncker Karlo xviij ß d vm goleringly; mer hab jch gebben miner frown zway gulden krûcz, ain ring mit aim robin vnd diemant, kost zûsamen xxj gulden; jtem mer sol juncker Karlo j lb vij ß d by aim ror; mer iiiij ß d vm zwo stefften an ain schnûr; jtem jch han dargelichen ij gulden ij ort zû dem ring mit dem palas vnd zû dem ring mit der trûe* [not readable]*; jtem von forig ringen lon ij gulden; <jtem jch han gen miner frowen j kettly, kost iij gulden>; j ring mit aim robin vnd diemant, kost iiij gulden; <ain krûcz von robin, kost xxiiij gulden>; ain ketten, kost xxij gulden minder ij ort; j ring mit aim robin vnd diemant, kost iiij gulden; mer hab jch miner frowen gebben j krûcz, kost viij gulden; mer viij stefft, kosten iiij ß d.*

[55] *Steffan Maignow*, ed. Signori and Müntz, 68/fol. 63r.

[56] *Steffan Maignow*, ed. Signori and Müntz, 68/fol. 64r. On Otto of Sonnenberg (1474–1491) see Franz Xaver Bischof, Brigitte Degler-Spengler, Helmut Maurer and Rudolf Reinhardt, "Die Bischöfe. Bistum Konstanz," in *Erzbistümer und Bistümer. Das Bistum Konstanz, das Erzbistum Mainz, das Bistum St. Gallen, Erzbistümer und Bistümer*, ed. B. Degler-Spengler, Helvetia Sacra I/2 (Basel and Frankfurt am Main: Helbing & Lichtenhahn, 1993), 366–71.

[57] *Steffan Maignow*, ed. Signori and Müntz, 91/fol. 101r. On Hugo of Hohenlandenberg (1496–1530) see "Die Bischöfe. Bistum Konstanz," in *Erzbistümer und Bistümer* I/2, 376–85; Peter Niederhäuser, "Kleriker, Kirchenfürst und Kunstmäzen – eine Annäherung an Bischof Hugo von Hohenlandenberg," in *Ein feiner Fürst in einer rauen Zeit. Der Konstanzer Bischof Hugo von Hohenlandenberg*, ed. Peter Niederhäuser (Zurich: Chronos, 2011), 17.

[58] *Steffan Maignow*, ed. Signori and Müntz, 84/fol. 90r. On Heinrich of Hewen, later the bishop of Chur (1491–1505), see Otto P. Clavadetscher and Werner Kundert, "Die Bischöfe. Bistum Chur," in *Schweizerische Kardinäle. Das Apostolische Gesandtschaftswesen in der Schweiz. Erzbistümer und Bistümer* I *(Aquileja, Basel, Besançon, Chur)*, ed. Albert Bruckner, Helvetia Sacra I/1 (Bern: Francke, 1972), 492–93.

pearls as well as a ring with diamonds and a ruby.[59] Shortly thereafter, he also ordered a gold ring with diamonds and three rubies worth twenty Gulden.[60] This was one of the most expensive rings Maignow made and sold in his twenty-year long career (table 3). This time, the bishop did not pay with money but with Meersburg wine. Shortly after Otto's death (in 1491), the final statement of accounts with the cathedral chapter reveals that at the time only half of the orders had been paid for.[61]

1–5 Gulden	6–10 Gulden	11–15 Gulden	20 Gulden
99	42	6	1

Table 3: Price range of rings (pieces with prices only)

Purely in terms of quantity, the number of rings made for the Bishop of Konstanz is rather modest compared to the stupendous amount of items ordered over the years by the two cathedral canons Johannes of Randegg (d. 1513) and Heinrich of Montfort (d. 1512) (table 4).

10	Junker Ludwig Eglin of Herten
11	Count Ulrich of Montfort
11	My Lady "Brisacherin"
12	Count Sigmund of Lupfen
12	Junker Kaspar of Randegg
12	Junker Ludwig Haidenhaimer
16	Junker Burckhard of Randegg
24	Count Heinrich of Montfort, Cathedral canon of Konstanz
30	Johann of Randegg, Cathedral canon of Konstanz

Table 4: Regular customers with ten or more ring orders in ascending order

The aforementioned Johannes of Randegg clearly had a particular proclivity for rings. On rings alone, he spent over one hundred Gulden over the years, which would likely have amounted to a substantial portion of his income.[62] The orders are similar throughout the years:

> I gave the [respected] Lord a ring with a ruby, which costs six Gulden, on Saturday after St. Nicholas Day [December 7] 1493, which his servant Melchior took. Moreover, Melchior also took an Agnus Dei for 1 ½ Gulden, on the eve of St Thomas Day [December 20] 1493. I also gave my Lord a small

59 *Steffan Maignow*, ed. Signori and Müntz, 68/fol. 64r. The settling of accounts followed on August 29, 1482, which shows that the bishop owed the goldsmith 28 Gulden, 69.

60 *Steffan Maignow*, ed. Signori and Müntz, 70/fol. 65r.

61 *Steffan Maignow*, ed. Signori and Müntz, 70/fol. 65r.

62 On which we have no information. For comparative numbers, see Sabine Arend, *Zwischen Bischof und Gemeinde. Pfarrbenefizien im Bistum Konstanz vor der Reformation* (Leinfelden-Echterdingen: DRW-Verlag, 2003), 93 and 95. Arend describes prebendary worth 60 to over 100 Gulden as "sizeable."

> ring with an amethyst on Thursday before the Day of Bartholomew the Apostle, [August 21] 1494, for 2 ½ Gulden. He sent that back to me, so I gave him another small ring with diamonds and two rubies, which costs three Gulden. I also gave my Lord a ring with a diamond and a ruby for five Gulden on Tuesday after St Nicholas Day [December 9] 1494.[63]

Like all other clients of the Konstanz goldsmith, Johannes of Randegg preferred diamond rings adorned with rubies (table 5).

40	diamond and ruby
30	diamond
25	ruby
16	sapphire
9	turquoise
7	ruby and turquoise

Table 5: Rings with gems with more than five mentions (167 rings out of a total 286)

As the years passed by, Johannes' rings became increasingly expensive and fancy, but he remained true to his favourite ring type.[64] Among the more exquisite pieces, costing five or more Gulden, several rings are prominent that consisted of a ruby, a sapphire, and a turquoise, as well as two rings with a diamond heart and a diamond spot:[65]

> I gave my Lord a ring with a ruby and turquoise for five Gulden on the day after St. Lawrence Day [*August* 11] in the year 1496; I also gave my Lord an Agnus Dei for 16 Shillings and one for six Shillings on the eve of the Holy Cross Day of Autumn (September 13) 1496; and I gave my Lord a turquoise ring for eight Gulden on the day before Johannes Baptista (June 23) 1497; and I gave my Lord two r ings for eight Gulden, of which he paid me three in cash on the Saturday following St. Joseph's Day (December 16) in 1497. One of the rings has a cameo,[66] the other a sapphire. I also gave my Lord a small ring with a diamond and a ruby for four Gulden on the day after St.

[63] *Steffan Maignow*, ed. Signori and Müntz, 28/fol. 19v: *Mer han jch gebben minem herren j ring mit aim robin, cost vj gulden, am samstag nach sant Niklas tag jm lxxxxiij iar, nam Melcher, sin knecht. Mer hat Melchior von mier tragen ain angnus de, kost ij gulden, an sant Tomas abbent jm lxxxxiij iar. Mer han jch gebben minem heren j ringly mit aim amotist am dunstag vor sant Bartlomes tag jm lxxxxiiij iar, cost iij gulden. Das schickt er mier wider vnd gab jm ain anders mit aim diemant vnd ij robinly, das kost iij gulden. Mer hab jch gebben minem heren ain ring mit aim diemant vnd robin vmm fûnf gulden am zinstag nach sant Niklas tag jm lxxxxiiij.*

[64] *Steffan Maignow*, ed. Signori and Müntz, 107/fol. 129r.

[65] Falk, *Edelsteinschliff und Fassungsform*, 15.

[66] According to the *Oxford English Dictionary*, a cameo is "[a] precious stone having two layers of different colours, in the upper of which a figure is carved in relief, while the lower serves as ground." See *Steffan Maignow*, ed. Signori and Müntz, 97/fol. 113r: *Am næchsten tag nach sant Marx tag jm lxxxxviij iar hab jch gebben juncker Rûland Muntbratten zwen ring, ain mit aim diemant punt vnd vier robin, vnd ain mit aim gamahû, sind zwai angesicht, vm zwainczig drig gulden zechen bechams.* Lightbown, *Medieval European Jewellery*, 23–32.

> Erhard's Day (January 9) in the year 1498; and I gave my Lord a small ring, which costs three Gulden, with a balas-ruby and a sapphire on the Holy Cross Day after Easter (May 3) 1498.[67]

Johannes of Randegg often ordered his rings before Christmas or New Year, which leads to the assumption that some of these pieces may have been intended as presents.[68] Amongst them was also a ring with a rose fashioned out of a ruby, worth four and half Gulden.[69] Other regular customers would increase their orders around Christmas and New Year, as well.[70] But the only item designated explicitly as a gift is the emerald ring the dean of the cathedral chapter, Heinrich of Hewen, bought for his sister-in-law Agnes of Lupfen,[71] as well as various wedding gifts.[72]

In addition to the many rings he purchased, Johannes of Randegg also acquired belt adornments, trims, buttons, coat rings, gold chains, and toothpicks, as well as pendants in the form of an Agnus Dei, hearts, and letters with which clerics and noblewomen decorated their prayer beads.[73] His "consumer behaviour" is almost identical to that of the noblewomen as concerns gold and silver jewellery.

---

[67] *Steffan Maignow*, ed. Signori and Müntz, 105/fol. 128v: *mer han jch gebben minem herren ain ring mit aim robin vnd tûrgus vm v gulden am næchsten tag nach sant Lorenczen tag jm lxxxxvj; mer han jch gebben minem herren ain angnusde vm xvj ß d vnd ains vm vj ß d an des hailgen crûcz abent am herbst lxxxxvj; mer hab jch gebben minem herren ain tûrgus ring vm viij gulden an sant Johans abent babtist jm lxxxxvij iar; mer hab jch gebben minem herren zwen ring vm acht gulden, daran hat er mier gebben drig gulden bar am samstag nach sant Jos tag jm lxxxxvij iar, der j ring hat j gamahû, der ander ain savir; mer hab jch gebben minem heren ain ringly mit aim diemant vnd robin vm iiij gulden am næchsten tag nach sant Erharcz tag jm lxxxxviij; mer han jch gebben minem herren ain ringly, kost iij gulden, palas vnd savir jst darin, an des hailgen crûcz tag nach ostern jm lxxxxviij.*

[68] *Steffan Maignow*, ed. Signori and Müntz, 26/fol. 18v, 26/fol. 19r, 27/fol. 19v, 44/fol. 44r, 102/fol. 126r, 103/fol. 127r, 105/fol. 128v.

[69] *Steffan Maignow*, ed. Signori and Müntz, 106/fol. 129r. See ibid., 11, 61, 82–84/fols 1v, 59r, 89r, 89v.

[70] Jan Hirschbiegel, *Étrennes. Untersuchungen zum höfischen Geschenkverkehr im spätmittelalterlichen Frankreich der Zeit König Karls VI. (1380–1422)*, Pariser historische Studien 60 (Munich: Oldenbourg, 2003), 161: "Noch häufiger als Spangen wurden Ringe – anneaux, verges, bagues – als Neujahrsgeschenk verwendet, in der Mehrzahl der Fälle in Verbindung mit einem Edelstein, meistens mit einem Diamanten in den gängigen Formen. Über 800 Ringe sind in den Rechnungen verzeichnet, verteilt über fast alle Jahre, wobei der Anteil am Gesamtwert aller Geschenke aber nicht einmal 3% beträgt. Ringe scheinen wie Diamanten ein typisches Massengeschenk gewesen zu sein, teilweise gleich dutzendfach verschenkt, was vielleicht – ganz banal – auch mit ihrer verhältnismäßig einfachen Handhabung zusammenhing: klein, leicht und problemlos auch in größeren Mengen zu transportieren. Nicht alle Ringe sind jedoch als ‚Billigware' anzusehen, denn immerhin 50 dieser Schmuckstücke erreichen Werte von über 100 l." See Battke, *Ringsammlung des Berliner Schlossmuseums*, 47–50; Cherry, "Medieval Rings," 54; Lightbown, *Medieval European Jewellery*, 66–78; *Spätmittelalter am Oberrhein. Alltag, Handwerk und Handel, 1350–1525* (Stuttgart: Thorbecke, 2001), 284, no. 569; *Der Schatzfund vom Fuchsenhof*, ed. Prokisch and Kühtreiber, 752.

[71] *Steffan Maignow*, ed. Signori and Müntz, 84/fol. 90r. Agnes of Lupfen married Peter of Hewen in 1477, ending a long-standing feud between the Lords of Hewen and the Lords of Lupfen, see Hans Stärk, "Heinrich von Hewen, Bischof von Konstanz," *Hegau* 31 (1974): 19–28.

[72] *Steffan Maignow*, ed. Signori and Müntz, 33, 39, 65, 74, 88, 95/fols 24r, 36r, 61r, 72r, 73r, 95v, 109r.

[73] *Steffan Maignow*, ed. Signori and Müntz, 25/fol. 18v and 28/fol. 19v.

The cathedral canon Heinrich of Montfort, on the other hand, practically only purchased rings,[74] preferably simple gold rings, or rings with a sapphire.[75] A diamond ring, a ruby ring, and a ring with a lion head,[76] worth eight and nine Gulden, were among the more exceptional pieces:

> I gave my esteemed Lord a small ring with a turquoise and a small ruby for two Gulden on the eve of St. Ulrich's Day (July 3) in the year 1498; I also gave my Lord a clasp (*haͤfftly*) for 16 Gulden on the Friday before St. Oswald's Day (August 3) 1498; I also gave my respected Lord two rings, one with a lion head, the other with a ruby, which both cost eight Gulden, on Saturday before St. Thomas Day (December 15) 1498; I also gave His Grace two rings, one with a diamond dot, the other with a ruby plate, both for nine Gulden, on St. Matthew's Day (September 21) 1499.[77]

Johannes of Randegg regularly paid his bills either in cash, or with corn or red wine from Ossingen or Thayingen (next to Schaffhausen), whereas Heinrich of Montfort's wines came from the neighbouring Meersburg.[78] Nevertheless, Randegg's debt grew continuously in the next years, as seen in the receipts he himself entered into the goldsmith's account book with surprising regularity (table 6).

1481	7 Gulden	1498	13 Gulden
1492	10 Gulden	1500	10 Gulden
1495	17 Gulden	1504	3 Pounds[79]

Table 6: Receipts made for the Cathedral Canon Johannes of Randegg in Stefan Maignow's account book

In 1498, Johannes was even forced to pawn a gold ring and a ring with a privy seal at short notice with Maignow.[80] The account book's last entry related to Jo-

---

74 See Karl-Heinz Burmeister, "Graf Heinrich VII. von Montfort-Rothenfels (1456–1512), Domherr zu Augsburg und Konstanz," in *Geschichte, Recht, Kultur. Festgabe zum 60. Geburtstag [für Karl Heinz Burmeister]*, ed. Alois Niederstätter and Karl Heinz Burmeister (Konstanz: Universitätsverlag Konstanz, 1996), 265–78.

75 In addition to this there were two chalices, collar rings, small gilded locks, and the aforementioned *häftli*: *Steffan Maignow*, ed. Signori and Müntz, 83 and 102/fols 89^{r}, 126^{r}.

76 *Schatzfund vom Fuchsenhof*, ed. Prokisch and Kühtreiber, 769.

77 *Steffan Maignow*, ed. Signori and Müntz, 104/fol. 127^{r}: *Jch hab gebben minem gnaͤdigen herren j ringly mit aim tûrgus vnd robinly vm zwen gulden an sant Ûrichs abbent jm lxxxxviij iar. Mer hab jch gebben minem gnaͤdigen herren ain haͤfftly vm sechzehen gulden am fritag for sant Oswalcz tag jm lxxxxviij iar. Mer hab jch gebben minem gnaͤdigen herren zwen ring, ain mit aim loͤwenkopf, ain mit aim robin, kosten bed ring acht gulden, am samstag vor sant Tomas tag jm lxxxxviij. Mer hab jch sin gnaden gebben zwen ring, ain mit aim diemant punt, den andern mit ainer robin taffel, bed ring vm nûn gulden, an sant Mateus tag jm lxxxxviiij.*

78 Other wines which Stefan Maignow accepted as payment came from Hilzingen, Sipplingen, and Stein am Rhein. *Steffan Maignow*, eds. Signori and Müntz, 26–28, 30, 83, 92, 104, 106/fols 18^{v}, 19^{r}, 19^{v}, 20^{v}, 89^{r}, 101^{r}, 127^{r}, 128^{v}, 129^{r}.

79 *Steffan Maignow*, eds. Signori and Müntz, 26, 105/fols 18^{v}, 19^{r}, 128^{v}, 129^{r} (2), 129^{v}.

80 *Steffan Maignow*, eds. Signori and Müntz, 27/fol. 19^{r}.

hannes of Randegg is from 1504, when he settled his accounts with Maignow's widow. In the meantime, his debts had decreased to three Heller pounds.[81]

In contrast, Heinrich of Montfort, the son of a count, settled his accounts with Stefan Maignow nearly annually between the years 1493 and 1499.[82] His entries had the same form throughout the years, a form strikingly different in detail to that of his colleague Johannes of Randegg and his relatives:

> Further, I, Heinrich, count of Montfort, cathedral canon of Konstanz and of Augsburg, have settled my accounts with Master Stefan Maignow, chief guild master, on St. Andrew's Day (November 30) of the year 1499, and after everything he gave me from the newest bill till today was calculated, and what I gave him was reduced, I remained on this day not more than 22 Gulden and 2 Kreuzer in debt. With my hand Heinrich, count of Montfort, cathedral canon, etc.[83]

As mentioned, despite the stupendous amount of goldsmith's workshops, the production of jewellery was certainly not "economically significant" in the fifteenth century. From the perspective of the consumers, the state of affairs is different: with cathedral clerics and landed gentry such as the Randeggs, their affinity for representative gold and silver jewellery is likely to have devoured a substantial amount of their budgets.[84] That finger rings played a central role should be sufficiently clear in the light of my remarks.[85] Gold rings with valuable gems visibly graced hands and meant not to work manually. They were an exclusive form of representation, like clothes and other jewellery, but also much fancied wedding or New Year's presents which helped establish or cement friendships.[86] Their high material value also made them secure objects of investment, which could easily be turned into money, if necessary. With characters such as Johannes of Randegg or Heinrich of Montfort, the preference for elaborate finger jewellery had traits which went far beyond common practice. The absolute numbers are impressive – the

---

[81] *Steffan Maignow*, ed. Signori and Müntz, 107/fol. 129^{v}.

[82] *Steffan Maignow*, ed. Signori and Müntz, 102–105/fols 126^{r}, 126^{v}, 127^{v}.

[83] *Steffan Maignow*, ed. Signori and Müntz, 105/fol. 127^{v}: *Jtem jch, Hainrich grauff zû Montfortt, thûmherr zû Costencz vnd Augspurg, hab gerechnett <vn> mitt maister Steffan Maygnaw, oberster zuff [sic], vff sant Andres tag anno domini jm nún vnd nûnczigestem jar, vnd /so/ alles gerechnett wirtt, was er mir geben hautt von der neusten rechnung <x> biß vff dissen tag, vnd die rechnung geschechen jst vnd dargegen auch gerechnett wirtt vnd abgezogen wirtt, was jch geben hab, so belib jch by aller rechnung bysz vff dienn [sic] for geschribnen tag vnd jar nitt mer schuldig dann zwen vnd zwayncziq gulden zwen crûczer. Mitt meiner hand, Hainrich g. z. Montfort, thümherr etc.* The slashes indicate additions and corrections added above lines.

[84] But they did not leave an account book.

[85] Petra Kathke, *Porträt und Accessoire. Eine Bildnisform im 16. Jahrhundert* (Berlin: Reimer, 1997) does not mention rings.

[86] Ulf Christian Ewert and Jan Hirschbiegel, "Nur Verschwendung? Zur sozialen Funktion der demonstrativen Zurschaustellung höfischen Güterverbrauchs," in *Luxus und Integration. Materielle Hofkultur Westeuropas vom 12. bis zum 18. Jahrhundert*, ed. Werner Paravicini (Munich: Oldenbourg, 2010), 105–21.

former with 24, the latter with 30 rings – but it is difficult to interpret them based on the sources at our disposal; ultimately, we do not know enough about the two clerics. But it is remarkable that clerics like Johannes of Randegg preferred the same pieces of jewellery as the noblewomen they were related to. Nevertheless, in the account book of the Konstanz goldsmith Stefan Maignow gold and silver jewellery prove to be a primarily male and clerical medium of representation.

(Translation by Srdjan Perko)

John Styles

Innovation and Obsolescence:

European Textiles for the Body and the Household, 1400–1800[1]

In Oscar Hammerstein's libretto for the musical and subsequently the film 'The Sound of Music', the favourite things he selected for his song of the same name were essentially timeless. Whether natural, like raindrops on roses, or manufactured, like brown paper packages tied up with strings, they represented perennial sources of consolation in a world of change, unwelcome change. Yet when I ask my teenage daughters about their favourite things, they are wont to emphasise the transitory and the temporary – 'just at the moment my favourite thing is …'.

Of course, timelessness and timeliness are not mutually exclusive as reasons for favouring one thing over another thing. On the contrary, they co-exist, and have long co-existed, in an uneasy but inescapable symbiosis. After all, nothing is permanent. Even objects of essentially the same kind can vary greatly in their longevity. Moreover, object lifecycles are not simply a matter of physical durability. My daughters' preference for what is current and modish indicates how object life-histories are shaped as much by taste and fashion as by the physical resilience of the materials from which they are made. And, as the notion of built-in obsolescence prompts us to recognise, the lifecycle of an artefact is something that, to a greater or lesser extent, is designed into it in the course of its manufacture. Makers may not necessarily succeed in determining how the artefacts they create are used, but they try nevertheless.

The period from the fifteenth to the eighteenth centuries witnessed a transformation in the lifecycles of one group of favourite things – textiles. Early-modern European textiles underwent a process of material and cultural re-sequencing. It culminated, during the seventeenth century, in the emergence of a new, annual fashion cycle, initially in France, but subsequently spreading out across Western Europe. It was systematically promoted in print, especially in periodical publications. It was characterized by backward linkages into textile marketing and manu-

[1] The research leading to these results has received funding from the European Research Council under the European Union's Seventh Framework Programme (FP/2007–2013) / ERC Grant Agreement n. 249512. The author would like to thank all the contributors to the HERA project 'Fashioning the Early Modern: Creativity and Innovation in Europe, 1500–1800'. He is especially grateful to Christopher Breward, David Celetti, Lesley Miller, Giorgio Riello, Michael Sonenscher, Corinne Thépaut–Cabasset, and Amanda Vickery for references and suggestions.

facturing. Although initially confined to a limited range of fabrics, and the garments and later furnishings into which they were made, in the course of the eighteenth century it increasingly came to shape public perceptions of the temporality of fashion change – the relationship between past, present and future fashions – across Europe.

Early-modern fashion in dress did not turn only on the characteristics of the fabrics worn – equally important were the ways fabric was cut to form garments, the ways garments were combined, and the dress accessories that supplemented them – but textiles were significant, above all because they were traded internationally on a much greater scale than either garments or accessories. The sixteenth and seventeenth centuries witnessed a tide of novelty in decorated fabrics made from a variety of materials – wool, linen, cotton and silk – sometimes employing novel techniques, such as machine knitting, lacemaking and printing with mordants. The main trend was a move towards fabrics that were lighter, more colourful, more highly patterned. It can be observed across the textile fibres.

Patterned silks, produced principally in Italy, but widely exported, were the most costly and high-status textiles in sixteenth-century Europe. Between the mid-fifteenth century and the early seventeenth century, their weave density fell by a third, reflecting a shift to lighter, thinner cloths.[2] A similar change can be observed in woollen broadcloths, which were often as expensive. Between the 1630s and the 1680s the weight of a typical coloured broadcloth made in Wiltshire, in the west of England, also fell by a third.[3] This reduction in the weight of existing fabrics was accompanied by the success of a variety of new, light fabrics made from combed, long-staple wool, sometimes mixed with silk or other fibres, known in English as stuffs or worsteds. They succeeded at the expense of heavier and less attractive competitors.[4] Initially a product of sixteenth-century Flanders, their manufacture burgeoned, spreading in the course of the next two centuries to Holland, England, France and beyond. By the later seventeenth century they were themselves facing competition in key markets from another lightweight, colourful, patterned fabric that was new to Europe – the painted or printed cotton calico imported from India, initially by the Portuguese in the sixteenth century and, after 1600, by the English and Dutch East India companies on an increasingly large scale.

---

[2] Luca Mola, *The Silk Industry of Renaissance Venice* (Baltimore: John Hopkins University Press, 2003), 88, 146–52.

[3] Julia de L. Mann, *The Cloth Industry in the West of England from 1640 to 1880* (Oxford: Clarendon Press, 1971), 14, 312–15. For Venetian perceptions of this trend in both English and Dutch woollens, see Domenico Sella, "The Rise and Fall of the Venetian Woollen Industry," in *Crisis and Change in the Venetian Economy*, ed. Brian Pullan (London: Melhuen, 1968), 120.

[4] Negley Harte, ed., *The New Draperies in the Low Countries and England, 1300–1800* (Oxford: Oxford University Press, 1997). For the displacement of heavier, traditional worsted fabrics, see Luc N. D. Martin, "Textile Manufactures in Norwich and Norfolk, 1550–1622" (Ph.D. thesis, University of Cambridge, 1991), 7, 60.

Textiles were not just becoming lighter in weight. The new fabrics cost less. The light silks – grosgrains, sarcenets, satins and damasks – cost only half to three-quarters of the price of the traditional heavy brocaded velvets they replaced.[5] But these new, light fabrics were also less durable. The Venetian ambassador to the French court complained in 1546 that the satins and damasks made by the Tuscans and the Genoese were 'cloths that cost little and last even less'.[6] In 1606 it was claimed, perhaps with some exaggeration, that the old Norwich worsteds of the mid-sixteenth century would have lasted six times longer than the new Norwich stuffs.[7] A century later, Daniel Defoe famously damned Indian calico as 'ordinary, mean, low-priz'd, and soon in rags'.[8] Cheaper, less durable fabrics were associated with an acceleration in turnover and a wider array of items for sale. They were also associated with a heightened sensitivity among consumers to novelty and variety. The Tuscan and Genoese silks criticized as cheap and flimsy by the Venetian ambassador in 1546 were made to 'suit the desires and tastes of the French'. They were 'exactly what that nation wants, because it would get bored if a garment lasted too long'.[9]

An emphasis on design innovation was a corollary of the acceleration in turnover. Almost all the new fabrics were distinguished by the speed with which patterns and colours changed.[10] Norwich was one of the main English centres for the new, light fabrics made from combed wool. In 1611, Norwich stuffs were already being described as being 'of infinite variety of sorts, figures, colours and prices.' The need for new patterns was constantly stressed. 'Our trade is most benefitted by our new inventions and the varying of our stuffes which is contynually profitable.'[11]

Much of this search for novelty in textile design was driven by fashion in clothing. In 1632, for instance, Dorothy, Lady Randolph wrote from London to the Suffolk gentlewoman Lady Jane Bacon:

> I have sent you some patterns of stuff such as is worn by many, but not much lace upon those wrought stuffs; but the newest fashion is plain satin,

[5] Elizabeth Currie, "Diversity and Design in the Florentine Tailoring Trade, 1560–1620," in *The Material Renaissance*, ed. Michelle O'Malley and Evelyn Welch (Manchester: Manchester University Press, 2008), 160.

[6] Quoted in Mola, *Silk Industry*, 96.

[7] Martin, "Textile manufactures in Norwich," 7.

[8] Daniel Defoe, *A Brief Deduction of the Original, Progress, and Immense Greatness of the British Woollen Manufacture* (London: J. Roberts and A. Dodd, 1727), 50.

[9] Quoted in Mola, *Silk Industry*, 96.

[10] Innovation in colour was, of course, encouraged by the availability of new dyestuffs from the Americas.

[11] Quoted in Ursula Priestley, "Norwich Stuffs, 1600–1700," in *New Draperies*, ed. Harte, 278.

> of what colour one will, embroidered all over with alcomedes [jewels and stones sewn into the cloth], but it is not like to hold past summer.[12]

Stuffs and satins were two of the new, lightweight fabrics, made from silk or wool-silk mixes, around which fashion change revolved in the 1620s and 1630s. In England, where sumptuary laws controlling dress ended in 1604, changes in fashions of this sort were not confined to the rich.

The early-modern fashion cycle in textiles did not, of course, originate in England. Insofar as we can trace its origins, they lie in the fine silks that began to be made in Italy in the later Middle Ages under the influence of imports from the Byzantine empire and the Muslim territories of the eastern Mediterranean. Italian-made silks came to be characterized by a cycle of ceaseless innovation in pattern and design. The rate of change may have been slower before the mid-sixteenth century, but it was already well-entrenched. Lisa Monnas has summarized these innovations, identifying a broad shift from orientalised animal silks in the fourteenth century, to combinations of animals and plants in the early fifteenth century, to the pomegranate cloths of gold of the middle to late fifteenth century, to foliate designs in the later fifteenth century, and to broader, bolder patterns in the sixteenth century. These changing fashions were driven by intense rivalry over export markets between the different silk-manufacturing city states – Lucca, Florence, Genoa, Venice. Each city state sustained particular specialisms, yet each endlessly stole the others' designs and each endeavored to secure a competitive advantage by generating new fashions.[13] By the mid-fifteenth century, a kind of proto-mercantilism had become the norm. Competitive import substitution was encouraged by Italian city governments, both to free the state from reliance on foreign textiles and to provide export opportunities.[14]

In the city states of fifteenth-century Italy we have a prototype of the kind of mercantilist competition in fashion that would become a distinctive element of the western European state system in the seventeenth and eighteenth centuries. By then, it was not, of course, confined to textiles. International rivalries over modes of dress extended to garments and accessories, most famously in the European-wide contest between Spanish and French styles in the seventeenth century. In textiles, however, a crucial refinement came in the 1660s and 1670s. It was in these decades that the French systematized the accelerated turnover of fashions associated with the new, lighter textiles. Lyon was newly emerging as the leading interna-

---

[12] Joanna Moody, *The Private Correspondence of Jane Lady Cornwallis Bacon, 1613–1644* (London: Fairleigh Dickinson Univ Press, 2003), 215.

[13] Lisa Monnas, *Merchants, Princes and Painters. Silk Fabrics in Italian and Northern Paintings, 1300–1550* (New Haven and London: Yale University Press, 2008), 19–20, 17.

[14] Luca Mola, "States and Crafts: Relocating Technical Skills in Renaissance Italy', in *Material Renaissance*, ed. O'Malley and Welch, 133–53.

tional centre for the production of decorated woven silks. A key element in its success was the introduction of an annual cycle of innovation in design.[15]

Jacques Savary in *Le Parfait Négociant*, published in Paris in 1675, made what is, perhaps, the first published comment on this innovation. He singled out 'patterned and coloured silks, in which fashions change from one year to the next', distinguishing them from silk and other fabrics not subject to fashion, such as those dyed plain black.[16] He pointed out the implications for business of what was both an intensification and a systematization of the fashion cycle. Annual fashion made timing crucial for sales, offering new opportunities, but also new dangers. 'Fashion generally encourages the sale of goods, and also increases their price'.[17] Profits on patterned silk fabrics were higher, but the loss was greater if they failed to sell. 'The French are naturally changeable, and most of the time they will not wear a fabric in a pattern or a colour that was current the previous year'.[18] If a fabric was for sale in Paris, it had to be the most fashionable. If it was for sale in the French provinces, or abroad, it should not be in the latest fashion, because that fashion would have not arrived and the merchandise would be too expensive. If, however, merchants were burdened with a stock of fabrics falling out of fashion, or no longer fashionable at all, it could always be sold in the provinces or abroad, although possibly at a loss.[19]

The French shift to annual fashion change soon prompted reactions from France's international competitors in the markets for patterned silks. For example, the directors of the English East India Company were quick to grasp its importance. In 1681 the Company was cultivating a new trade in woven silks from Bengal. The aim was to compete directly with European patterned silks. The directors wrote to their Bengal agents requiring

> that in all flowred Silkes, you Change the fashion and flower as much as you can every yeare, for English Ladies and they say the french and other Europeans will give twice as much for a new thing not seen in Europe before though worse, than they will give for a better Silk of the same fashion worn the former yeare.[20]

---

[15] Peter Thornton, *Baroque and Rococo Silks* (London: Faber & Faber, 1965), 20–21; Carlo Poni, "Fashion as Flexible Production: The Strategies of the Lyon Silk Merchants in the Eighteenth Century," in *World of Possibilities: Flexibility and Mass Production in Western Industrialization*, ed. Charles Sabel and Jonathan Zeitlin (Cambridge: Cambridge University Press, 1997), 69–70.

[16] Jacques Savary, *Le Parfait Négociant ou instruction generale pour ce qui regarde le commerce*, (Paris: Louis Billaine, 1675), I, 61. In the French original, the phrase is 'des étoffes façonnées, et de couleurs dont les modes changent d'une année à l'autre'. Carlo Poni identifies Savary's remarks as the earliest reference to annual fashion change; Poni, "Fashion as flexible production," 69–70.

[17] Savary, *Parfait Négociant*, II, 13.

[18] Savary, *Parfait Négociant*, I, 305.

[19] Savary, *Parfait Négociant*, II, 13, 37.

[20] Henry Dodwell, ed., *Records of Fort St George: Despatches from England, 1680–1682* (Madras: Government Press, 1914), 51.

We should not exaggerate the extent of the change represented by the shift to annual fashion. The western European climate, with marked contrasts in temperature between winter and summer, meant that clothing had long been subject to change according to season. The new, annual cycle of fashion innovation incorporated these seasonal rhythms.[21] Moreover, the range of textiles subject to a strict annual design cycle remained narrow. The extent of annual changes in design could be quite small.

Nevertheless, what we observe in embryo in the patterned silks of the second half of the seventeenth century is the kind of pre-programmed, routine innovation cycle that still shapes fashion today. It set the timetable for design. By the early eighteenth century, the specialist silk designers based in Lyon customarily made visits once a year to Paris in order to gather new ideas.[22] It also set the timetable for marketing, enabling the forthcoming season's designs to be sold in advance as a collection by circulating samples among distant customers.[23] Finally, it shaped the complicated scheduling necessary for weaving the fabrics ordered in advance. In the eighteenth century, making a single gown length of patterned silk at Lyon could take over four months.[24] It required the manufacturer to assemble finance, designs, dyestuffs in particular colours, yarns in particular counts, and workers with particular skills. All this was regulated according to the annual cycle.

Why did the annualization of the fashion cycle emerge in France during the late seventeenth century? Carlo Poni, the historian of the silk industry, presents the annualization of the fashion cycle principally as a tool of the mercantilist economic policies pursued by Jean-Baptiste Colbert, Louis XIV's finance minister in the 1660s and 1670s.[25] Colbert promoted French manufacturing in three main ways. First, existing industries were improved to make them internationally competitive, particularly by state regulation of quality standards. Second, tariff barriers were erected to exclude goods from the French market manufactured by competitors. Third, new industries were set up to capture foreign markets and reduce the need for imports.

Luxury and fashion goods loomed large here. In patterned silks, the objective was for Lyon to supplant Italy in the design and manufacture of the dominant

---

[21] Corinne Thépaut-Cabasset, "Garde-robe de souverain et réseau international: l'exemple de la Bavière dans les années 1680," in *Se vêtir à la cour en Europe (1400–1815)*, ed. Isabelle Paresys and Natacha Coquery (Villeneuve-d'Ascq: Université Lille 3 et al., 2011), 184.

[22] Lesley Ellis Miller, "Paris-Lyon-Paris: Dialogue in the Design and Distribution of Patterned Silks in the Eighteenth Century," in *Paris: Studies in the History of the Skilled Workforce*, ed. Robert Fox and Anthony Turner (Aldershot: Ashgate, 1998), 154–57.

[23] Lesley Ellis Miller, "Innovation and Industrial Espionage in Eighteenth-Century France: An Investigation of the Selling of Silks through Samples," *Journal of Design History* 12 (1999): 271–92.

[24] Lesley Ellis Miller, "Les matériaux du costume de cour," in *Fastes de cour et cérémonies royales: Le costume de cour en Europe (1650–1800)*, ed. Pierre Arizzoli-Clémentel and Pascale Gorguet-Ballesteros (Paris: Rmn-Grand Palais, 2009), 82.

[25] Poni, "Fashion as flexible production," especially 69–71.

western European fashion fabric. Carlo Poni argues the shift to annual fashion change was crucial to achieving this objective. Drawing on Jacques Savary's 1675 account, he emphasizes the temporal interaction of quality and price in fashion markets where early entrants command what economists term a positional rent. At the start of the fashion cycle, the latest fashions enjoyed a huge competitive advantage and a correspondingly high price. Towards its end, prices could be slashed to offload goods in marginal markets, while, at the same time, underselling competitors. An annual fashion cycle allowed this sequence to be managed with predictability and precision. It was a variant of the Colbert's programme of quality enhancement, but one in which quality turned on timing as much as on materials.

It took a foreigner to sum up the benefits of the new system for the French economy. Ernst Ludwig Carl was a councillor to the Margrave of Bayreuth in Germany. He visited France early in the eighteenth century and wrote a report on the experience for his employer:

> Only France has discovered a valuable secret in changes of fashion; as goods fall out of use in the kingdom, neighbouring nations eagerly adopt them. Peru and Mexico also absorb a great number, while garments and clothing discarded by the rich end up in the hands of the poor at a cheap price; without all this, frequent changes of fashion might have been prejudicial to the realm; instead, such changes have, in practice, been an opportunity to perfect the arts and enrich the state, by manufacturing many superfluous and unnecessary things to send abroad.[26]

Lyon's shift to annual fashion change in the 1660s and 1670s represented an aggressive rationalization and acceleration of the existing product cycle for Italian patterned silks. The objective was to out-compete Italian manufacturers in international trade. It succeeded. By 1675, Savary insisted, Italian courtiers, male and female, considered themselves well-dressed only if they wore French silks. This was despite the high quality of Italian-made equivalents. Savary's explanation of the Italian élite's craving for French silks alerts us to a second, key element in the shift to annual fashion change. 'The reason is that it is the Court of France which sets the fashion for all the princes of Europe'.[27]

The idea that, under Louis XIV, the royal court acted as a stage for displaying French luxury products is a familiar one. However, the regulation of appearance at court was much more than just an exercise in mercantilist marketing, promoting French taste. It was profoundly political, an exercise in the systematic projection of royal power, designed to evoke awe and encourage submission among Louis XIV's French subjects and his European neighbours. Just as French manufacturing was remodelled during the first two decades of Louis' personal rule in the 1660s and

---

[26] Ernst Ludwig Carl, *Traité de la Richesse des Princes et de leurs Etats* (Paris: Theodore Le Gras, 1722), II, 492–93. For Carl and fashion, see Michael Sonenscher, "Fashion's Empire: Trade and Power in Early 18th-Century France," in *Luxury Trades and Consumerism*, ed. Fox and Turner, 231–54.

[27] Savary, *Parfait Négociant*, I, 64.

1670s, so too was court dress and its management. Louis transformed his and his queen's formal dressing (*levée*) and undressing (*coucher*) into daily state rituals. The courtiers responsible for the royal wardrobes – the *grand maître de la Garde-robe* and the *dame d'atours* – became major court officials. Crucially for the move to annual fashion, these officials were made responsible for ordering fabrics and clothing for the king and the queen, according a yearly cycle. The royal wardrobes underwent an annual *réforme*, at which new sets of clothes for the coming winter and summer replaced the previous year's garments. The same officials removed the discarded items and were then entitled to exercise the privilege of selling most of them for their own profit.[28]

Courtiers were expected to follow the annual pattern set by the king and queen. Louis insisted that women appearing at court should wear the voluminous, stiff gown made from the most expensive patterned silks, later known as the *grand habit*, not the looser mantua then coming into vogue. Yet the silk fabrics and the ornament of the *grand habit* were permitted to change according to fashion, as long as its form remained fixed. Hence regulation of court appearance was fused with regulation of fashion innovation. Hierarchy and novelty were reconciled in the service of Louis XIV's ceremonial politics. Both were rendered subservient to a shared logic of control.

Fashion was not, of course, the only practice to undergo a regularization of innovation in the course of the seventeenth century. The same process applied to news, not only in France but across Western Europe. In what John Sommerville has termed 'the news revolution', the newspaper and periodical press re-organized the circulation of news according to new, regular periodicities – annual, monthly, weekly, and ultimately, by the middle of the seventeenth century, daily.[29] The irregular circulation of political news by correspondence and messenger began to be replaced, from the end of the sixteenth century, by printed periodicals published at fixed intervals, transforming news into a product. It is no co-incidence that for both fashion and news, this regularization of novelty happened in the course the seventeenth century. The two parallel changes were linked.

In exploring these linkages, it is useful to draw on Roland Barthes' argument that fundamental to the fashion system in capitalist societies is a distinction between, on the one hand, the real, actual garment and, on the other, the garment as it is imagined or represented. It is, perhaps, more useful for our purposes to conceive this as a three-fold distinction between, first, clothes as material objects in the process of manufacture, second, clothes as imagined objects that undergo a process of meaning-making through print and image in the course of their distribution

[28] Corinne Thépaut-Cabasset, "Le service de la Garde-robe: une création de Louis XIV," in *Fastes de cour*, ed. Arizzoli-Clémentel et Gorguet-Ballesteros, 28–33.

[29] John Sommerville, *The News Revolution in England* (Oxford: Oxford University Press, 1996).

and marketing, and, third, clothes as material objects that are purchased and worn.[30]

Barthes focuses on the second of these three stages, and specifically on the way fashion magazines create semiotic meaning through text and image. However, this second stage in the fashion system plays a key role not only in attaching meaning to clothes, but also in constructing the periodicity of the fashion cycle. Before the seventeenth century, information about clothes and fashion had for centuries been communicated in words, whether printed, written, or spoken, but the rise of the periodical press provided a new vehicle for intervening in the timing of the relationship between production of fashion and its consumption. Fashion news, like all the other kinds of news, could be subjected to a periodic routine.

Sommerville argues that the seventeenth-century news revolution fundamentally changed the character of politics by bundling up news about affairs of state into artificial weekly chunks. Fashion news too was amenable to temporal reconstruction. We should not be surprised, therefore, that the shift to an annual pattern of fashion innovation in Lyon silks in the 1660s and 1670s coincided with the appearance in Paris of the first periodical to devote substantial space to fashion, the *Mercure Galant*.[31] Published as a monthly for more than thirty years, its subject matter was principally social and literary, but between 1672 and 1701 it regularly featured fashion as news. Fashion news was organized around a two-season cycle, with a substantial article on new fashions usually appearing twice a year, in spring and autumn, although in textiles the difference between the winter and the summer fashions might amount to little more than the thickness of the fabric.[32] Great emphasis was placed on what was worn at court. Details were provided about each season's new patterned silks, as well as information about the Parisian retailers who supplied the silks. In addition, for a period in the 1670s there were engraved fashion plates, which included images of the silk piece goods fashionable for the current year, cross-referenced to textual descriptions of the fabrics concerned.

Gradually, in the course of the eighteenth century, the *Mercure Galant* spawned imitators across Western Europe. Dissemination of fashion news in printed periodicals became widespread. It was not confined to specialist monthly or bimonthly fashion magazines, such as the *Journal des Luxus und der Moden* in Germany from 1786. The same temporal rhythms governed the presentation of fashion in periodical publications of many other kinds, from engravings in annually published pocket diaries to advertisements placed by shopkeepers in the weekly newspapers printed

---

30 Roland Barthes, *The Fashion System* (London: University of California Press, 1985). Also see the useful discussion of Barthes in Michael Carter, *Fashion Classics from Carlyle to Barthes* (Oxford: Berg, 2003), chapter 8.

31 Corinne Thépaut-Cabasset, ed., *L'Esprit des modes au Grand Siècle* (Paris: CTHS, 2010); Reed Benhamoud "Fashion in the 'Mercure': From Human Foible to Female Failing," *Eighteenth-Century Studies* 31(1997): 27–43.

32 Thépaut-Cabasset, *L'Esprit des modes*, 25.

in English provincial towns.[33] In the process, fashion innovation became icreasingly (though by no means entirely) subservient to regular chronological sequencing. Fashion became a routine. Public expectations of the temporality of fashion adjusted accordingly. People developed a more acute, shared sense of its contemporaneity, of the sum of what constituted current fashion, while becoming attuned to when current fashion would become old fashion and new fashion appear.[34]

In the boom in fashion studies that has swept the academic world during the last twenty-five years, it is one conception of fashion that has predominated: fashion as identity – subcultural, national, sexual, religious, ethnic, and so on. Thinking about fashion in terms of identity has been especially influential in the study of early-modern Europe, not least through the influence of Stephen Greenblatt's hugely successful *Renaissance Self-Fashioning: From More to Shakespeare.*[35] Yet focus on identity has become so intense that other ways of conceptualizing fashion in the period are in danger of being overlooked, especially fashion as a process of change. Fashion is inseparable from novelty and innovation, as it is from their inevitable mirror image, obsolescence and decline. It is as much, if not more, about the material sequencing of change as it is about the material ordering of identities.

Periodicity remains at the heart of the modern fashion system. It shapes the way we think about fashion, as recent debates over 'fast fashion' and 'slow fashion' demonstrate.[36] Early-modern Europe was the birthplace of the forms of innovation management and built-in obsolescence that, in an intensified form, provoke debate today. That is not to say we should interpret their early-modern invention as a first step on the road to a unified, undifferentiated, capitalist modernity, a modernity in which fashion is a matter of consumer choice and personal self-expression – in the words of Oscar Hammerstein, '*my* favourite things'. A vision of modernity did inspire Louis XIV's remodelling of France's politics and economy in the later seventeenth century. Louis sought to rationalize, to standardize and to centralize, as the new annualized fashion cycle attests. But this was the early-

---

[33] Anne Buck and Harry Matthews, "Pocket Guides to Fashion: Ladies' Pocket Books Published in England 1760–1830," *Costume* 18 (1984): 35–58. For examples of advertisements in late eighteenth-century English provincial newspapers that announce the season's fashions for the year of publication, see "Spring Fashions, R. Lawrence," *Reading Mercury*, 3 May 1790 and "Home News: Winter Fashions," *Norfolk Chronicle*, 19 November 1791.

[34] For an enhanced sense of contemporaneity as an outcome of the early-modern news revolution, see Daniel Woolf, "News, History and the Construction of the Present in Early Modern England', in Brendan M. Dooley and Sabrina A. Baron, *The Politics of Information in Early Modern Europe* (London: Routledge, 2001), 80–108.

[35] Stephen Greenblatt, *Renaissance Self-Fashioning: From More to Shakespeare* (Chicago: University of Chicago Press, 1980).

[36] For 'fast fashion,' see Simona Segre Reinach, "China and Italy: Fast Fashion versus *Prêt à Porter.* Towards a New Culture of Fashion," *Fashion Theory* 9 (2005): 43–56, and C. Scott Hemphill and Jeannie Suk, "The Law, Culture, and Economics of Fashion," *Stanford Law Review* 61 (2009): 101–50. For 'slow fashion,' see Kate Fletcher, *Sustainable Fashion and Textiles: Design Journeys* (London: Taylor & Francis, 2008), especially chapter 7.

modern form of modernity termed by Steve Pincus, in his discussion of late-seventeenth-century England, 'Catholic modernity', absolutist, intolerant, regulatory, hierarchical.[37] In its early-modern origins, the modern fashion cycle was profoundly authoritarian.

[37] Steve Pincus, *1688: The First Modern Revolution* (New Haven: Yale University Press, 2009), chapter 6.

Ottó Gecser

Some Like It Hot:*

Piquant Taste between the Middle Ages and Modern Times

> Why has Tabasco Sauce become so popular the world over? It's simple: put it on any food you like, and it'll make you like it even more! Because Tabasco Sauce brings out a food's flavor while adding a peppery punch of its own. Splash it on everything from Mexican food to Italian, seafood to sandwich spreads, Eggs Benedict to Bloody Marys![1]

Such instructions for use combined with the fact that hot sauces constitute a separate category of contemporary food products suggest that there is a widespread tendency to make any savory dish (or even drink) spicy. Many people prefer almost everything like this, and not only individuals: hot or spicy is a distinctive feature of several kinds of ethnic food from Mexican to Indian as well.

The excessive use of spices – in the sense of exotic condiments imported to Europe from faraway lands – frequently appears as a hallmark of the Middle Ages as well. In the formulation of Wolfgang Schivelbusch, "[p]repared foods were virtually buried under spices; food was little more than a vehicle for condiments which were used in combinations we nowadays would consider quite bizarre."[2] Major narratives of the transition between the medieval and the modern in terms of food preferences point to the drop in the use of spices as one of the emblematic areas of change. This drop is usually explained with reference to the declining prestige of these exotic ingredients as objects of conspicuous consumption following the Portuguese exploration of the sea route leading to their South Asian places of cultivation.[3] Some connect the previous suitability of spices for showing off to

---

* This article is based on research I made at the Herzog August Bibliothek in Wolfenbüttel, with a grant by the Federal State of Lower Saxony, and at the Institute for Advanced Study in Princeton, with the support of the Herodotus Fund. If not indicated otherwise, all translations and emendations of the quoted sources are mine.

1 http://www.tabasco.com/tabasco-products/sauces/tabasco-original-red-sauce (last accessed 2 October 2018).

2 Wolfgang Schivelbusch, *Tastes of Paradise: A Social History of Spices, Stimulants, and Intoxicants*, trans. David Jacobson (New York: Vintage, 1993), 4.

3 Stephen Mennell sees in spices a barrier to further "social competition through the kitchen and the table" because through them "dishes became rather undifferentiated and broadly 'tasted the

their high price: "When spices began to fall in price and to appear on all tables, so that they were no longer a symbol of wealth and luxury," writes Fernand Braudel, "they were used less and their prestige declined."[4] Others point to a process of disenchantment, to the stripping of the spices of their mythic origins which made them highly desirable in the Middle Ages.[5]

Whichever is the case, the same discovery that made spices cheaper and less exotic – combined with that of Columbus on the other side of the globe – led to the diffusion of the chili pepper in Asia and, thus, made possible the emergence of distinctively hot cuisines there.[6] Moreover, it is the recent popularity of Asian and South American ethnic foods that has brought the spicy back to mainstream Western culinary taste after the limited success of chili in some areas of Europe – including Calabria, Hungary, and the Balkans – and among some higher status British diners, as an ingredient of *curry*, in the colonial era.[7]

When the chili first came to Europe, with Columbus himself, the Old World was still very much favorable to spices. The aim of this paper is to understand how

---

same'." It seems to me, however, that his explanation also presupposes the loss of their previous value which had made spices appropriate instruments of social competition in the Middle Ages. See Stephen Mennell, *All Manners of Food: Eating and Taste in England and France from the Middle Ages to the Present* (Oxford: Blackwell, 1985), 54. To my knowledge it is only Rachel Laudan who attributes the decline of the spicy to a factor entirely unrelated to conspicuous consumption and the geographical discoveries, namely new (Paracelsian) ideas of digestion and health. See her "A Kind of Chemistry," *Petits Propos Culinaires* 62 (1999): 8–22.

4 Fernand Braudel, *Civilization and Capitalism, 15th–18th Century*, vol. 1: *The Structure of Everyday Life: The Limits of the Possible*, trans. Miriam Kochan and Sîan Reynolds (London: Collins, 1981), 221. To be sure, declining overall prices do not necessarily imply loss of appeal in showing status, since more equal access to (former) luxuries can also lead to their re-stratification in terms of quality from "premium" to "economy". Paul Freedman, *Out of the East: Spices and the Medieval Imagination* (New Haven: Yale University Press, 2008), 221, makes a similar point about English tea culture.

5 Bruno Laurioux, *Une histoire culinaire du Moyen Âge* (Paris: Champion, 2005), 197–211; Freedman, *Out of the East*, 225.

6 On the global spread of the chili, see Jean Andrews, *The Pepper Trail: History and Recipes from Around the World* (Denton: The University of North Texas Press, 1999), 3–33; Clifford A. Wright, "The Medieval Spice Trade and the Diffusion of the Chile," *Gastronomica* 2 (2007): 35–43; Sucheta Mazumdar, "The Impact of New World Food Crops on the Diet and Economy of China and India, 1600–1900," in *Food in Global History*, ed. Raymond Grew (Boulder, CO: Westview, 1999), 58–78.

7 For the fate of the chili in Calabria, Hungary, and the Balkans, see Vito Teti, *Storia del peperoncino: Cibi, simboli e culture tra Mediterraneo e mondo*, 2nd ed., Virgola 118 (Rome: Donizelli, 2015); László Kőszegi, "A paprika útjai Közép-Európába – a kibővült kutatási lehetőségek tükrében" [Routes of paprika to Central Europe – in the light of new research possibilities], *Ethnographia* 123 (2012): 255–77; Gabriella Schubert, "'Pfeffer' und 'Paprika' im Südosten Europas: Eine sprach- und kulturhistorische Betrachtung," *Zeitschrift für Balkanologie* 28 (1992): 104–30 (I am grateful to Snežana Petrovic of the Serbian Academy of Sciences for this reference); and Sándor Bálint, *A szegedi paprika* [The paprika of Szeged] (Budapest: Akadémiai, 1962). For the curry, see Lizzie Collingham, *Curry: A Tale of Cooks and Conquerors* (Oxford: Oxford University Press, 2006); and Stephanie R. Maroney, "To Make a Curry the India Way: Tracking the Meaning of Curry across Eighteenth-Century Communities," *Food and Foodways* 19 (2011): 122–34.

Europeans received it, why they received it like that, and to what extent were their reactions different from its "post-modern" appreciation today. In the first section, I will explore the immediate context in which chili was perceived by sixteenth-century Europeans, namely the consumption of pepper and other hot spices in the Late Middle Ages. In the second section, I will survey the earliest references to chili until the end of the sixteenth century, and reconstruct a pattern of its reception in terms of regional and social differences and their links to mediaeval taste.

Pepper and Its Cognates in the Late Middle Ages

The two main types of sources through which historians have studied in a systematic fashion the consumption of spices (as more or less separate or separable from their commerce) are *cookbooks* and *household accounts*. Both take various forms which, nevertheless, have the same function, that is, recording and transmitting culinary recipes in the one and everyday expenditures in the other case.[8] Both types of sources have their own biases.

As to household accounts, here the problems are connected, first of all, to the fact that spices can be preserved for long; thus if we do not have all years covered for an extended period of time, we do not know for how long given amounts of spices purchased at one time lasted. Additionally, we tend to ignore for how many persons it was bought, not to mention the exact purposes of its purchase. Was it for flavouring food or colouring it? For making candies, perfumes, or medicines? Was it entirely for the use of the household in question or for giving away as gifts to outsiders as well?

A rare example where most of these unknowns are known is an ordinance of Humbert II, the last Dauphin of the Viennois, for provisioning the house of his mother, Beatrice of Hungary, in his absence for war in 1345. It is not a balance drawn after having made the relevant purchases but a plan of how to make them, that is not an account in the strict sense. Nevertheless, such a plan must have taken into consideration the accounts of previous years in order to be realistic, even if we can suppose that such a high-standing aristocrat as Humbert wanted to avoid running out of foodstuffs and, thus, he ordered to buy more than what seemed necessary.

The document lists the members of Beatrice's household by function, altogether thirty, and then specifies that the following is "necessary for the said Lady, our mother, together with the aforesaid persons and some thirteen [more] each

[8] See Christopher Dyer, "Do Household Accounts Provide an Accurate Picture of Late Medieval Diet and Food Culture?," in *La vie matérielle au Moyen Âge: L'apport des sources littéraires, normative et de la pratique; Actes du colloque de Louvain-la-Neuve, 3–5 octobre 1996*, ed. Emmanuelle Rassart-Eeckhout et al., Publications de l'Institut d'Études Médiévales: Textes, études, congrès 18 (Louvain-la-Neuve: Institut d'Études médiévales de l'Université catholique de Louvain, 1997), 109–25; and Bruno Laurioux, *Les livres de cuisine médiévaux*, Typologie des sources du Moyen Âge occidental 77 (Turnhout: Brepols, 1997).

year."[9] In other words, the yearly provisions are calculated for ca. 43 persons which include the members of the household plus others who may be guests or local paupers or both. Of pepper, ginger, and other spices it orders to buy ca. 37 kg for them, that is, ca. 0.86 kg per person.[10] Since candied spices are ordered separately, without specifying the quantity but arranging for it almost the same amount of money as for the spices themselves,[11] we can assume that the latter item was not for making candies and, possibly, not even for making medicine; nothing indicates, however, that it was not used for making perfumes, apart from cooking.

But, at any rate, is 0.86 kg per person per year very much? In the USA, the *per capita availability* of spices in 2015 was ca. 1.7 kg (3.7 lbs);[12] food waste in the USA is estimated at 30–40%,[13] which means that ca. 1–1.2 kg of the amount available per capita was actually consumed. Moreover, modern statistics of spice consumption do not include sugar because today sugar does not count as spice. It was not the case in the Middle Ages, however. Thus, if the spice provisions of the household of Beatrice of Hungary contained sugar as well, then the figure of 0.86 kg per person per year must have been doubly over-calculated from our perspective: once for aristocratic generosity and once for including sugar.

Cookbooks are even vaguer on quantities than household accounts. Dosage was apparently not regarded as a necessary part of the recipe as such; rather, it was seen as something that depended on the taste and medical characteristics of the persons for whom a dish was made. And what was true of main ingredients, it was all the more so of spices, the dosage of which – with regard to salt and pepper at least – even modern cookbooks tend to entrust to the cook (cf. "add salt and pepper to taste"). As a consequence, cookbooks are more informative about typical combinations of flavours and the popularity of specific spices in those mainly aristocratic milieus from which the recipes originated, than about quantities used.

---

[9] "Summa dictarum personarum in numero, inclusa Domina: XXX. Extimantes esse necessaria pro dicta Domina matre nostra cum personis praedictis et trezena quolibet anno, videlicet..." Jean-Pierre Moret de Bourchenu, marquis de Valbonnais, *Histoire de Dauphiné et des princes qui ont porté le nom de dauphins*, 2 vols (Geneva: Fabri et Barillot, 1722), 2:519 (with slightly different punctuation). For the interpretation of the word *trezena*, see the editor's note, ibid., 523.

[10] "De speciebus piperis, gingiberis, et aliarum per annum circa unum quintale, valent: LXVI. flor. VIII. gross." Ibid. I have relied on the exchange rate between quintals and kilograms given in Laurioux, *Une histoire culinaire*, 195n. Laurioux (ibid., 194–95) calculates the per capita ratio for thirty persons, not considering the *trezena* (see the quotation in note 9 above).

[11] "Pro confectibus specierum per ann. L. flor." Valbonnais, *Histoire de Dauphiné* 2, 519.

[12] "Coffee, tea, cocoa, and spices," in *Food Availability (Per Capita) Data System*, USDA, Economic Research System, www.ers.usda.gov/data-products/food-availability-per-capita-data-system (last accessed 2 October 2018).

[13] USDA, Office of the Chief Economist, http://www.usda.gov/oce/foodwaste/faqs.htm (last accessed 2 October 2018). In 1966, the per capita availability of spices was only 0.54 kg (1.2 lbs) and it has grown constantly ever since; on the other hand, in 1966 the rate of food waste must have been much lower too.

Recipes of the fourteenth and fifteenth centuries contain altogether a dozen and a half different spices: cardamom, cassia, cinnamon, cloves, coriander, cubeb (*piper cubeba*), cumin, curcuma, galangal, ginger, grains of paradise (melegueta pepper), mace, nutmeg, black and white pepper (*piper nigrum*), long pepper (*piper longum*), saffron, spikenard, and sugar.[14] Some of them (cubeb, grains of paradise, black and white pepper, long pepper) were hot, some (galangal and ginger) only if uncooked, others not at all. "Spicyness" or "hotness" is sometimes recommended explicitly in medieval recipes, implying that it was not the rule. An Anglo-Norman recipe collection written around 1300, for example, writes about a dish made with cloves, mace and cubebs that "let it taste strongly with spices" (*qu'il savoure bien d'espices*), or about another one made with cloves and cubebs that "it should be hot" (*doit estre chaud*).[15]

One of the advantages of cookbooks as historical sources is that they permit statistical comparisons of recipes in terms of the relative frequency of their ingredients and thus help revealing some of the underlying culinary preferences. If, relying on the data gathered by Bruno Laurioux, we compare the frequency of regular pepper, melegueta pepper and saffron in fourteenth- and fifteenth-century recipe collections from different regions of Europe we can observe some interesting regional patterns in cooking for high-status diners (see table 1).[16]

Recipe collections	Regular pepper	Grains of paradise	Saffron
French (N=11)	13 (0–45; 17)	19 (0–68; 19)	23 (14–39; 9)
English (N=15)	21 (0–38; 11)	2 (0–8; 2)	38 (12–69;12)
Iberian (N=3)	20 (13–22; 5)	2 (0–3; 2)	17 (14–20; 3)
German and North European (N=10)	17 (2–37; 12)	2 (0–17; 5)	19 (0–39; 12)
Italian (N=14)	12 (3–22; 6)	2 (0–4; 1)	33 (16–64; 13)

Table 1: Frequency of selected spices in medieval cookbooks from different regions of Europe (average percentage of recipes containing the spice in question with range and standard deviation, all rounded up to integers; source: see note 16)

The Iberian figures based on limited evidence may not be relevant, but the frequencies of regular pepper in French, English, as well as German and North European cookbooks are characterized by wide range and high standard deviation suggesting big differences between the cooks who compiled these collections:

---

[14] Laurioux, *Une histoire culinaire*, 158–60.

[15] Constance B. Hieatt, "Medieval Britain," in *Regional Cuisines of Medieval Europe: A Book of Essays*, ed. Melitta Weiss Adamson (London and New York: Routledge, 2002), 19–45, at 26 and 37.

[16] Laurioux, *Une histoire culinaire*, 443–50. Laurioux analyzes the data differently.

some of them recommended the use of pepper in a large part of the dishes described, while others only in a small part. This result can be compared to Helmut Klug's finding in his study of another corpus of German cookbooks concerning their flavouring practice that regular pepper is mentioned in merely 10% of all recipes but the generic term *würze* occurs in 40% of them; the referents of *würze* may or may not have included pepper depending on the circumstances in which the meals were prepared.[17] Following this lead, it may be possible to explain (away) the big intra-regional differences in Laurioux's data by supposing that cookbooks with low frequencies of pepper only indicate it among the ingredients when it was deemed necessary but it could still be added to other meals as well.

Another possible explanation is that pepper was a divisive spice among high-status diners in, at least, some areas of Europe. In France, for example, grains of paradise show a higher level of average use with similarly big differences between cookbooks, while saffron was even more frequent with much lower differences. In England saffron is strongly preferred to pepper with limited consistency, while grains of paradise are consistently disliked. Elites of Germany and Northern Europe – as far as Laurioux's data is concerned – were moderately enthusiastic about both pepper and saffron with significant intra-regional differences, and uniformly indifferent about grains of paradise. Their Italian counterparts had consistently low interest in regular pepper (and even lower and even more consistently in grains of paradise) but tended to appreciate saffron very much albeit with major disagreements between recipe collections. In general, saffron seems to have been a more popular and less divisive spice than regular (let alone melegueta) pepper. Considered that saffron is far stronger in colour than in taste, the use of spices in the kitchen may have been aimed more at making food *look* attractive than *feel* pungent.[18]

A major implication of these statistics is that inter- and intra-regional differences in the recommended use of (these) spices are too big for permitting the reconstruction of long-term changes – on the basis of recipes, at least. Household accounts, however, if they are interrogated not for the quantities consumed but for the selection of spices purchased, show declining interest in pepper in the French elite, parallel to an increasing penchant for *grain de paradis* also prized by a number of French cooks, as we have seen above.[19] Saffron purchases of French aristocratic households were also plummeting in the course of the fifteenth century but

[17] Helmut W. Klug, "*gewürcz wol vnd versalcz nicht*: Auf der Suche nach skalaren Erklärungsmodellen zur Verwendung von Gewürzen in mittelalterlichen Kochrezepten," *Medium Aevum Quotidianum* 61 (2010): 56–83, at 80.

[18] Cf. Christopher Woolgar, "Fast and Feast: Conspicuous Consumption and the Diet of the Nobility in the Fifteenth Century," in *Revolution and Consumption in Late Medieval England*, ed. Michael Hicks (Woodbridge UK and Rochester NY: Boydell, 2001), 7–25, at 20–22; Klug, "*gewürcz wol vnd versalcz nicht*," 70–74.

[19] Laurioux, *Une histoire culinaire*, 187–88. Its popularity in the French elite can be traced in toll registers as well (ibid., 287n).

whereas the retreat of pepper was accompanied by its democratization, that of the saffron witnessed its mounting price.[20]

Much of these changes, of course, cannot be studied on the basis of household accounts alone; the latter need to be supplemented by scattered references in various other sources and, more systematically, by documents of the spice trade. From the thirteenth century onwards, we can see pepper appearing in social contexts well below the elites like colleges of students in Trets (Provence) and Toulouse, a military garrison in Edinburgh, a hospital in Neubourg (Normandy), or even among peasants and artisans in Montauban.[21] A medical commentary composed in Leuven around 1480 and falsely attributed to Arnau de Vilanova calls pepper-sauce "the sauce of peasants," and adds that "[t]hey, indeed, mix pepper-sauce with beans and peas."[22] On the other hand, no similar evidence for a tendency towards democratization is known to me from Central and Northern Europe. Given the low level of European market integration (measured by price correlations between various local markets) in the fifteenth century, and the dependence of price differences on geographical distance as demonstrated by Kevin O'Rourke and Jeffrey Williamson,[23] pepper may have remained less accessible to those on the lower rungs of the social ladder in much of the German-speaking areas, and the Kingdoms of Poland and Hungary; or, levels of accessibility may well have been quite patchy everywhere, depending very much on one's location even in France which offers most of the evidence of democratization analyzed in the literature so far.

All these difficulties in the source material notwithstanding there remains the fact that Europe's pepper imports were growing incessantly throughout the fifteenth and the sixteenth centuries and, according to C. H. H. Wake, more so before ca. 1500 than afterwards. Moreover, the spice trade in general, and that of the expensive Moluccan spices (nutmeg, mace, cloves) in particular, grew much more than pepper imports already before Vasco da Gama's discovery of the sea route to

---

[20] Ibid., 187.

[21] Ibid., 190.

[22] "[P]onuntur quinque ex quibus potest fieri salsamentum. [...] Tertium est piper et est salsamentum rusticorum. Commiscent enim piper cum fabis et pisis." *Commentum Arnaldi de Villa Nova super Regimen Salernitanum*, in Arnau de Vilanova, *Opera nuperrime recognita ac emendata* (Venice: Scotus, 1505), fols. 150a–72d, at fol. 157r. Cf. Laurioux, *Une histoire culinaire*, 191; Freedman, *Out of the East*, 43; and Ernest Wickersheimer, "Autour du Régime de Salerne," *Le Scalpel* 50 (1952): 1–12.

[23] Kevin H. O'Rourke and Jeffrey G. Williamson, "Did Vasco da Gama Matter to European Markets?" *Economic History Review* 62 (2009): 655–84.

India,[24] suggesting that elites were shifting their resources from pepper to finer spices less associated with low-status consumers.[25]

Unfortunately, quantities of spices for sale in fifteenth-century Europe can be known from ports of entry (Venice, Genoa, Barcelona) alone, thus it seems impossible to know the ratios of distribution between different parts of the continent. For the sixteenth century, however, we have estimates to this effect from two insiders of the trade, the Augsburg merchant Konrad Rott, and the consul of the Hanseatic League in Lisbon, Hans Kampferbek. According to them, most of the pepper imported by the Portuguese ended up in Central and Northern Europe, and the least of it went to the Hispanic Peninsula.[26] If the supposed trend towards democratization in the fifteenth and sixteenth centuries is correct, then the main European consumers of pepper after ca. 1500 must have been below-the-elite social groups residing in German-speaking areas and some of the surrounding territories.

Where does chili, the new hot spice from America, fit in this picture of democratization and regional difference? Who were most interested in it? Those in the North or those in the South? Those high on the social ladder or those below them?

The Arrival of the Chili

In the accounts of his first voyage, one of the most important issues discussed by Christopher Columbus was the economic use of the islands discovered by him. In his letter to the "most Christian and lofty and powerful sovereigns" of 4 March 1493, he mentions "spicery of a certain pepper to fill as many ships as Your Highnesses may order to be loaded."[27] Earlier in the same text he also gives the local Taino name of this "certain pepper" as *agí*, while in his letter to the Chancellor of

---

24 "[T]he increase in pepper imports was at most about 64% in the fifteenth century, and more likely under 45% (as against upwards of 177% for spices), and about 27% in the sixteenth century. What the pattern for the spice trade as a whole was for the sixteenth century is not known, though [...] the trade in Moluccan spices [...] appears to have grown as much as 500% between 1500 and 1620." C. H. H. Wake, "The Changing Pattern of Europe's Pepper and Spice Imports, ca. 1400–1700," *The Journal of European Economic History* 8 (1979): 361–403, at 392.

25 The real (grain-deflated) price of both pepper and the fine spices was declining all over Europe after the Portuguese's joining the trade. See O'Rourke and Williamson, "Did Vasco da Gama Matter," 667–69.

26 Hermann Kellenbenz, "Autour de 1600: Le commerce du poivre des Fugger et le marché international du poivre," *Annales: Économies, Sociétés, Civilisations* 11 (1956): 1–28, at 7–11; Stefan Halikowski Smith, "Demystifying a Change in Taste: Spices, Space, and Social Hierarchy in Europe, 1380–1750," *The International History Review* 29 (2007): 237–57, at 241–42.

27 "Especería de una pimienta, quantas naos Vuestras Altezas mandaren cargar y almastiga quanta mandaren cargar." The letter is edited and translated in Margarita Zamora, *Reading Columbus* (Berkeley: University of California Press, 1993), 181–97; the quotations are from pp. 186 (Spanish) and 194 (English).

the Exchequer of Aragon, Luís de Santángel, he relates about the islanders that they endure cold winters "with the help of meats which they eat with much and excessively hot spices."[28]

A year later, another Italian in Spanish royal service, the humanist Pietro Martire d'Anghiera (1457–1526), sent a sample of the new hot spice, brought home by Columbus in the form of seeds, to the papal vice-chancellor, Ascanio Sforza (1455–1505); in the attached letter he called it "more pungent to the taste than Caucasian pepper," and warned the vice-chancellor to taste them "with caution; not that they are harmful, but they are very peppery, and if you leave them a long time in your mouth, they will sting the tongue. In case you should burn your tongue a little in tasting them, take some water, and the burning sensation will be allayed."[29] Apparently, Pietro Martire did not expect his correspondence partner to have been accustomed to particularly hot food.

This is how the "pepper" that has come to be known as *chili* (its name in Nahuatl) made its entrance into the Old World. By the end of the sixteenth century, it was apparently known and used almost everywhere in Europe. Fernandez de Oviedo (1478–1557), the governor of Santo Domingo at the time, wrote in the seventh book of his *Historia general y natural de las Indias* first published in 1535, that the *axi* or *pimienta de los indios* "is shipped to Spain and Italy, and other regions as a very good spice [...] and merchants and other persons are sent for it from Europe, and they look for it eagerly for their own greed and appetite."[30] Similarly, Leonhart

---

[28] "[C]on la ayuda delas viandas que comen con especias muchas y muy calientes en demasia." Richard Henry Major (ed., trans.), *Select Letters of Christopher Columbus, with Other Original Documents, Relating to His Four Voyages to the New World* (London: The Hakluyt Society, 1870), 13. My translation; Major translates it as "by eating meat with a variety of excessively hot spices."

[29] "Grana quaedam rugosa diversorum colorum Caucaseo pipere acutiora [...] [Si] ex granis [...] gustare volueris, illustrissime Princeps, tenuiter admoto labello, pertingito: sunt enim, quamvis non noxia, ob nimiam tamen caliditatis acuitatem, acria et linguam, si in ea diu morentur, expungunt; sed statim, si forte eius degustatione lingua concoquatur, epota aqua, asperitas illa tollitur." Pietro Martire d'Anghiera, *De orbe novo decades*, 2 vols., ed. Rosanna Mazzacane and Elisa Magioncalda (Genoa: Dipartimento di Archeologia, Filologia Classica e Loro Tradizioni, Università di Genova, 2005), decade 1, bk. 1, p. 49 and decade 1, bk. 2, p. 71–73. The quotations in the main text are taken from *De Orbe Novo: The Eight Decades of Peter Martyr D'Anghera*, trans. Francis Augustus MacNutt (New York: The Knickerbocker Press, 1912), 65 and 84. "Caucasian pepper" refers to regular pepper since according to Pliny, *Hist. Nat.* 12, 14 (trans. H. Rackham, Loeb Classical Library 370, [Cambridge, MA: Harvard University Press, 194], 19): "trees resembling our junipers that bear pepper occur everywhere [in India – O.G.], although some writers have reported that they only grow on the southern face of the Caucasus." Similarly, Isidor of Seville writes that pepper „grows in India on the side of Mount Caucasus exposed to the sun." *Etym.* 17, 8; quoted in Freedman, *Out of the East*, 133.

[30] "Llévasse á España é á Italia é á otras partes por muy buena especia [...] é desde Europa envian por ello mercaderes é otras personas, é lo buscan con diligencia para su propria gula é apetito." Gonzalo Fernández de Oviedo y Valdés, *Historia general y natural de las Indias, islas y tierra-firme del mar océano*, ed. José Amador de los Rios, 4 vols. (Madrid: Imprenta de la Real Academia de la Historia, 1851–1855), bk. 7, ch. 7, vol. 1, p. 275.

Fuchs (1501–1566) observed in 1542 that "[i]t is found almost everywhere in Germany now, planted in clay pots and earthen vessels" and "many use this instead of true pepper."[31] His fellow German botanist, Hieronymus Bock (1498–1554), called it *Teütscher Pfeffer* already in 1539.[32] According to Bartolomé de las Casas (1484–1566), writing around 1552, it "is known in all of Spain [and] it counts as a healthy spice as stated by our physicians."[33] The Seville doctor and author of a very successful handbook of American plants, Nicolas Monardes (1493–1588), adds (in a contemporary English translation) that it "serueth not onely for Medicine, but it is otherwise most excellent, the which is knowen in all Spayne, for there is no Gardeyne, nor Orcharde, but that it hath plentie thereof in it."[34] Carolus Clusius (Charles de l'Écluse, 1526–1609), remembers "to have also seen it grown in the greatest abundance, in the 1585th year of Christ, in the suburban gardens of the famous city of Brno in the March of Moravia; and the farmers made a considerable profit from it, since the common people used it frequently."[35] A few years later it appears to have been ubiquitous in (Southern) Italy as well, as implied in the comment of the Neapolitan polymath, Giovanni Battista della Porta (1535–1615),

---

[31] "In Germania iam in fictilibus ac testaceis satum passim fere provenit. Perpaucis anteannis Germanis incognitum fuit. [...]. Valenter excalfacit atque desiccat, id quod seminis immensa acrimonia et foliorum amaritudo evidentissime monstrat, ut certe non temere plerique hoc semine loco veri Piperis utantur." Frederick G. Meyer, Emily E. Trueblood, and John L. Heller, *The Great Herbal of Leonhart Fuchs:* De historia stirpium commentarii insignes, *1542 (Notable Commentaries on the History of Plants)*, 2 vols. (Stanford: Stanford University Press, 1999), 1, 622 (English), 2,731 and 735 (Latin, with slightly different punctuation).

[32] Hieronymus Bock, *New kreütter Buch: Von vnderscheydt, würckung und namen der kreütter so in Teütschen landen wachsen* etc. (Strasbourg: Rihel, 1539), pt. 2, ch. 117, fol. 86v–87r.

[33] "[E]s en toda España conocida. Tiénese por especia sana, según acá dicen nuestros medicos." Quoted in Janet Long-Solis, *Capsicum y cultura: La historia del chilli* (México: Fondo de Cultura Económico, 1986), 34.

[34] "[N]o solo sirve a medicina, pero es excelentissima, la qual es conocida en toda España, porque no ay jardin, ni huerta, ni maceton que no la tenga sembrada." Nicolas Monardes, *Primera y segunda y tercera partes de la Historia medicinal de las cosas que se traen de nuestras Indias Occidentales que sirven en Medicine* etc. (Seville: Escrivano, 1574), fol. 24v translated as *Ioyfull newes out of the newfound world wherein are declared the rare and singular vertues of diuers and sundrie herbs, trees, oyles, plants, [and] stones* etc., by John Frampton (London: Norton, 1580 [1577]), fol. 20r–v. Clusius confirms its widespread use in Spain on the basis of his own observations as well: "Piper igitur Americanum diligentissime coli observabam, dum per Hispaniam peregrinabar anno Christi millesimo quingentesimo, sexagesimo quarto, in multis eius Regni provinciis, praesertim vero tota Castella vetere et nova, cum ab hortulanis, tum a mulieribus in aedium suarum pensilibus hortis; etenim per totum annum eo utebantur recente et sicco pro condimento in cibis." Carolus Clusius, *Curae posteriores, seu plurimarum non ante cognitarum aut descriptarum stirpium, peregrinorumque aliquot animalium novae descriptiones* (Leiden: Raphelengius, 1611), 54. See also Rebecca Earle, *The Body of the Conquistador: Food, Race and the Colonial Experience in Spanish America, 1492–1700* (Cambridge: Cambridge University Press, 2012), 137–38.

[35] "Memini etiam videre anno Christi M. D. XXCV. maxima copia cultum in suburbanis Brunnae celebris Marchionatus Moraviae urbis hortis, e quo cultores non contemnendum quaestum faciebant; erat enim apud vulgus frequens eius usus." Clusius, *Curae posteriores,* 54.

that "we plant and cultivate it in our gardens and in pots both for its visual appeal and for cooking."[36]

Clusius' comment on the social status of its consumers will be of interest for us later on, but now it is worth coming back to the problem of how the pungency of the chili was initially perceived. We have seen that for Colombus the spices used by the American natives were "excessively hot," and that Pietro Martire warned Ascanio Sforza to taste chili seed with due caution. A century later, a Capuchin friar, a certain Fra Gregorio da Reggio, who became the main chili expert of the period growing 25 different types in the Bolognese convent of his order, described a method of how to make red pepper less hot:

> This pepper was not merely not used as a medication but it was not added to food either, because of the outstanding pungency that comes with it. Nonetheless, human talent has apparently found a method through which its defectiveness can be amended, so that it could be put to use without any inconvenience as a condiment of food, and also applied as a medication if prepared in the following way: we pick the ripen hulls or pods of this pepper with the stems on and dry them in the shade; when we want to utilize them, we put them with flour in a vessel similar to the one used by apothecaries for drying almonds and pine nuts to be coated with sugar, and slowly dry them on the fire; then we clean off the flour, and remove the stems; then, with a pincer, we cut them in small pieces and weigh them together with the seeds, and add to each ounce of pods and seeds one pound of finely ground flour, knead the whole together with yeast in the manner of bread, and leave the dough to leaven; when it is leavened well, we bake it in the oven; if set, we cut them in slices, and bake them again in the manner of toasts; finally, we pound them in a copper or other kind of mortar and let them through a sieve.[37]

---

[36] "Nos hortis nostris, et vasculis, tum plantae spectaculo, tum culinis, eam serimus, et colimus." Giovanni Battista della Porta, *Villae libri XII* (Frankfurt a M.: Wechel, 1592), bk.10, ch. 51, p. 714. Vito Teti goes out of his way to show that chili appears in the works of the Calabrian philosopher Tommaso Campanella but it does not seem sure for me that what is meant by him is chili pepper indeed, and not just the regular one. See Teti, *Storia del pepperoncino*, ch. 5.

[37] "Non modo in medicamenti usum receptum non erat hoc piper, sed neque in cibum etiam admittebatur, propter insignem illam acrimoniam qua praeditum est. Nihilominus videtur humanum ingenium rationem invenisse qua eius malignitas corrigeretur, ut in usum recipi posset sine ullo incommodo ad cibos condiendum, atque etiam pro medicamento usurpati, hoc modo preparatum: maturae huius piperis vesicae sive siliquae leguntur cum suis pediculis, et in umbra siccantur; quando quis uti volet, reponat in vase illi simili quo utuntur pharmacopolae ad resiccandos amygdalarum et nucis pinae nucleos quos saccharo operire volunt, cum farina, et exsiccet lento igne; deinde a farina purgentur, et a pediculis suis liberentur; deinde cum forcipe minutissime cum suis seminibus incisae ponderantur, atque singulis siliquarum cum semine unciis, pollinis farinae libra additur, pinsuntur simul omnia cum fermento panis instar, et fermentari haec massa sinitur; probe fermentata in clibano coquitur, cocta in taleas scinditur, et denuo coquitur, instar biscocti; postremo in aheneo mortario aut alio tenuissime teritur et per cribrum transmittitur." Fra

Independently of Fra Gregioro, and in much less detail, the Roman doctor and botanist, Castore Durante (1529–1590), writing around 1585, also described the same method:

> It is used in all condiments of food because its taste is better than that of regular pepper; and in order to make it more enjoyable, its pods are pounded together with the seeds, added to a dough and prepared as toasts, which mixed with the usual spices enhances their flavor pretty well."[38]

Interestingly enough, in the sixteenth century, I found this method in Italy alone.[39] Others either did not portray chili as excessively hot, or they did but also regarded it as poisonous. Spanish authors – including Fernandez de Oviedo and Monardes – are in the first group while northerners – like the Flemish physician and botanist Rembert Dodoens (1517–1585), his German colleague, Joachim Camerarius the Younger (1534–1598), or the English herbalist, John Gerarde (1545–1612) – are in the second.[40] Some of the northerners saw Spain as the place of Europe where it was typically eaten in spite of its supposedly unhealthy character. According to Gerarde, for example,

> in Spaine and sundrie parts of the Indies they do use to dresse their meate therewith, as we do with Calecute pepper [i.e. regular pepper – O.G.]: but

---

Gregorio had sent his work to Clusius and it was published in the latter's *Curae posteriores* on pp. 50–57; the quotation is from p. 56.

38 "Si usa in tutti i condimenti de i cibi, perche è di miglior gusto, che il pepe comune, e per farlo più piacevole, si pestano le sue guaine insieme col seme, e s'incorporano con pasta, e se ne fa pan biscotto, il quale accompagnato con le spetie communi le moltiplica con non ingrato sapore." Castore Durante, *Herbario nuovo di Castore Durante medico e cittadino romano con figure che rappresentano le vive piante, che nascono in tutta Europa, e nell'Indie Orientali e Occidentali* etc. (Rome: Iacomo Bericchia and Iacomo Tornierij, 1585), 344.

39 It does pop up, however, in late eighteenth-century Hungary: "Some also grind it and, kneaded together with flour, bake it like a bread, which they use for flavoring." ("Némellyek porrá törve és lisztel egybe-gyúrva kenyérnek-is sütik, mellyel azután bors hellyett füszerszámoznak"). István Mátyus, *Ó és Új diaetetica az az: az életnek és egésségnek fenn-tartására és gyámolgatására, Istentől adattatott nevezetesebb természeti eszközöknek való elszámlálása.* [Old and new dietetics, or an account of the most notable natural means given by God for sustaining and safeguarding life and health] 6 vols (Bratislava: Landerer, 1787–1793), vol. 4, 339. The use of chili (*paprika*) as a condiment in Hungary is not attested before the eighteenth century, even if the plant is known to have been grown already between the 1570s and 1590 in the garden of Boldizsár Batthyány at Stadtschlaining/Szalónak in modern-day Austria; see Dóra Bobory, *The Sword and the Crucible: Count Boldizsár Batthyány and Natural Philosophy in Sixteenth-Century Hungary* (Newcastle upon Tyne: Cambridge Scholars Publishing, 2009), 98–99.

40 See Rembert Dodoens, *Stirpium historiae pemptades sex, sive libri XXX* (Antwerp: Plantin, 1583), 705; Camerarius in Pietro Andrea Mattioli and Joachim Camerarius, *De plantis epitome utilissima Petri Andreae Matthioli Senensis [...]. Novis iconibus et descriptionibus pluribus nunc primum diligenter aucta a D. Ioachimo Camerario, medico inclytae Reipublicae Noribergensis* (Frankfurt am Main: Feyerabend, 1586), 348; John Gerarde, *The Herball or Generall Historie of Plantes* (London: Norton, 1597), 293.

> (saith my author [i.e. Dodoens]) it hath in it malitious qualitie, whereby it is an enimie to the liver and other of the entrails.[41]

The idea of regarding chili as poisonous was based on its identification with *Zingiber caninum* which is said to kill dogs in Avicenna's *Canon*.[42] This identification we do not find in the above mentioned Spanish or Italian authors, not because they did not know their Avicenna, but because they probably knew their chili consumed more frequently around them. According to Monardes, it is

> used in al manner of meates and pottages, for that it hath better tast then the common Peper hath. Beaten in peeces, and cast into broth it is an excellent sauce, they doe use it in al thinges that the aromatike spices are used in, which are brought from Maluco, and Calicut. It doeth differ from that of the East Indias, for that costeth many ducates, and this other doth cost no more but to sowe it, for that in one plant you have spice for one whole yere, with lesse hurte and more profite."[43]

In other words, it is not only better than regular pepper but it is also more economical. It is something you are supposed to eat only for its culinary and medical qualities not being suitable for showing off. That chili, in spite of the enthusiasm surrounding it, never made it to early modern Spanish cookbooks,[44] confirms the latter point.

This brings us back to Clusius' comment on the chili pepper cultivated in Brno: "the common people used it frequently." His account is corroborated by the protestant parson and author, Johannes Coler, who saw it sold a few years before 1596 in Frankfurt a. d. Oder for four silver groats (*Groschen*) a pound, that is much less than regular pepper which came for at least sixteen groats a pound, and reported that "the simple folk regards it as their best pepper."[45] Monardes, by contrast,

---

41 Gerarde, *The Herball*, 293; see also Iacobus Theodorus Tabernaemontanus, Hieronymus Bauhin, and Caspar Bauhin, *Iacobi Theodori Tabernaemontani New vollkommen Kräuter-Buch [...]. Vormahls durch D. Casparum Bauhinum [...] gebesseret. Jetzt widerumb auffs newe übersehen [...] durch Hieronymum Bauhinum* etc. (Basel: König and Werenfels, 1664), 1242–43.

42 Avicenna, *Canon medicinae*, 5 vols. (Venice: Pierre Maufer, 1486), bk. 2, tract 2, ch. 748 (without continuous foliation).

43 Monardes, *Ioyfull newes*, fol. 20v. Probably the same is implied in Della Porta's assertion that "[p]iperis vice, quod ex India nobis defertur, herbae cuiusdam siliquis, et granis, quod suo piperis gustu iura commendet, quam saepissime utimur." Della Porta, *Villae*, 714.

44 Jeanne Allard, "Les produits des «Indes Occidentales» dans la cuisine espagnole au siècle d'Or," in *Des Indes Occidentales à l'Amérique Latine*, ed. Thomas Calvo and Alain Musset (Lyon: ENS Éditions, 1997), 137–42 at 139–40.

45 "Ein Pfund Pfeffer umb sechzehen Groschen oder ein halben Taler, wenn er gans ist. [...] Ich hab auch zu Franckfurt an der Oder eine art des Pfeffers gesehen [...] den nennen sie auch Türckischen Pfeffer; [...] wird das Pfund umb 4 silber Groschen, oder 1 Ortstaler geben; das halten einfeltige Leute vor Iren besten Pfeffer." Johannnes Coler, *Oeconomia oder Hausbuch: Zum Calendario oeconomico et perpetuo gehörig*, 6 vols. (Wittenberg: Hellwig, 1593–1601), vol. (pt.) 3, bk. 9, ch. 34 (with slightly different punctuation, without page numbers). Cf. Kőszegi, "A paprika útjai," 266–67.

plainly did not belong to, and his audience hardly consisted of members of the "common people" or the "simple folk," and the consumers he is talking about are just Spaniards without further qualification in terms of social status. His enthusiasm for the chili was shared by those who came to know it in America. According to Fernandez de Oviedo "Christians do not like it less, and are no less devoted to it than the Indians […] and to tell the truth, the *ají* is better with meat and fish than the best pepper."[46] Similarly, Cervantes de Salazar also affirms in his *Chronicle* that in America the "Spaniards use it no less than the Indians."[47] Knowledge of and taste for chili pepper were surely transmitted by Spaniards from America to their relatives and acquaintances back home much before the publication of such learned accounts. Relation of personal experience must have played a part in making the allegedly poisonous character of chili difficult to believe and its diffusion not limited to the lower echelons of society most sensitive to the price of spices.

In Northern Europe, on the other hand, potential consumers of higher status were much less connected to sources of first-hand information. Indeed, many of them thought that chili had come from India (where, as a matter of fact, it had been introduced by the Portuguese). Matthias de L'Obel (Lobelius) and his assistant, Pierre Pena, wrote in 1571 that "this very beautiful plant started to be imported to Europe from Goa and the shores of Calicut in our times."[48] According to Fuchs, "[i]n German it is called *Chalechutischer* or *Indianischer Pfeffer*."[49] It may well be the case that the merchants from all over Europe mentioned by Fernandez de Oviedo spread the chili first among the poor of the North as a cheap substitute for pepper and the botanists like Fuchs encountered it first in this capacity. In Germany, chili could apparently be sold better if masked as regular pepper. "Some of our merchants and spice sellers, who are so much after the penny," writes Hieronymus Bock,

> know how to retail bastard pepper, which lacks all pungency and taste, efficiently, since they pound and mix seeds of the new hot German pepper

---

46 "[N]o es menos agradable a los cristianos, ni hacen menos por ello que los indios [...] y en la verdad, el ají es mejor con la carne e con el pescado que la muy buena pimiento." Fernández de Oviedo, *Historia general*, 1: 275–76.

47 "El agí sirve de especia en estas partes; […] es apetitoso, y de manera que los más guisados y salsas se hacen con él; usan dél no menos los españoles que los indios." Francisco Cervantes de Salazar, *Crónica de la Nueva España*, [ed. Manuel Magallón] (Madrid: The Hispanic Society of America, 1914), bk. 1., ch. 6, p. 15.

48 "Coepit nostra memoria ista perpulchra planta adferri ex Goa, et Calecutiis oris in Europam." Matthias de L'Obel and Pierre Pena, *Stirpium adversaria nova: Perfacilis vestigatio, luculentaque accessio ad priscorum, praesertim Dioscoridis et recentiorum materiam medicam* etc. (London: Thomas Purfoot, 1571), 134.

49 "Germanice dici potest *Chalechutischer oder Indianischer Pfeffer*." Meyer, Trueblood, and Heller, *The Great Herbal of Leonhart Fuchs*, vol. 1, 621 and vol. 2, 731. The chili arrived in Goa in the first half of the sixteenth century under the name "Pernambuco pepper" which refers to the Brazilian context where the Portuguese had become familiar with it; see Mazumdar, "The Impact of New World Food Crops," 60–61.

> (which we [Bock, or the botanists in general – O.G.] call *Siliquastrum* and *Zinziber caninum*) with the feeble tasteless bastard pepper, which they call among themselves "refuse", whereupon this pepper, feeble in itself, becomes rather hot and piquant, and they sell and distribute it as pepper of the highest quality.[50]

The account implies that this fake pepper *could* be sold as pepper of the highest quality, which suggests that many of the consumers were far from being pepper connoisseurs and what mattered to them was pungency and prestige. "German pepper" apparently failed to have the latter quality, while regular pepper continued to enjoy it since – as we have seen above – most of its import targeted Central and Northern Europe.

Conclusion

Having soon become a cheap domestic product all over Europe, chili pepper could not attempt to dethrone regular pepper as a new luxury like grains of paradise did in the elite cuisine of fifteenth-century France. But it was not entirely relegated to the status of a cheap and despised substitute either. In Spain, and partly in Italy, probably because of the personally related experiences of compatriots in America, it was regarded by many as genuinely better than regular pepper. It was neither trickling down from above nor creeping up from below. It spread as a socially rather undifferentiated condiment. In Central and Northern Europe, on the other hand, it emerged as a spice of the "common people" or the "simple folk."

Such a North–South difference in the reception of the chili is not necessarily the consequence of comparable differences in medieval taste. It could be argued (rather tentatively, of course) that Northern and Central Europeans were more into regular pepper than others in the sixteenth century because they had less of it in the Middle Ages due to higher prices. But it seems that chili became widely accepted not in those areas where regular pepper reigned supreme. Should we assume, on the other hand, that those who had (or could have had) more pepper in the Middle Ages were more accustomed or even more attracted to exceptional

---

[50] "[U]nsere kauffleüt unnd wurtzkremer zům theil, die dem pfennig so hart nach stellen, wissen den Basthart Pfeffer, welcher on alle scherpffe und geschmack ist, wol zůvertreiben, ursach sie stossen und mischen den newen hitzigen Teütschen pfeffer samen (den wir Siliquastrum unnd Zinziber caninum nennen) under den toerichten ongeschmackten Basthart pfeffer, welchen sie bei inen Gerbelier nennen, als dann würt der selbig toericht pfeffer ganz hitzig unnd zanger, und für den aller besten pfeffer verkaufft und vertreiben." Hieronymus Bock, *Teütsche speiszkammer: Inn welcher du findest was gesunden unnd krancken menschen [...] zur Kost und artznei gereichet werden sollen* (Strasbourg: Rihel, 1550), fol. 95r. For contemporary debates around the spice trade and its supposed moral and economic impact in Germany, see Christine R. Johnson, *The German Discovery of the World: Renaissance Encounters with the Strange and Marvelous* (Charlottesville and London: University of Virginia Press, 2008), 123–65.

pungency than those who had less of it, we cannot account for the fact that all early commentators from Italy found the chili excessively hot.

Moreover, if we try to go beyond the realm of the tentative and the hypothetical, tendencies in medieval taste for pungent spices are quite difficult to reconstruct, as we have seen above. And even if the consumption of high quantities had been true, the food of medieval elite groups was not an early variant of Tex-Mex. "Contemporary Italian or European food," write Alberto Capatti and Massimo Montanari about the late twentieth century,

> has a predominantly analytical character, which means that it tends to distinguish between flavors (sweet, salty, tart, sour, or spicy), reserving a separate place for each, both in individual dishes and in the order of courses served at a meal. Linked to this practice is the notion that the cook should respect as much as possible the natural flavor of each food: a flavor that is distinct and different and should be kept separate from other flavors [...] Renaissance cuisine, like that of the Middle Ages or – to go back further – the cuisine of ancient Rome, had developed a model of cooking based mainly on the concept of artifice and the mixture of flavors. Here the preparation of individual dishes and their presentation at various points throughout the meal disclose a synthetic rather than an analytical logic: in other words, the tendency to keep things together rather than to separate them.[51]

On this account, modern western (*hautes) cuisines* are analytic rather than synthetic, while medieval *hautes cuisines* were synthetic but not necessarily spicy in the modern sense. Even if adding hot sauces like Tabasco to any savory dish has the consequence of leveling tastes, the analytic character of modern cooking can be detected even here as these condiments have relatively few ingredients. Their flavour mainly depends on the type and quality of red pepper used for making them. Among sixteenth-century writers it is only Castore Durante who explicitly recommends using chili pepper together with the traditional spices. Others seem to refer to using it in ways that deny the synthetic taste of medieval cuisine, as *the* spice of the meal. In this sense, even if its journey to mainstream European taste lasted for centuries, the early appreciation of chili in southern Europe was more a harbinger of (post)modern food-ways than a reflection of medieval ones.

[51] Alberto Capatti and Massimo Montanari, *Italian Cuisine: A Cultural History*, trans. Áine O'Healy (New York: Columbia University Press, 2003), 86–87.

Janine Maegraith

Communal Favourite Things:

Food Gifts in Seventeenth-Century Bohemia[1]

Gift giving as a social practice embedded within the early modern economy has been recognised in various anthropological and historical studies.[2] The interconnectedness of gifts in local economies alongside market transactions, credit, inheritance, and other forms of exchange also suggests their importance for consumption studies. Food constituted one of the main expenses of a household in early modern Central Europe, and especially in times of crisis alternative forms of food acquisition to smooth out temporary shortages was vital. Food gifts could act as support but also as a means to create or strengthen social bonds or to back political negotiations. The potential of gifts for food history emerged from the works by Natalie Zemon Davis and Felicity Heal, amongst others.[3] As an alternative form of transaction and the allocation of foodstuffs, food gifts can also complement and question current narratives in historiography: do early modern ego-documents reveal periodical consumption changes in their region as postulated by Wilhelm Abel, for example? What expectancies did people have in terms of food consumption? Does the social hierarchy in the consumption of specific foods, as described in the literature, correspond with actual practice? Looking at food gifts also enables us to analyse communal consumption and sociability, which

---

[1] I would like to thank Veronika Čapská, Craig Muldrew and Ingrid Matschinegg for their valuable comments and the Silesian University of Opava for inviting me for a visiting fellowship in 2013, during which I could pursue much of my research. The slightly different version of the article appeared in Czeck in Janine Maegraith, "Sdílení oblíbených věcí. Dárcovství jídla a dějiny konzumu v severovýchchodních čechách 17. Století" [Communal favourite things. Food gifts and consumption history in seventeenth-century Northwest Bohemia], *Dějiny–teorie–kritika* 2 (2017): 226–67.

[2] Marcel Mauss, *The Gift: The Form and Reason for Exchange in Archaic Societies*, trans. W. D. Halls (New York and London: W. W. Norton, 1990) [Mauss's 1925 *Essai sur le Don*]; Natalie Zemon Davis, *The Gift in Sixteenth-Century France* (Madison: University of Wisconsin Press and Oxford: Oxford University Press, 2000); Felicity Heal, "Food Gifts. The Household and the Politics of Exchange in Early Modern England," *Past and Present* 199 (2008): 41–70; Ilana Krausman Ben-Amos, *The Culture of Giving: Informal Support and Gift-Exchange in Early Modern England* (Cambridge: Cambridge University Press, 2009); Craig Muldrew, *The Economy of Obligation. The Culture of Credit and Social Relations in Early Modern England* (Basingstoke and New York: Palgrave, 1998); Hans Peter Hahn, *Materielle Kultur. Eine Einführung* (Berlin: Reimer, 2005), 89–99, and others.

[3] Davis, *The Gift*, esp. 34–36, 40–42; Heal, "Food Gifts," 41–70.

recently experienced an increase in scholarly interest, especially in the context of alcohol consumption.[4] Finally, looking at changes over time or distribution of food gifts, personal strategies can be addressed: How did people deal with crises and scarce food supplies? How did their practices change when they experienced social decline?

While inventory studies allow an insight into people's everyday lives and well-being – and the analysis of kitchen tools, crockery, supplies and crops have revealed various aspects of food history – they necessarily leave some questions unanswered.[5] They remain static documents which allow a snapshot of a specific time and household but limited dynamic insights. Only long-term quantitative analyses of inventories can reveal changes over time, but the decisions of the individuals remain obscure.[6] However, the very existence of inventories drawn up to regulate inheritance matters or to specify the allocation of marital property points to other ways of acquiring goods, such as inheritance, marriage or, as mentioned in some inventories and wills, by gifts. Therefore, using ego-documents to supplement what we know from serial documents is an important way to learn more about the individual's experiences and decisions.[7] For example, did the presence of a butter-churn in a household mean that butter was made on a regular basis or only occasionally? Or was the object simply inherited and not used? Was some of the butter produced at home shared with others and given to neighbours, family members or friends as a gift? Or was some of it sold on the market? The analysis of ego-documents and of food gifts can contribute to such debates and potentially reveal the meaning that material goods had for people.

Gift giving, exchange, and sharing of goods were, alongside commercial transactions and inheritance, marital property transfer, charity, home production,

---

[4] On hospitality and sociability see Gabriele Jancke, *Gastfreundschaft in der frühneuzeitlichen Gesellschaft. Praktiken, Normen und Perspektiven von Gelehrten* (Göttingen: V & R unipress, 2013); on England see, e. g., Mark Hailwood, *Alehouses and Good Fellowship in Early Modern England* (Woodbridge: Boydell Press, 2014).

[5] On inventory studies with regard to kitchen tools and crockery see, e.g., Sarah Pennell, "'For a crack or flaw despis'd:' Thinking about Ceramic Durability and the 'Everyday' in Late Seventeenth- and Early Eighteenth-Century England," in *Everyday Objects: Medieval and Early Modern Material Culture and Its Meanings* (Farnham: Ashgate, 2010); Sheilagh Ogilvie, Markus Küpker, and Janine Maegraith, "Frauen und die materielle Kultur des Essens im frühneuzeitlichen Württemberg: Ergebnisse aus Wildberger Inventaren," *Zeitschrift für Württembergische Landesgeschichte* 71 (2012): 229–54.

[6] See Janine Maegraith and Craig Muldrew, "Consumption and Material Life," in *Oxford Handbook of Early Modern European History*, ed. Hamish Scott (Oxford: Oxford University Press, 2015), vol. I, 369–97, here 372 and 390–91.

[7] Jancke's study on early modern hospitality is an excellent example of the use of ego-documents and showing their potential, see Jancke, *Gastfreundschaft*, 30–31. See for the use of diaries for early modern England, for example, Craig Muldrew, "The culture of reconciliation: community and the settlement of economic disputes in early modern England," *The Historical Journal* 39 (1996): 915–42; Amanda Vickery, *The Gentleman's Daughter. Women's Lives in Georgian England* (New Haven, CT: Yale University Press, 1998).

and credit relations firm components of the complex early modern *mixed economy,* which consequently had several different levels of obligations. This heterogeneity of practices proved successful especially during times of crisis. A crisis and shortages of money and goods could then be bridged with informal support from neighbours, friends and kin. However, obligations and reciprocity remained fundamental criteria. The author of the memoir discussed here wrote in 1642, after he had received much-welcome food gifts, how he hoped to be himself in a positon again to give to others.[8] Gifts created obligations and maintained networks of relations besides those formed by credit and market exchanges. In addition, food gifts point to the frequent communal consumption of these gifts.

In this article I will analyse the social and economic context in which food gifts were exchanged. The focus on everyday foodstuff in the context of a rural town, and not on urban consumption and luxuries, suggests a quotidian perspective and the analysis of its changes. Food was undoubtedly a favourite thing and often consumed communally. The memoirs of Michel Stüeler provide an ideal basis for this approach: they allow an insight into the everyday social and economic life of an artisan in a rural town in central Europe during the Thirty Years War. And the analysis of the recorded food gifts serves as an experiment to complement the history of food in this period.

The memoirs of Michel Stüeler (1583–1656)

It all began with a bad gift. In 1616, the new Emperor Matthias donated the free mining town of Graupen, today's Krupka, in northwest Bohemia, together with its woods, levies and jurisdiction, to his *burggrave* Adam von Sternberg, who became the new landlord of the said town.[9] This was a hard blow for the formerly free burghers, who had as recently as 1584 bought themselves out of subservience and retained the status of a free town until 1615. The burghers of Graupen – now subjects of Sternberg – tried to hold on to the privileges that had previously been confirmed, but they were contested and the burghers spent the next century in negotiations to win back their privileges, and in law suits against their new

[8] Jan Kilián, ed., *Paměti krupského měšťana Michela Stüelera (1629–1649)* [Erinnerungen des Graupener Bürgers Michael Stüeler (1629–1649)] (Teplice: Regionální muzeum v Teplicích, 2013). The memoirs are written in German, and Kilián's introduction and notes are in Czech. It has recently also been published as a German edition: Jan Kilián, ed., *Michel Stüelers Gedenkbuch (1629–1649): Alltagsleben in Böhmen zur Zeit des Dreißigjährigen Krieges* (Göttingen: V&R unipress 2014). I am grateful to Veronika Čapská for referring this edition to me, and to Jan Kilián and Tomáš Rataj's generosity in allowing me access to the PDF document of the text.

[9] See on the history of the town and its handover to Adam von Sternberg esp. Hermann Hallwich, *Geschichte der Bergstadt Graupen in Böhmen* (Prague: Credner, 1868), 151–55; Jan Smetana, "Graupen (Krupka, Bezirk Teplitz)," in *Handbuch der historischen Stätten: Böhmen und Mähren* ed. Joachim Bahlcke, Winfried Eberhard and Miloslav Polívka (Stuttgart: Kröner, 1998), 172; Kilián, *Michela Stüelera*, 19–37.

landlord. In the eyes of the burghers of Graupen, this really was a bad gift which tainted the relationship with their new landlord and coloured their daily lives. The conflicts and continuous efforts to regain the privileges found its way into the local historiography, a town chronicle of 1680 compiled by the town clerk Michael Johann Weiner and his scrivener Johann Wagner (*Weinersche Chronik*), and a history of the *Bergstadt Graupen,* which used passages of the memoir kept by Michel Stüeler.[10] Stüeler had kept his *Gedenckbuch* between 1615 and 1656, shortly before he died, but only the middle part covering the years 1629 to 1649 survives.[11] In 2013, Jan Kilián published a comprehensive edition of the second part of the memoir (1629–1649) with the original German and a Czech translation, and included the results of his extensive research on the persons mentioned by Stüeler.

Although the original memoir does not survive and the edited part contains some gaps, the ego-document constitutes a valuable historical document giving an insight into a person's perspectives.[12] Bräuer's analysis of town chronicles in the neighbouring region of Saxony-Lusatia sets out their methodological constraints when used to research historical events.[13] But in this contribution the memoir is approached as an ego-document which was probably not intended to be published: the author kept records continuously and close to the time in question; he recorded everyday events as well as political negotiations and was in both very impulsive; he revealed his confessional inner conflict, his sexuality and his opposition to the landlord; and he disclosed his opinions about others in colourful language, calling his fellow burghers names from *Schelm* (rascal) and whore to

---

[10] On the *Weinersche Chronik* by Johann Michael Weiner (1642–1726), his scrivener Johann Wagner, and the use of the *Gedenckhbuch,* see Kilián, *Michela Stüelera*, 46–47, 52–54, and 840; Hallwich, *Graupen*, vi–vii, 209–16, esp. 213. The chronicle was used by Hallwich (but he did not yet know Stüeler's memoir) and during his time it was located in the Graupen town archives. It is now in the archives of Teplice, Státní okresní archiv v Teplicích, Archiv Města Krupky, Inv. č. 56, Pamětní kniha 1426–1853, kniha č. 1 (tzv. Weinerova kronika). [State District Archives in Teplice, Archives of the Town Krupka, inventory no. 56, Memorial Book 1426–1853, book no. 1 (the Weiner chronicle)].

[11] The manuscript was last used in 1680 for the *Weinersche Chronik* and was only rediscovered at the end of the nineteenth century. The second part was transcribed, but the whereabouts of the original manuscript remain unknown. See on the history of the *Gedenckhbuch* Kilián, *Michela Stüelera*, 46–52, 840.

[12] The following years or parts are missing: 21.10.1632 until March 1633; 4.9.1634 until 26.12.1634; 18.1.1639 until 1.1.1640; 12.8.1645 until April 1646; 1649 incomplete. On ego-documents and a collection and discussion of various documents see Gabriele Jancke, *Selbstzeugnisse im deutschsprachigen Raum (Autobiographien, Tagebücher und andere autobiographische Schriften), 1400–1620. Eine Quellenkunde*, in collaboration with Marc Jarzebowski, Klaus Krönert and Yvonne Aßmann. (13. 8. 2008), URL: http://www.geschkult.fu-berlin.de/e/jancke-quellenkunde (last accessed October 2, 2018).

[13] Helmut Bräuer, *Stadtchronistik und städtische Gesellschaft: Über die Widerspiegelung sozialer Strukturen in der obersächsisch-lausitzischen Stadtchronistik der frühen Neuzeit* (Leipzig: Leipziger Universitätsverlag, 2009), esp. 253–54.

thief.[14] All this indicates that the memoir was for private use, although its existence was probably known to others. As mentioned above, shortly after Stüeler's death it must have come into the hands of the town clerk Weiner, who used it for the town chronicles.

Michel Stüeler, born around 1583, was a tanner by profession and his social sphere constituted the town's middle class. He held several offices such as Master of Krupka's Guild of Tanners, *Bergmeister* (supreme mining administrator), forest warden and member of the council of elders from 1628.[15] As an office holder, he was at times also involved in the inspection of the local butchers and bakers and the fish ponds. He therefore had some control over the quality of food as well as access to special foodstuff such as fish and game. In addition, he owned land and his rural by-employment was considerable. He was himself involved in the negotiations with the landlord, and recorded current political events. With this unique document he also created a memoir of all the demographic events of his family, friends and neighbours, the agricultural year, crop prices and weather conditions, local tin mining, his municipal offices, his craft, beer brewing and wine making, confessional matters, purchases and inheritance cases, and gift giving. He also recorded all his consumption activities: when he bought any household goods such as a mortar for the kitchen or clothing for himself and his family, for example, and the day he started using them. In 1643, for example, he wrote: "[I] bought 3 ells of black cloth for trousers and stockings from Tobias Götlich, at 37 Kreutzer an ell. Simon Kolschitter made them [the trousers]. [...] God grant me his grace and bless me. Amen." Less than two weeks later he records: "[I] have put on the black garb trousers. God the heavenly King give me his grace and bless me in them. Amen. Cost me 36 Bohemian Groschen."[16] The mention of his purchases, the price and when he started wearing them indicates the personal meaning the goods had for him, even more so when we consider that all his entries on consumption activities are followed by a brief prayer. But just as important as buying goods on the market were gifts. Gifts could be anything from food items such as butter or apples, to pewter dishes and clothing items. He sometimes recorded the value of the gifts, indicating their entangled symbolic, social and economic significance especially in times of crisis. This is valuable information which is rarely found in inventories apart from occasional wedding presents or

---

[14] Kilián, *Michela Stüelera*, 104 (27.9.1630), 172 (4.1.1632), 714 (8.3.1649). Kilián states that Stüeler's records were kept close to the time, see 839.

[15] On biographical notes on Stüeler see Kilián, *Michela Stüelera*, 39–46.

[16] Kilián, *Michela Stüelera*, 540 (25.11.1643): "[...] 3 Elen schwarz tuch zu Hosen und Strümpffen kauft von der Tobias Götlichin, die Ele pro 37 Kr. Simon Kolschitter gemacht. [...] Gott gebe mir sein Gnad und Segen. Amen." Ibid., 542 (6.12.1643): "[...]die schwarzen Gewandthosen angezogen. Gott der himmlische König geme mir sein Gnad und Segen darinnen. Amen. Kostet mich 36 böhm. Groschen. [...]" All translations into English in this contribution are mine. With *tuch* and *Gewandt* he was probably referring to woollen cloth.

bequeathed objects.[17] All of these events were interwoven in his daily routine and invoke a detailed picture of economic, social and religious life in the first half of the seventeenth century. The entries follow a similar structure: Stüeler began each year with a prayer for a good year, and organised all the entries by month and day. At the end of the year he composed a brief résumé in which he stated the harvest and grain prices, health issues, demographic and family matters, and major political events, all concluded by a brief prayer.

Graupen suffered enormously from the consequences of the Thirty Years War, and the memoir reflects the author's personal experiences. Stüeler described the quartering of soldiers, troops marching through the town, looting and the heavy burden of war contributions. He also noted down the number of plague victims, many of which were his family members and close acquaintances. By 1649, the population had according to Hallwich decreased to 100 families from just over a 1,000 inhabitants in 1626.[18] After 1634, when the town was hit by destruction, fire and the plague, we can observe Stüeler's economic decline, which worsened in the 1640s. To make ends meet, he then had to sell pieces of land or precious objects such as his tanner's boiler.[19] During this period, the town also faced re-catholicisation. Graupen had been Lutheran since around 1576, and saw its first Catholic priest installed in 1624. However, the community resisted until after 1628, when according to Hallwich re-catholicisation was established in Graupen.[20] But still, a continuing confessional ambiguity is reflected in Stüeler's entries, which would form an ideal basis for more thorough studies on the context of re-catholicisation than is possible in this contribution. The memoir invokes a detailed picture of these events and gives testimony on the way people retained their social and economic lives in spite of war and diseases. And one important part in this was played by an integrated gift economy.

Gift economy and the history of consumption

Natalie Zemon Davis presented a fascinating analysis of gift giving in sixteenth century France taking Marcel Mauss' thoughts further. She explored gift giving as a "gift mode" or "register" with its own "repertoire of behaviour" and showed its

---

17 In southern Tirol, for example, local court records show frequent references to gifts. With a separate marital property regime in place, the respective property of the spouses had to be identified after the death of a spouse in order to administer the separation of the marital property and the endowment of the widowed spouse. In those records, the widow's trousseau, for example, was described as her own property brought into the marriage, including all objects which had been given to her as a gift. In some cases, these gifts were named as well. See, e.g., Brixen, Stadtgericht, Verfachbuch 3, 1539, fols 19v–21v, a widow's endowment contract which mentions that her husband had given her a small silver bowl as a gift.

18 Hallwich, *Graupen*, 167 and 190. 1648, two-thirds of the houses were deserted.

19 Kilián, *Michela Stüelera*, 434 (7.5.1641).

20 Hallwich, *Graupen*, 165–66, 170.

embeddedness in economic life: the gift mode existed alongside the mode of sales and of coercion.[21] Whether gifts were given voluntarily or were part of a system governed by expectation and obligation and if this changed over time, remains a stimulating question. In this paper I have been inspired by Zemon Davis' approach and will look at specific gift practices. I will explore them for a small town and within a social stratum of municipal office holders and artisans, and how this persisted through a time of crisis. Stüeler articulated his thoughts on gift exchanges and thus on the question of reciprocity. And he also offers ways to explore their entanglement within the local economy. I will focus on food gifts to examine their importance within a wider network of exchange, which normally is not captured in serial documents and other sources for food history.

Felicity Heal analyses food gifts in her article on households and political exchange in early modern England in the light of the circumstances that constituted food as a gift rather than a commercial item. She uses household accounts of the nobility and finds that food gifts, the most basic form of offering and its role in hospitality and relief of need, were critical in the maintenance of social bonds in early modern society. Apart from neighbourly exchanges, she points to the seeking of patronage, local political relationships and political bonds. But she also points out that the gift and the market economy existed alongside each other and that both carried a moral dimension and linked obligations: reciprocity and creditworthiness respectively.[22] The question of obligation points to Craig Muldrew's work and his emphasis on an economy built on different levels of obligation.[23] Although not with a focus on food gifts as such, Valentin Groebner's work on Basel municipal account books offers an analysis of gift-giving in an official environment. Especially gifts of wine revealed ambivalence: Groebner viewed them as predominately political gifts which could easily turn into bribes.[24] The question of informal support and gift-giving is examined for early modern England by Ilana Krausman Ben-Amos, who adopts a wider definition of 'giving'.[25] However, the above-mentioned works all analyse distinctive societies and social groups different from the one represented in Stüeler's memoir, so that comparisons have to be approached with caution.

I have adopted an inclusive definition of 'gifts' based on the definition in Grimm's German dictionary, meaning all transactions of goods or services which were given without the expectation of payment but with the intention of making a

[21] Davis, *The Gift*, 9.

[22] Felicity Heal, "Food Gifts."

[23] Muldrew, *Economy of Obligation.* Also discussed in Jancke, *Gastfreundschaft*, 308–11.

[24] Valentin Groebner, *Liquid Assets, Dangerous Gifts: Presents and Politics at the End of the Middle Ages,* trans. Pamela E. Selwyn (Philadelphia: University of Pennsylvania Press, 2002), 22–24, for gifts of wine.

[25] See Krausman Ben-Amos, *Culture of Giving.*

gift.[26] The expression used in the memoir was not *schenken* (to bestow, to gift) but *verehren,* which in its early modern meaning could be translated as: to honour somebody with something.[27] Stüeler also used the term *Gabe* especially in connection with gifts bestowed by God, which would be closer to the term *donatio.* Jacob Grimm offered an etymological study of gift-giving in which he anticipated some of Mauss' aspects such as reciprocity and the gift in return. He also highlighted the importance of food and drink in this context.[28] Marcel Mauss also looked at gift-giving in Germanic law and found a long tradition of temporary postponement of the gift in return and the obligation to reciprocate. As Mary Douglas stressed in her introduction to the translation of Mauss' *The Gift*, there are no free gifts, and this also reflects Stüeler's understanding.[29] In addition, the analysis of the practice of gift giving might point to a more fluid boundary between payment and gift giving. Especially when looking at economically challenged societies such as Central Europe during the Thirty Years War, the meaning of reciprocity acquires a different emphasis.[30] Much has been written on the theory of gift-giving and on the legacy of Mauss' work.[31] In this study I will contrast some of the results with the view of the author of the memoir and how he perceived gift-giving in his own society.

Gift giving practices in Stüeler's memoir[32]

The most important gift of all was God's gift of grace – for Stüeler this manifested itself in God's gift of health, prosperity or agricultural produce.[33] In his annual résumé, he recorded a summary of the harvest's outcome and thanked God

---

26 "Geschenk, 1. sache, die geschenkt wird, freiwillige gabe." See *Deutsches Wörterbuch von Jacob und Wilhelm Grimm,* 16 Bde. in 32 Teilbänden. Leipzig 1854–1961. Quellenverzeichnis Leipzig, 1971. Online version http://woerterbuchnetz.de/DWB/?lemma=geschenk (accessed October 2018).

27 See *Deutsches Wörterbuch von Jacob und Wilhelm Grimm*, online version http://www. woerterbuchnetz. de/DWB?lemma=verehren (accessed October 2018).

28 Jacob Grimm, "Schenken und Geben," in idem, *Kleinere Schriften*, vol. II (Berlin: Ferd. Dümmler, 1865), 173–210.

29 See Mary Douglas, "Foreword," in Mauss, *The Gift.*

30 See also Jonathan Parry, "The Gift, the Indian Gift and the 'Indian Gift'," *Man*, new series 21, 3 (Sept. 1986), 453–73.

31 See, for an overview, Hans Peter Hahn, *Materielle Kultur. Eine Einführung* (Berlin: Reimer, 2005), 91–99; Dirk Quadflieg, "Tauschen und Geben," in *Handbuch Materielle Kultur. Bedeutungen, Konzepte, Disziplinen*, ed. Stefanie Samida, Manfred K. H. Eggert, and Hans Peter Hahn (Stuttgart and Weimar: Metzler, 2014), 117–24.

32 Several different gift-giving practices can be determined from Stüeler's records. The set of practices chosen here could be broken down into more specific ones. However, the present choice should suffice for the study of food gifts. On the complexity of giving practices see also Ben-Amos, *Culture of Giving*, 9–10.

33 See also Davis, *The Gift*, 100 (ch. "Gifts and the Gods").

for his plentiful gifts.[34] Those gifts varied, of course, and in some years the harvest turned out less plentiful. But the universal belief that all things had their origins in God's generosity was mirrored in the description of transactions, whether purchases, making debts or giving gifts, to which Stüeler added a brief prayer. This view conditioned the view that these gifts – just as a common good – should be shared with others.

Gift giving practices	Description	Number	Total
Alms			7
Rewards			19
Demographic events			24
	Weddings	8	
	Baptisms	3	
	Funerals	9	
	Wills	4	
Seasonal gifts			30
	Christmas	10	
	New Year	10	
	Easter	7	
	Pentecost	3	
Family / kin			14
General gifts, unrelated			46
Church related, parish priest			17
Borrowed			5
Municipal and office related			39
	Following an official act	18	
	Guild related	4	
	Office related	17	
Denied gifts			18
Political gifts			26
	Negotiation gifts	21	
	War related, military	5	
Sum			245

Table 1: Stüeler's gift giving practices, 1629–1649

[34] See for example, Kilián, *Michela Stüelera*, 114 (Dec. 1630): "Dem Allmechtigen Gott sei Lob, Preis, Ehr und Danck gesaget für alle seine reichen Gaben, [...]."

Alms and charity

Charitable relief and giving alms to the poor had a religious intention, the expectation being that such gifts would be reciprocated with prayers for the giver, and that they would contribute to one's salvation.[35] Alms to the poor could arguably also be seen as gifts to God.[36] They were part of the gift-giving culture, for example when Stüeler donated some of his harvested grapes to the poor and thanked God for the year's bountiful gift of wine;[37] or when he gave away two loaves of bread on baking day to two single women.[38] But they were also linked to official acts such as the inspections of the bakers, after which the bread of those bakers who did not meet the regulations was distributed amongst the poor. In this case no reciprocity was expected other than gratitude. People also considered the poor in their wills. During the funeral of the apothecary's widow, for example, the whole municipal administration received a meal, there was communal drinking, and the poor were given bread and wine.[39] The gift of bread and wine conveyed a religious meaning as the Eucharistic gifts.

However, almsgiving in this context revealed another hidden meaning. The town of Graupen had been Lutheran for over 48 years when it was faced with re-catholicisation in the 1620s, and most burghers had converted by 1628. But the entries of the analysed memoir show the inner conflicts which remained: theological differences between the confessions influenced everyday decisions such as observance of certain saints' days or Lent. "Doles at death" as seen in the example of the funeral of the apothecary's widow was also a practice amongst Protestants and might indicate a continuity of former practices.[40] But almsgiving accounts for a comparatively small number of the recorded gift-giving events. This might have several reasons: Stüeler never personalised the poor, and the *arme Leute* remain in most cases without name. But their fate always seemed close to his, and the author often described how people were made poor by accidents, military raids, robbery, fire or exaggerated demands by the authorities.[41] This stands in

---

[35] On charity and informal relief see, e.g., Robert Jütte, *Poverty and Deviance in Early Modern Europe* (Cambridge: Cambridge University Press, 1994), 139–40; Davis, *The Gift*, 100–03, 110.

[36] Davis, *The Gift*, 103.

[37] Kilián, *Michela Stüelera*, 362 (4.–6.10.1638).

[38] Kilián, *Michela Stüelera*, 350 (1.7.1638).

[39] Kilián, *Michela Stüelera*, 112 (17./22.12.1630): "Nach Begrebnüs ist ein ganzer Rath und die Adjuuanten gespeiset worden, und den armen Leuten Wein und Brot ausgeteilet worden; ist 1 ½ Vas Wein aufgangen. Gott sei ihr genedig." (After the burial the whole municipal council and adjutants were given a meal, and wine and bread was distributed amongst the poor; 1 ½ barrels of wine was consumed. God rest her soul.)

[40] See Diarmaid MacCulloch, *Reformation. Europe's House Divided 1490–1700* (London: Allen Lane, 2003), 578–79.

[41] Stüeler recorded after a military raid in Teplice: "Dieser Hans Panir [Johan Banér, Swedish Field Marshal] hat das Rote Haus, das Seestedel abgebrent und viel umliegente Torffer, hat viel arme Leute gemacht, und außn Lande gezogen. Gott wird ihn straffen." (This Johan Banér burnt down

contrast to his description of all other gift transactions where givers and recipients are always named – these were the people Stüeler interacted with on a regular basis, such as family members, neighbours, other guild members and community officials, and who formed his social sphere or "reciprocal voluntary cycles of exchange," as Douglas puts it.[42] In Protestant communities, poor relief was organised on community and church level, which might be the reason why Stüeler hardly ever mentioned beggars. The poor receiving alms were probably institutionalized in the local *Spital* (hospital). I would argue that personal alms-giving had not been curtailed during the Protestant period but continued within a social realm of exchange after re-catholicisation. Therefore the attitude to charity after re-catholicisation does not reveal confessional differences.[43] Charity could then be seen in the context of informal help within personal social spheres, and donations to the poor in cases of a plentiful harvest or when food was left over. In addition, he was a very pious man and contributed to church life especially with his musical skills. His piety is reflected in gifts exchanged in this context, between the parish priest and himself or to the parish community. Torn between Protestantism and Catholicism, Stüeler's relationship with the local priests remained troubled. But his piety won him the sympathy of some priests, who allowed him to teach at the girls' school. Only when he showed Protestant tendencies was he banned from this task. On one occasion, after the priest allowed him to teach again in 1647, they celebrated the renewed social bond over pike and carp, wine and beer until late at night.[44] Stüeler's relationship to the Catholic faith as well as the clergymen remained ambiguous. In the case of alms and charity, reciprocity was not necessarily linked back to the giver. Although the poor were expected to pray for the giver, in some cases such gifts could act as reciprocities of previous help received from somebody else. This indicates an expectation to help in form of a cycle of charity if one has the means to do so. Even alms were no "free" gifts.

Rewards

A more common mode of gift giving seems to have been a reward for a favour, a service or for concluding an official task. They often had the character of counter-gifts for services rendered. This has been discussed by Davis, who gives

---

the red house, the lake barn and many surrounding villages, he made many people poor, and he went away again. God will punish him.) Kilián, *Michela Stüelera*, 386 (20./22. 3. 1640).

[42] Mary Douglas, "Foreword," in Mauss, *The Gift*, xx.

[43] See Robert Jütte, who also argues that the Reformation did not have an effect on individual alms-giving, Jütte, *Poverty and Deviance*, 139; recently Ilana Krausman Ben-Amos showed this for early modern England, Krausman Ben-Amos, *Culture of Giving*.

[44] Kilián, *Michela Stüelera*, 662 (2.12.1647): "Pfarrherr mir vorgönnet Schul zu halten, und mit ihme gessen von ein Hechte und von Karpfen, Wein und Bier getruncken bis die Nacht umb 10 Uhr." (The priest allowed me to teach again, and [I] ate with him of some pike and carp, drank wine and beer until late at night around 10 p.m.)

examples of wine being given as a "tip" for services or in addition to wages.[45] Servants would receive a small gift for delivering goods, or Stüeler and his fellow office holders would be served a meal accompanied by wine after conducting the measurement of a field. Communal drinks were a frequent way to reward a group of people after the conclusion of an official act. The communal aspect was important, and the rewards thus mostly consisted of food and drink. In 1642, for example, the pastor had a new *Marther* or religious monument raised and 12 burghers helped with this task. The pastor rewarded them with 18 *Seidel* [c. 8.64 litres] beer, 12 *Seidel* [c. 5.76 litres] wine, cheese and buttered bread, which they consumed together.[46] Communal consumption was intended in invitations to meals or contributions to communal meals with dishes of *Sauerkraut*, for example.[47]

Demographic events

Gifts related to demographic events such as weddings, baptisms, funerals or in wills occupy an important place in this gift-giving culture.[48] Invitations to weddings would entail communal meals and drinks, but wedding gifts would often consist of household goods. Gifts were expected during weddings, which could pose a problem for the invited guests: In times of need, Stüeler decided not to attend because he had nothing to give, and this would have meant a breach of the exchange of gifts. In 1643, for example, Stüeler recorded two marriages of fellow burghers, neither of which he attended because he had no money.[49] Baptisms did not necessarily include gifts, but in the 1640s the pastor exempted Stüeler from the baptism fees for his children, which Stüeler himself termed as a gift. Forgiveness or exemption as a form of charity and thus of gift-giving is an important component of early modern economies which does not surface very often. Craig Muldrew discussed the forgiveness of debts and its importance for the poor and for luckless traders, and emphasized their unofficial significance for poor relief and neighbourliness; contemporary sources even described such forgiveness as a form of charity.[50] In Stüeler's memoir, forgiveness of debts also appears in connection with punishments and fines being forgiven, and this is a good example to highlight the

[45] Davis, *The Gift*, 53–54; see also Groebner, *Liquid Assets*, 55–59 (on additions to wages).

[46] Kilián, *Michela Stüelera*, 472 (20.5.1642): "Het er uns vorehret 18 S. Bier, 12 S. Wein, Kes und Butterbrot." (He gave us as a gift 18 Seidel beer, 12 Seidel wine, cheese and buttered bread.)

[47] See Davis, *The Gift*, 35. She described the custom in early modern France of neighbours bringing a dish to dinner and termed it a kind of sixteenth century "pot-luck."

[48] See also Mauss, *The Gift*, 78, on Germanic law and the *Gaben* at baptisms, first communions, engagement parties, weddings etc.

[49] Kilián, *Michela Stüelera*, 538 (8.11.1643): "Bin uf keine gezogen, habe kein Geld gehabt." (I did not go to any of them. I had no money.)

[50] Muldrew, *Economy of Obligation*, 304–07.

ambiguity of gift-giving practices: seasonal gifts and official acts could also be a form of charity.[51]

Seasonal gifts

Seasonal gifts at Christmas, New Year, Easter and Pentecost were mainly recorded during the later period of c. 1641 to 1649, and the majority of them, especially for Easter and Pentecost, were food gifts consisting of bread or meat. These gifts especially indicate an increasing need of support. Stüeler was grateful for them and in some cases he even recorded his frustration at not being able to give and thus support others himself. Stüeler recorded in his memoir in 1642:

> Easter-day was nice and bright, and I had no money to buy myself a pitcher of beer. Gorge Bruch gave us a jug of pasties, Casper Sadlerin gave me a small piece of pork and two liver sausages, and Michel Pazelt sent me two pounds of beef. He owed me for selling grass from the pasture. God give that I can give to poor people again.[52]

This entry reveals several aspects: the neighbourliness and support he received with food gifts, and his idea of reciprocity. Reciprocity, in his understanding, meant that, as soon as he was able to do so, he would help his neighbours and friends with gifts in return. This position was God given, however, and created a moral obligation to give or share with others.

Family gifts and general gifts

Gift-giving was common amongst close family members and Stüeler recorded gifts he received from his wife, such as a silver wedding ring, or the clothes and fabric he bought for her. Clothes, but mainly food gifts, were exchanged with his children, his brother-in-law and with the latter's father.[53] Family gifts were not necessarily connected to a specific event but could result from his wife's visit to his

[51] In 1630, Stüeler has Michel Koler sentenced for stealing wood. But Koler's wife pleaded for his release and his punishment was forgiven except for the cost of the wood. Kilián, *Michela Stüelera*, 92 (4.2.1630). "Den 7. dito ist er des gefengnüs entledigt worden, aus grosser Bit wegen seines Weibes ist die Straf ihm geschenckt worden. Das Holz hat er müssen zalen pro 1 SS." (On the 7th he was released from prison, because of the pleading of his wife his punishment was forgiven [lit.: given to him as a gift]. For the wood he had to pay 1 SS.) See also Groebner on officials' power to grant forgiveness and the ambivalence of such gifts, Groebner, *Liquid Assets*, 59–63.

[52] Kilián, *Michela Stüelera*, 466 (Easter 1642): "Der Ostertag ist schon und helle gewesen, und habe kein Geld gehabt, daß ich mir hette können eine Kanne Bier kauffen. Gorge Bruch hat uns einen Krug vol Patjesten geben, Casper Sadlerin hat mir ein Stückel Schweinefleisch und 2 Leberwürste bracht, und Michel Pazelt hat mir 2 lb Rindfleisch geschickt. Ist mir schuldig gewest vor Gras uf der Wiese vorkaufft. Hat mir ein Flecken geschickt und die Gorge Pruchin auch ein Flecken geschickt. Gott bescher mir auch wieder, daß ich armen Leuthen kan geben. Amen."

[53] C. 14 instances could be identified as family gifts. But a more detailed analysis would be necessary to identify all of Stüeler's kin.

cousin, from which she would return with gifts of grain and poultry or just a random gift of a handkerchief from his daughter.[54]

Most of the cases were gifts not connected to a specific, seasonal or demographic occasion but given within a wide range of contexts. They formed part of a gift network between social equals and kin and perpetuated obligations or answered expectations.[55] For example, a gift to conclude a successful commercial transaction, gifts from other artisans, for example the finishing of a table by the carpenter which was given as a gift, a mulberry tree from a friend, dishes of food as contributions to communal meals, or even grain and vegetable seed. They point to the existence of a system of reciprocal exchange.

Gifts in disguise

Closely linked with neighbourliness and forgiveness might be a disguised form of gift-giving which Stüeler termed borrowing. During the 1640s he saw himself compelled to ask family members and neighbours to 'lend' him a loaf of bread or some grain. In 1645 he borrowed some grain, with which he baked bread two days later.[56] Reciprocity or even the return of a 'borrowed' loaf of bread at a later date could not have been expected in such a difficult economic situation, and it might have been the case that these items were part of an anticipated forgiveness or in fact gifts in the form of alms, with the difference that Stüeler did not have to call them alms and thus retained his position in his social sphere. Should he find himself in a better economic position again he would reciprocate. His careful recording of such practices, the collection of evidence of cycles of giving and receiving, could indicate this intention.[57]

Gifts denied

Although gift exchange might have been regarded as morally obligatory, it was not legally binding and could therefore be denied.[58] Stüeler recorded 18 cases where he was denied a gift, mostly food gifts, all of which were after 1641. It is probable that people denied him a gift out of their inability to give themselves. Nevertheless, Stüeler found denials unacceptable and regarded them as rudeness, *eine Grobheit*. In one case he called Caspar Rach, butcher and member of the

---

[54] Kilián, *Michela Stüelera*, 522 (13.7.1643) and 628 (7.9.1646).

[55] See also Davis, *The Gift*, 34.

[56] Kilián, *Michela Stüelera*, 612 (13./15.7.1645). *Korn* refers here to rye.

[57] This can be found in other diaries as well and would include invitations to dinners, visits as well as gift-giving. See, e.g., *Gabriela Sobková z Kornic, provdaná ze Spens-Booden. Deníkové rodinné záznamy (1784–1808)* [Gabriela Sobková of Kornice, married of Spens-Booden. Diarial Family Records (1784–1808)], ed. Veronika Čapská and Veronika Marková (Prague: Scriptorium 2009). I am grateful to Veronika Čapská and Chrisitane Holm for their suggestions.

[58] See Groebner, *Liquid Assets*, 13.

council of elders, a 'reckless, wicked dog' after he refused to give him some meat around Christmas 1649.[59] This reveals his understanding of gifts and the expectations which were linked with them. He expected social equals to respond to a request for a gift. But there was a fine line between requesting a gift and begging, which could create an awkward situation for the person asking for a favour.[60] Stüeler asked on several occasions for a gift or to 'borrow' something, which was similar to asking for support but circumvented the pitfall of begging. Denial could mean breaking a gift-giving and reciprocation cycle.

Political gifts

The discussed gifts, given or denied, were exchanged within the community and most of them within Stüeler's own social sphere. But linked with the "bad gift" mentioned at the beginning were gifts which accompanied the negotiations to gain back the town's privileges, to fight off the landlord's demands for dues or to petition for the right to keep the Protestant faith. These were political gifts that the delegations would take to the meetings to influence the parties towards a more favourable outcome, but mostly to no effect. Hallwich describes how in 1627 the Protestant magistrates wrote a petition to protest against re-catholicisation, specifically a Corpus Christi procession held in Graupen by the Jesuits, and sent Stüeler and another burgher to Prague to negotiate with the authorities. But, as Hallwich puts it, although they took six pewter bowls with them, the audience did not go well: the delegation was detained and forced to accept Catholicism.[61] In most cases, political or negotiation gifts consisted of gifts of food: venison, poultry, wine, fruit, nuts, and cheese, representing local produce. After many failures they became more of a habit; Stüeler recorded that he gave the delegation four kinds of wild fowl as gifts for the landlord, but that again nothing was achieved.[62] These gifts of food were meant to strengthen the negotiations and had more the symbolic character of a courtesy or a "token" as Heal termed it. They were too small to be considered as bribes and remained unreciprocated.[63] Many gifts were exchanged in the context of Stüeler's role within the municipality and as an office holder. The conclusion of an official act such as the measurement and division of a field or the fishing of the municipality ponds was often followed by

[59] Kilián, *Michela Stüelera*, 738 (24.12.1649): "Casper Rach mir nicht wollen 1 lb Fleisch borgen, der leichtfertige schlimme Hundt."

[60] See Heal, "Food Gifts," 61–62.

[61] Hallwich, *Graupen*, 168: "sie hatten keine gute Audienz, trotz sechs zinnernen Schüsseln, mit denen das Bittgesuch beschwert worden war." (They did not have a good audience, in spite of the six pewter bowls with which the petition was reinforced.) Hallwich refers to the above mentioned Weinersche Chronik, which in turn probably used Stüeler's own memoirs.

[62] Kilián, *Michela Stüelera*, 154 (22.10.1631), "und nichts ausgerichtet."

[63] See Heal, "Food Gifts,"63, 67. Groebner's findings involved much larger quantities and values and are not directly comparable in this case.

the gift of food or communal drinks. Communal was also the meal celebrating the master examination of a fellow craftsman. As a forest warden, Stüeler would frequently receive gifts of game, most of all venison. Such gifts can be regarded as additions to official payments or rewards, and they signify the belonging to a specific social group. This becomes clear with change over time: political, municipal, and office-related gifts declined especially during the 1640s, reflecting Stüeler's decreasing involvement in official acts as well as the increasing difficulties of the municipality of a now subjected town during the war.

This complex culture of gift-giving shows how the practice permeated everyday life. It constituted an important component of the exchange and acquisition of goods within a mixed economy. This corresponds with Natalie Zemon Davis' analysis of sixteenth century French society, but it also shows local nuances and social idiosyncrasies. No precious and exotic gifts appear in Stüeler's descriptions; books hardly feature as gifts in the memoir, as they carried a denominational meaning and were thus too politically charged.[64] Nor were there any gifts made of precious metals as described by Groebner for Basel.[65] The gifts described in Stüeler's records were quotidian, affordable, but nonetheless special to the recipient.

Food gifts

Gifts in seventeenth-century Graupen were predominantly food gifts: 163 food gift exchanges were identified, compared with 86 gift exchanges of other items such as money in 42, clothing items in 19, pewter dishes in 13, and other household items in 12 cases.[66] Given the importance of food and food procurement, it is not surprising that food was also exchanged as gifts and that it made up a large proportion of gift giving. Using local produce made such gifts affordable as well as special as they originated from the giver's own work. Their consumption was often communal and gave them additional meaning in terms of creating or maintaining social bonds.[67] When examining the nature of the food gifts, almost all components of the then diet emerge, and the diversity of the foodstuffs and drinks exchanged allows an insight into the preferences for and availability of food during

[64] According to Hallwich and probably Stüeler, in 1627 the houses of the burghers were searched for Protestant books, which were confiscated. See Hallwich, *Graupen*, 169. Stüeler records in 1635 that he had silver locks attached to his prayer book "Paradies-Gärtlein" by Johann Arndt, which was a gift by Andres Baumgarten. The "Paradiesgärtlein" was a Protestant book. Kilián, *Michela Stüelera*, 256 (18.5.1635).

[65] See for descriptions of some costly gifts Groebner, *Liquid Assets*, 28.

[66] The predominance of food gifts corresponds to Davis' findings for city neighbours who also used food as primary gifts, especially wine. Davis, *The Gift*, 35. Frequent gifts of money are slightly surprising, see Grimm, "Schenken und Geben," 176, where he stressed the prevalence of movables as gifts.

[67] See for example Davis, *The Gift*, 35–36; Heal, "Food Gifts,"44.

the first half of the seventeenth-century in northern Bohemia. By far the most frequent food gift consisted of meat and alcohol, followed by bread, flour and grain. These gifts mirror the staple foods of the time.

Food gifts	Description	Number	Total
All food gifts			163
Meat			62
	Game	35	
	Meat (red)	18	
	Poultry	12	
Fish			14
Bread			25
Grain, flour			12
Garden vegetables	Sauerkraut, peas, salad		5
Fruit	Apples, pears, cherries, grapes		13
Nuts			2
Honey			1
Dairy products	Milk, cheese, butter		6
Alcoholic drinks			44
	Wine	26	
	Beer	9	
	Cider	1	
	Communal drink	25	

Table 2: Food gift items[68]

Meat

Meat occupies a significant part in food history, as it was regarded an important source of protein and energy but also as a social indicator.[69] Looking at changing levels of meat consumption can, according to Roman Sandgruber, serve as an

[68] The numbers represent the result from a first analysis and are therefore tentative. The numbers of the food items exchanged do not add up to the 163 overall food gift exchanges, as the recorded gift-giving instances sometimes name several object categories simultaneously.

[69] See J. G. Krünitz, *Oekonomische Encyklopädie oder allgemeines System der Staats- Stadt- Haus- und Landwirthschaft 1773–1858*, http://www.kruenitz1.uni-trier.de/, entry for "Fleisch" (accessed October 2018).

indicator for changing living standards and social stratification.[70] It is assumed that meat consumption in southern and Central Europe was relatively high during the fifteenth and sixteenth century but fell especially in the countryside during the mid-sixteenth century. Wilhelm Abel showed that during the sixteenth century food consumption changed to a more grain-based diet with less animal protein such as meat due to population growth, increasing food prices and stagnating or even decreasing spending power,[71] as food prices rose sharply after 1550 and by 1600 common people were limiting their spending on meat. This brought about social changes. The diet of the middle classes became more varied, and bread and cake replaced missing meat, but common people could not replace meat with bread and had to complement their diet with vegetables, pulses and flour-based foods.[72] The northwest German territories, however, experienced a very different development, with cattle imports from Eastern Europe being replaced by local husbandry.[73] After the Thirty Years War, meat consumption remained low in many regions until the eighteenth or beginning of the nineteenth century, especially for common people and in the countryside.[74] Different kinds of meat were associated with different social statuses, with venison, veal and poultry, for example, generally believed to be reserved for the elite and pork for the common people.[75] How do those general findings correspond with the information we get from gifts of meat in Stüeler's memoir? Did northern Bohemia experience a similar decrease in meat consumption?

Meat was either home-produced, exchanged, given as a gift or bought at one of the town butchers. Hallwich published the numbers of the masters of the guild crafts for 1635 and 1648. Although the town was in economic decline from the mid-1630s, the number of butchers increased from three to six, and the number of

---

[70] As indicators of a decline in living standards in early modern Austria he specified for example the decline in meat consumption and increase in flour-based dishes and bread. See Sandgruber, Leben und Lebensstandard, 174; Robert Jütte, "Diets in Welfare Institutions and in Outdoor Poor Relief in Early Modern Western Europe," *Ethnologia Europaea* 16 (1988): 117–35.

[71] See Wilhelm Abel, *Stufen der Ernährung* (Göttingen: Vandenhoeck & Ruprecht 1981), 32–33, 40 and 64.

[72] Günter Wiegelmann, *Alltags- und Festspeisen in Mitteleuropa. Innovationen, Strukturen und Regionen vom späten Mittelalter bis zum 20. Jahrhundert* (Münster, New York, Munich, and Berlin: Waxmann, 2006), §§ 34, 37, 44. See also Allen Grieco, "Lebensmittel und soziale Hierarchien im spätmittelalterlichen und frühneuzeitlichen Europa," in *Der lange Weg in den Überfluss: Anfänge und Entwicklung der Konsumgesellschaft seit der Vormoderne*, ed. Michael Prinz (Paderborn: Schöningh, 2003), 37–46, here 46.

[73] Wiegelmann, *Alltags- und Festspeisen*, 36–37.

[74] Gunther Hirschfelder and Manuel Trummer, "Food and Drink," in *European History Online (EGO)* (Mainz: Leibniz Institute of European History, 2013-08-20.), http://www.ieg-ego.eu/en/threads/backgrounds/food-and-drink [2015-09-04], § 24 (accessed October 2018); Fernand Braudel, *The Structures of Everyday Life. The Limits of the Possible* (New York: Harper 1981), 104, 199; Hans Jürgen Teuteberg and Günter Wiegelmann, *Nahrungsgewohnheiten in der Industrialisierung des 19. Jahrhunderts* (Münster 2005), 103–04.

[75] See Grieco, "Lebensmittel," 43–45.

bakers from three to eight.[76] This change might have been a sign for an increase in market activity following a decrease in home production, as can be seen in Stüeler's case, but this would have to be further investigated. Stüeler himself was a municipal inspector of the butchers and bakers, and was required to check their produce for quality and size.[77]

Another way to acquire meat was hunting. However, during the Middle Ages hunting rights were converted into a sovereign right and were then conferred on the landlords.[78] The burghership of Graupen claimed the privileges they had acquired when they had bought themselves out of subservience, before the Emperor gave them away to the *burggrave* Sternberg. One of those privileges was hunting game in their forests. In 1636, Sternberg reiterated to the rebellious town that all their privileges had been annulled and renewed his demands, one of which was the tribute of stags and wild boars to be delivered to his kitchen annually – retroactively for the last years and in future.[79] In 1637, the municipal council (*Magistrat*) petitioned to have its original privileges re-established, which was confirmed by Emperor Ferdinand III. However, this seemed to have intensified the fierce dispute between Sternberg and the town of Graupen, which dragged on for decades.[80] The burghers of Graupen insisted on their right to hunt and to consume game. But this meant that to a certain degree the privileges of Graupen's landlord were disregarded. Consequently, game and especially venison played an important and ambivalent role in gift-giving. Felicity Heal emphasized the role of venison as a gift not only to best friends and equals, but also as a reward or for maintaining patronage networks. However, hunting was controlled by the authorities, which could lead to a "clandestine trade" in game.[81] In one case, Stüeler recorded that, after a stag was shot, the municipal council had to pay a large fine to the landlord for doing so.[82] Graupen sent the landlord some venison and wood grouse as a gift in six instances; but whether those "gifts" were in fact the official dues is not clear from Stüeler's entries. The boundary between gifts and

---

76 Hallwich, *Graupen*, 191.

77 See also Hallwich, *Graupen*, 173; according to him this office was reintroduced in Graupen in 1631.

78 See Gerhard Köbler, *Lexikon der europäischen Rechtsgeschichte* (Munich: Beck, 1997), 202, entry "Jagd", 355.

79 See Hallwich, *Graupen*, 181.

80 See Hallwich, *Graupen*, 183 and Kilián, *Michela Stüelera*, 320–22. Stüeler mainly mentions the beer brewing privileges.

81 Heal, "Food Gifts," 55, 57–59.

82 For example in 1629, Kilián, *Michela Stüelera*, 68 (15.6.1629): Michel Kinel shot a stag; 70–72 (1.7.1629): the municipal council was fined 300 Taler and the money had to be borrowed from the regent.

dues was fluid and the intention of the town's gifts to the landlord could have been to evoke his reciprocation.[83]

Wild boars, which were claimed by the landlord, do not feature as gifts in the memoir, but stag meat and especially venison do. Between 1643 and 1648, Stüeler received stag meat as a gift from the *Bergmeister* Michel Pazelt four times. And in two cases he complained that a stag was shot but that he did not get a share of its meat.[84] Roe venison was given as a gift more frequently than stag meat, with 20 instances, of which Stüeler received the meat eleven times and gave it to the priest on one occasion. Hare with four, and grouse with six instances featured less often as gifts. Stüeler was a forest warden – not with a license to hunt, but he was notified about any game shot by the hunter. Game might have served as an informal additional payment for office-holders, since Stüeler still received some game from members of the municipal council in 1646.[85] These kinds of gifts are also described by Groebner as part of the regular payment of municipal office-holders.[86] In this context, venison becomes an ambivalent gift, an indication of the burghers of Graupen's continuing resistance to the donation of their town to the landlord Sternberg and the withholding of their privileges. However, the municipal office-holders who would get a share of game represented the local elite and venison was a privileged food. Within the town's community this might have articulated a shared identity.[87]

Meat in the form of chicken, pork, lamb, veal, beef, sausage, and unspecified meat appeared in 30 instances as a gift for the New Year, Easter and Pentecost, in communal meals and just as gifts. The descriptions of the meat gifts also have information on the methods for preparing meat. Interestingly we find roast meat among the gifts, indicating a costly way of preparing meat which was normally reserved for the elite.[88] Boiled meat or stews, on the other hand, do not appear, but Stüeler recorded dishes of meat, which imply they were prepared and not raw, or he received sausages and smoked meat.[89] In the historiography, smoked or salted meat is usually associated with the lower classes. It might point to the fact that slaughtering happened rarely and that the rations were conserved to go a long way. In addition, slaughtering was a seasonal affair, mostly in autumn or winter. The

[83] See for gifts (often food gifts) moving between peasants and landlord, Davis, *The Gift*, 40–41; Heal found that gifts to landlords reminded them of their duties to reciprocate, and that rent payments could be relabelled as gifts, see Heal, "Food Gifts," 52–53.

[84] Kilián, *Michela Stüelera*, 522, 570, 622, 690 (stag meat as a present); 620, 726 (no share of a shot stag). Stüeler had been *Bergmeister* or the supreme mining administrator himself 1633–1637, and handed the office over to Michel Pazelt in 1638.

[85] Stüeler was forest warden from 1629 onwards; see Kilián, *Michela Stüelera*, 837.

[86] Groebner, *Liquid Assets*, ch. 2, 50, 55–59.

[87] See Heal, "Food Gifts," 55. Her chapter is tellingly called "Friends and Venison."

[88] Roasts as gift appear four times, Kilián, *Michela Stüelera*, 452, 498, 666, 738. See Hirschfelder and Trummer, "Food and Drink," § 19.

[89] Kilián, *Michela Stüelera*, 372, 602 (*Gericht*, dish); sausage as gift: 466, 666, 712, 738.

cold season not only meant that the life stock was well fed after the summer pasture, but the cold also helped with conserving the meat.[90]

Some of the meat was home produced. Households with enough means and land kept chickens, pigs, and a cow or two, and not only made dairy products at home, but they would also slaughter a cow or calf for meat. Southwest German inventories, for example, show that households of rural towns kept one or more cows for transport, meat, and home dairy production.[91] Looking at agricultural labourers' inventories in early modern England, Muldrew showed that more than half of them listed cattle, mostly cows, usually for home dairy production.[92] Stüeler also kept a pig, cows and oxen, and recorded many references to husbandry, dairying and when he slaughtered a calf.[93] With increasing difficulties, Stüeler had to give up keeping pigs and cows in the 1640s and kept a goat instead, which was cheaper.[94] Henceforth he kept goats and recorded when he slaughtered one.[95] However, goat's meat was not mentioned as a gift which might indicate that it was regarded as a cheaper type of meat not esteemed highly enough to be given as a gift.

Meat as a gift appeared throughout the period but during the 1640s the nature of the meat gifts changed. Stüeler experienced increasing hardship and reduced his home production of meat. The priest, for example, sent him a piece of roast veal for Christmas in 1641, and at Easter 1643 he received two pounds of veal from his friend and office-holder Michel Weiner. In addition, on the same day the money he and his friend collected as cantors was turned into wine and drunk communally, and the priest lent him money for bread. "It was a lovely day," he recorded.[96]

---

[90] See Ingrid Matschinegg, "Tiere in der Stadt. Begegnungs- und Problemzonen zwischen Menschen und Tieren in europäischen Städten des Spätmittelalters," *Österreich in Geschichte und Literatur* 3 (2016): 48–62, here 54.

[91] In Württemberg they were found in some cases to have been paid for on credit, as revealed by a study on household debts, see Sheilagh Ogilvie, Markus Küpker and Janine Maegraith, "Household Debt in Early Modern Germany: Evidence from Personal Inventories," *Journal of Economic History* 72 (2012): 160, 163.

[92] Craig Muldrew, *Food, Energy and the Creation of Industriousness: Work and Material Culture in Agrarian England, 1550–1780* (Cambridge: Cambridge University Press, 2011), 250.

[93] Kilián, *Michela Stüelera*, 386 (2.3.1640): [Hat] "mein Elisabeth 9 Kese gemacht zum Anfange von der Kuh. Gott der Allmechtige gebe sein Gnadt und Segen. Amen." (My Elisabeth [his wife] made nine cheeses, the first from the new cow. God the almighty give his grace and blessing. Amen.) In 1631, e.g., he had two calves slaughtered, Kilián, *Michela Stüelera*, 134 (1./8.5.1631).

[94] The last entry in which Stüeler recorded that he had a pig slaughtered was in 1637, Kilián, *Michela Stüelera*, 310 (13.1.1637). In 1640 he bought a cow for 9 *Reichstaler*, which died shortly afterwards. Kilián, *Michela Stüelera*, 416 (18.11.1640). The next year he bought a goat for 2.5 Reichstaler, Kilián, *Michela Stüelera*, 444 (3.9.1641).

[95] For example, Kilián, *Michela Stüelera*, 632 (30.11.1646): "Den 30. dito ein junge Zieg geschlacht, Caspar Arnolt ½ vorkaufft pro 9 böhm. Gr. Habe sie selber geschlacht." (On the 30th I slaughtered a young goat, sold half to Caspar Arnolt for 9 Bohemian Groschen. I slaughtered her myself.)

[96] Kilián, *Michela Stüelera*, 452 (25.12.1641): "hat mein Gefatter Pfarr ein Stücke Kelberpraden geschickt mit seiner Magd." (my fellow pastor sent me a piece of roast veal with his maidservant);

Stüeler expected to have meat at certain events such as Easter and Pentecost. He recorded the lack of meat at Pentecost in 1646 but was then given a piece of *Schwarzfleisch* (smoked pork) and some flatbread by the *Bergmeister* Michel Pazelt.[97]

Up until 1649, meat constituted an important food gift and meat was expected to be part of the diet at least at religious holidays and festivities. This is also confirmed by the increased number of butchers in 1648. Stüeler's memoirs contain many references to meat consumption and it could be deduced from his entries that meat consumption was still quite high in this area around 1629, before the consequences of the war made its production increasingly difficult. Judging from Stüeler's entries, meat was badly missed on certain occasions, and food gifts played an important part in filling those gaps to a certain extent. Changes in meat consumption affected people's lives and ego-documents can help us to understand changing perceptions during transition times such as the end of the Thirty Years War.

Some examples show how gifts could reveal denominational tendencies or even express resistance to re-catholicisation. For example, meat gifts during Lent could expose the giver's non-observance of the fasting period. Stüeler recorded an episode where the parish priest criticized the breaching of Lent. In 1648 the parish priest was invited to dinner by the nobleman Karel Maximilian Bleyleben. The priest accused his host of serving and eating meat during Lent, which led to a violent dispute during which the knight attempted to throw the priest out of the window. Another nobleman was able to prevent this defenestration and the priest vowed never to accept an invitation from him again.[98]

This episode reveals that as late as 1648, 20 years after Catholicism had officially been reinstated in Graupen, either some practices still appeared to be remnants from former Protestant approaches or approaches to Lent varied within the Catholic community. Diet restrictions during Lent were one indicator, and

---

508 (4.4.1643) "Cornet mir 5 bo. gr. vorehret, der Pfarrherr 3 ggr geliehen zu Brot. Ist ein schoner Tag gewesen, haben ubersingen vor 1 fl Wein ausgetruncken beim Michel Pazelt, und hat Michel Weiner mir 2 lb Kalbfleisch geschickt." (Cornet gave me 5 Bohemian Groschen as a gift, the pastor lent me 3 Groschen for bread. It was a lovely day, we drank wine worth 1 Gulden we collected from singing at Michel Pazelt, and Michel Weiner had sent me 2 pounds of veal.)

[97] Kilián, *Michela Stüelera*, 618 (20.5.1646): "als der Pfingstag habe ich kein Fleisch gehabt. Der Vater Michel Pazelt hat mir ein Stücke Schwarzfleisch und einen Fleck geschickt." (on Pentecost day I had no meat. The father [of] Michel Pazelt sent me a piece of smoked meat and a flatbread [or pancake].)

[98] Kilián, *Michela Stüelera*, 682, 25-3-1648, "[...] hat ihn [Bleileben] der Pfarr angeredet, daß er in der Fasten Fleisch speiset; sind uneins mit einander worden, hat ihn der Bleilöbe wollen zum Fenster nausser stürzen, wen ein fremder Edelman nicht mit Gewalt hette gewehret. Geschwind der Pfarrherr heimgangen, vorredet, er wolle niemehr zu Gaste mehr kommen. [Die Pfaffen sein es werdt.]" (the priest reproached Bleileben for eating meat during Lent; they had a disagreement, Bleileben would have thrown the priest out of the window had not another nobleman prevented him with force from doing this. The priest quickly went home and vowed he would never come to him again as a guest. [for what ranting priests are worth.].)

meat during Lent was in breach of the Catholic doctrine at the time. In this context, meat gifts could become 'subversive gifts'. In one instance, a woman brought the elderly Mennichen couple, friends of Stüeler, some meat in February 1644. This was just at the beginning of Lent and the gift transaction was observed by Michel Kinel, a church warden, who went into the house, confiscated the meat and gave it to the local *Spital*.[99] Kinel probably suspected that the giver and recipients were adherents of the Protestant faith, and intervened. But this was also an intervention in an act of neighbourly support for the elderly couple, who no doubt would have cherished some meat. Interesting to note is the aspect of visibility, which Groebner had pointed out as being the requirement for a gift to be legitimate.[100] In this case, the gift was not intended to be invisible or dangerous, but the neighbours were expected not to tell, which is why Stüeler called Kinel a traitor in his memoir.

Meat gifts points to several aspects of food history: Game constituted an important food gift within Stüeler's social context of municipal office-holders or the town's middle class. Similar to Heal's and Davis' results, the type of meat reflected social status when game was involved. But the meat gifts comprised any type of meat, from game and veal to pork. This only partially corresponds to the historiography on meat consumption, which often refers to contemporary treatises stating that the peasants preferred pork and the urban elite especially veal and poultry.[101] Meat consumption might, however, have been very different in rural towns, which combined agricultural and urban contexts and where some meat was home produced. Meat gifts also acquired political meaning: during Lent, meat gifts could be subversive, indicating religious dissent or continued practices, and gifts of venison could be interpreted as resistance against the landlord's demands. But most of all, meat gifts could act as informal support.

Dairy products

Although regarded as an important source for protein, dairy products have attracted little attention in Central European historiography.[102] As mentioned

---

[99] Kilián, *Michela Stüelera*, 550 (13.2.1644): "hat ein Weib von Behancken den Paul Mennichen Eltern ein wenig Fleisch bracht. Michel Kinel dieses gesehen, ins Haus gelauffen, das Fleisch genommen und in Spital getragen. Der Vorrether wie sein Vater, wird auch von der Stadt vorwiesen." (A woman from Pyhanken [Běhánky] brought the parents of Paul Mennichen a little bit of meat. Michel Kinel saw this, went into the house, took the meat und carried it to the *Spital*. The traitor like his father will be expelled from town.) Stüeler was obviously angry and the entry might hint that Michel and Davit Kinel were regarded as traitors because of denominational differences or for another reason. They were his neighbours.

[100] Groebner, *Liquid Assets*, 1, 35, 70; see also Douglas, "Foreword", in Mauss, *The Gift*, xviii.

[101] See Hirschfelder and Trummer, "Food and Drink", § 20; Grieco, "Lebensmittel", 43–45.

[102] Wiegelmann mentions the importance of dairy as a substitute fat in the diet for the missing meat, see Wiegelmann, *Alltags- und Festspeisen*, § 44; but Braudel discusses the meaning of dairy products in more detail, see Braudel, *Structures*, 210–13.

above, Stüeler, like many of his fellow burghers, at times kept cows or goats, and his wife oversaw home dairy production. But unlike meat, dairy products hardly appear as gifts in Stüeler's memoir, being mentioned in only six cases. Stüeler got a jug of milk with bread as an Easter gift, for example, and the priest donated a meal consisting of beer, wine, cheese and buttered bread to Stüeler and his colleagues, who did some repair work for him.[103] The rarity of dairy gifts could indicate that dairying served predominantly home consumption or was for selling on the market. In 1647, Stüeler asked his daughter for some butter since she had just been making some. But she refused to send him any, probably because it was meant for home consumption as well as for the market – or maybe their relationship was troubled. But Stüeler could not understand how a daughter could leave her old and sick father in hardship and called her a "reckless child" whom God would punish.[104] Clearly, her behaviour did not fit his gift-giving expectancies. In addition to its rarity – cheaper lard was used more often than butter – people were not allowed to make butter every day. When the priest caught the wife of a municipal official churning butter on the feast day of Saint Lawrence, he ordered the court to have the butter churn confiscated, the maid servant incarcerated for the day, and the cream given to the poor.[105] The priest's harsh reaction can be explained with the ongoing re-catholicisation process; the disregard of certain religious days was one indicator of hidden Protestantism or a reluctance to embrace Catholicism. Food gifts rarely included dairy products, although they were home produced and therefore 'present'. But perhaps instead it was bought fresh on the market, or it lacked a certain symbolic meaning to serve as a gift, or other sources of protein such as meat and fish were regarded as more significant as gifts.[106]

Fish

Fish constituted an important part of Lent food. But similarly to meat, fresh fish is regarded as a privileged food in historiography, allowing social differences to be determined.[107] Access to rivers was in many places controlled by the landlord, and fishponds by the owner of the land, mostly the municipality, and therefore regulated through property rights.[108] But fish could also be purchased on markets, and inventories show to some extent kitchen tools referring to fish indicating that

[103] Kilián, *Michela Stüelera*, 554 (28.3.1644), 472 (20.5.1642).

[104] Kilián, *Michela Stüelera*, 652 (23.7.1647).

[105] Kilián, *Michela Stüelera*, 268 (10.8.1635).

[106] Davis mentions butter and goat's milk as gifts between peasants and landlords, Davis, *The Gift*, 41.

[107] See for example Hirschfelder and Trummer, "Food and Drink," § 7; also Groebner, *Liquid Assets*, 27; Grieco, "Lebensmittel," 42.

[108] Ernst Cahn, *Das Recht der Binnenfischerei im deutschen Kulturgebiet von den Anfängen bis zum Ausgang des 18. Jahrhunderts* (Frankfurt/Main: Vittorio Klostermann, 1956), 70 and § 17; Gerhard Köbler, *Lexikon der europäischen Rechtsgeschichte* (Munich: Beck, 1997), 202, entry "Fischereirecht."

it was prepared at home. In Bohemia, fish farming thrived and was very important. The municipality of Graupen took great care of the fish ponds in its authority. Hallwich mentions the municipality's acquisition and retaining of the property and fishing rights of the fishponds around Graupen.[109] And Stüeler describes how the town officials fished the ponds regularly after which the members of the municipality distributed some of it amongst themselves, mainly carp and pike.[110] In the 1640s, when Stüeler was no longer involved in the fishing of the ponds, he was still given fish as a gift by members of the municipal council. In April 1649, for example, after members of the municipal council had fished the town's middle pond, Stüeler received a carp and some small fish as a present from the mayor.[111] He also received fish as a gift from the parish priest on several occasions – not necessarily during fasting days but predominantly during the years 1646 and 1648, when Stüeler probably needed such support most.[112] Gifts of fish, a privileged food, similarly to meat and especially game gifts, were aimed at affirming social bonding even at a time when Stüeler experienced economic decline. They smoothed out shortages of provisions and were in some cases consumed communally.

Bread

Bread or flour-based foods – depending on the region – is seen as the most important part of the daily diet in Central Europe between the sixteenth and eighteenth centuries, accounting for up to 75% of calories intake.[113] Günter Wiegelmann identified a regional difference in the German lands, with bread and gruel consumption in the northwest, predominantly bread consumption in the central German area, and in the southeast, including Austria, mainly flour soups and gruel, which required less fuel for their preparation than bread.[114] According to Stüeler's notes, bread consumption prevailed in northern Bohemia at that time; he does not mention gruel or similar dishes. His records contain references to grain and flour, bread, *Semmel* (rolls), and *Fleck,* which is probably a form of flatbread or

---

[109] See Hallwich, *Graupen*, 134, the fishponds had been common property since 1580.

[110] Kilián, *Michela Stüelera*, 154 (18.10.1631). He recorded that they gave every member of the municipal council four carps and two pikes after they fished the middle pond. Then they drank wine together.

[111] Kilián, *Michela Stüelera*, 598 (21.3.1645); 716 (23.4.1649): "Ein Rath den Mittelteich gefischet. Michel Mathe Bürgemeister hat mir ein Karpen und ein Messel kleine Fische geben." (A member of the municipal council fished the middle pond. Michel Mathe the mayor gave me a carp and a *Messel* small fish.)

[112] Kilián, *Michela Stüelera*, 630 (22.10.1646), 662 (2.12.1647), 664 (27.12.1647), 682 (10.4.1648), 702 (22.10.1648).

[113] Hirschfelder and Trummer, "Food and Drink", § 25.

[114] Wiegelmann, *Alltags- und Festspeisen*, §§ 32–33, 36–37.

pancake. The importance of bread as a food gift with 25 instances, and twelve referring to grain or flour, corresponds to these findings.

Bread was a staple food, and town bakers supplied it on the market. As mentioned earlier, one of Stüeler's offices was to inspect the bakers' bread to make sure they offered the correct size for the appropriate price. He was appointed to do the same with the town's butchers and their wares, and the municipality's interest in controlling the size and quality of bread and meat suggests their significance. But bread was also baked in households that could afford the fuel. Stüeler had an oven, access to fire wood, and shared his oven with others.[115] When baking bread, he also gave some of it as a gift to others. In 1638, for example, he gave two loaves to two single women.[116] He recorded baking bread ten times, nine of which were from 1641 onwards. Obviously, he did not record every instance of baking bread. But like gifts of bread, they were mentioned mainly in the 1640s, indicating bread's increased importance for Stüeler in accordance with his economic need. However, cakes and other sweet pastries are curiously absent from his memoirs.

Bread with its intrinsic religious meaning constituted an important gift item. Wine and bread were given out as alms, and bread and *Flecken* were given as gifts between friends and neighbours to smooth out times of need. Stüeler felt this need during the 1640s and enjoyed many gifts of bread. In some cases, it was refused, probably because the giver's situation was not much better. Sometimes, bread was even the only food available. In 1641, after the godfather of one of his children refused to lend him money, Stüeler wrote that he and his wife only had a small piece of bread and some salt for dinner, but that they did not die from it.[117]

Grain and flour could also be given as a gift, and the twelve instances recorded indicate scarcity, all being given between 1641 and 1649. During the 1630s, Stüeler seemed to have produced enough grain for his own subsistence or to make enough money out of the crops. With troops constantly marching through, this situation changed dramatically. Only for the last year of his memoirs, at the end of 1649, did he mention that the grain yield was sufficient.[118]

---

[115] In 1647, for example, he mentions that Caspar Rach had baked bread at his place, Kilián, *Michela Stüelera*, 640 (21.2.1647): "Caspar Rach mir ein Brot leihen vorsaget, und hat den Tag zuvor bei mir gebacken." (Caspar Rach refused to borrow me a loaf of bread, and had baked [bread] at mine the day before.)

[116] Kilián, *Michela Stüelera*, 350 (1.7.1638): "1/4 Korn Neues backen, ein Brotel der Katen, 1 Brotel der Schwart Annen darvon geben. Gott helf, daß ich es in Gesundheit mit den Meinigen vorzehren möge. Amen." (Baked a quarter of rye new [bread], one loaf I gave Katen, and one bread to Schwart Anna. God grant that I can consume it in good health with mine. Amen.)

[117] Kilián, *Michela Stüelera*, 430 (25.4.1641): "hat Gorge Janich Kopferschmied als mein 3fechtiger Gfatter 2 bo. Gr. Vorsagt zu leihen. Habe den selben Abent mit mein Weibe nur ein kleines Stückel Brot und Salz gehabt, bin nicht darvon gestorben." (Gorge Janich, coppersmith, promised as my godfather to lend me 3 Bohemian Groschen. The same evening, my wife and I only had a small piece of bread and some salt for dinner, but did not die from it.)

[118] Kilián, *Michela Stüelera*, 738 (after 24.12.1649). Entries at that time are fragmented.

The memoir conveys the importance of bread as a gift and a staple food. It shows that in this region bread consumption dominated over gruels and other flour-based foods. As alms it also carried a religious meaning. Bread gifts were an important means to enable the author to share it with others, and, like meat, they were often offered as support in times of need.

Vegetables, fruits and nuts

The consumption of vegetables, fruits and nuts in early modern societies left fewer traces than other foodstuffs which were taxed or traded, such as bread, alcohol and meat. What was grown in gardens or gathered in the forests was seldom recorded. Inventories show graters for vegetables and salads, and supplies of dried fruits. In Württemberg, where inventories also recorded land, many burghers had a small garden attached to their small house and some had an orchard.[119] But exactly what edibles people grew is difficult to establish. Vegetables, fruits and nuts have therefore been discussed less intensively in the historiography than meat and bread. Wiegelmann, for example, does not discuss vegetables much.[120] Gunther Hirschfelder and Manuel Trummer maintain that the rural population ate turnips, cabbages, beans and peas, and possibly leeks, celery and pumpkins. They also point out that there were social differences regarding the type of vegetables consumed, with the poor primarily reliant on pulses and the wealthier having the option to buy fresh vegetables.[121] Correspondingly, Robert Jütte described how peas and lentils complemented a peasant's diet in the mid sixteenth century.[122] Allen Grieco emphasizes the social distinction visible in vegetable consumption. He finds that most of the late medieval and Renaissance physicians' treaties emphasized that certain foodstuffs belonged to certain social groups, and thus determined that consumption patterns were dependent on social stratum. The importance of vegetables in the diet of the common people contrasted with the high animal protein diet of the elite. For many people vegetables served as a substitute for other foodstuffs which were hard to get or too expensive, such as meat. The treatises, though, speak of the necessity for the lower social classes to eat vegetables – not of the economic constraints which led to a low protein diet. Grieco highlights the importance of gardens in this context, small plots of land which could help supplement the diet of rural people.[123]

---

119 See, for Württemberg inventories, Ogilvie, Küpker and Maegraith, "Household Debt," 159. On information on vegetables and the importance of gardens for producing vegetables and fruit in England see also Muldrew, *Food,* 106–11.

120 Wiegelmann, *Alltags- und Festspeisen.* In § 46 he discusses the northern German mixed stew of meat and vegetables around 1800.

121 Hirschfelder and Trummer, "Food and Drink", §§ 3 and 7.

122 Jütte, *Poverty and Deviance*, 139, 72–73.

123 Grieco, "Lebensmittel", 45–46.

In Stüeler's memoirs, garden vegetables were not important gift items, accounting for a total of about five instances. Sauerkraut was given three times and peas and lettuce were mentioned once.[124] At first glance, this corresponds to the historiography. But vegetables, their cultivation and harvest played an important role in the memoir. Stüeler minutely recorded when he sowed which vegetables. In spring 1641, for example, he recorded several days in a row how he and his wife sowed lettuces, beans, radishes, onions, beetroot, cabbages, cucumbers, carrots and saffron seeds in three of their gardens.[125] In one instance, somebody even stole his seedlings from his garden.[126] Seeds were usually home produced but could also be bought or given as a gift by friends and neighbours. His accounts on gardens are a valuable addition to the historiography of food, as they convey a sense of the varieties eaten and of the meaning the items had for the consumers. They might not have had a meaning as gifts, but the amount of time and labour put into his vegetable gardens shows that they were very important to Stüeler and an essential part of his diet.

However, local fruit and nuts, to which the author gave just as much attention, were given as gifts more frequently, especially pears and apples, ranging from alms to negotiation gifts. In 1636, for example, he received two *Scheffel* pears from his foster-child's garden, and in 1640 his father-in-law gave him half a *Pott* of pears and apples as a gift.[127] The tending of the orchards and the outcome of the fruit harvest were given prominent space in the memoir. They could be valuable reserves in times of bad harvests and dearth. In his résumé of 1640, for instance, Stüeler wrote that it had been a particularly bad year; the grain and wine-grape yield had been small, and everything had been eaten by mice, and the enemy had also caused a lot of damage by burning, robbery and theft. But there had been plenty of fruit and nuts, including cherries.[128] Fruit offered a welcome diversity in people's diet. At the end of June 1649 Stüeler was happy to record that, thanks to God, he and his wife enjoyed the first cherries of the year.[129] What is surprising though is that although cherries, peaches, apples and pears are mentioned, no fruit cakes appear as gifts. Fruit cakes were probably consumed at home, and dried fruits served as a source of sweetness in the absence of sugar or honey.[130] Fresh fruits and nuts were therefore favourite things and items of gift exchange between neighbours and family, but also served as a negotiation gift. The members of the municipality sent Stüeler and others to the colonel, who had asked for the payment

---

124 A dish of *sauerkraut* was given in three instances, Kilián, *Michela Stüelera*, 170 (1.2.1632), 372 (30.12.1638), 504 (11.3.1643).

125 Kilián, *Michela Stüelera*, 432 (April and May 1641).

126 Kilián, *Michela Stüelera*, 474 (10.6.1642).

127 Kilián, *Michela Stüelera*, 296 (27.8.1636), 406 (1.9.1640).

128 Kilián, *Michela Stüelera*, 416.

129 Kilián, *Michela Stüelera*, 724 (29.6.1649): "die ersten Kirschen gessen außn Weingarten, Gott Lob."

130 Honey and cider appeared only once as a food gift, Kilián, *Michela Stüelera*, 596 (15.3. 1645).

of three horses, with half a *Tonne* of wine, a quarter of fruit and half a quarter of nuts along with their petition to prevent this demand for additional payments.[131]

While vegetables featured rarely as gifts, fruits and nuts were exchanged more often especially during and after harvest time. The latter were probably regarded as more special with their sweetness or source of oil and for being ready for consumption. All of them, however, highlight the importance of gardens for the home production of supplementary foodstuffs and confirm Heide Wunder's thesis of complementary food strategies.[132]

Beer and wine

Beer and wine were essential components of the diet with alcohol being an important supplier of carbohydrates. This has been discussed for early modern England by Craig Muldrew especially in regard to beer.[133] In Graupen, both were produced locally and the rights to brew and sell beer and to make wine were of great importance to the municipality. Around Graupen there were more than a dozen vineyards, and barley and wheat were integral parts of local crops. Alcohol therefore had nutritional as well as economic significance, and dues for wine and beer constituted part of the municipality's income.[134] The town obtained the privilege to brew wheat and barley beer in 1584. Beer communally brewed with home produced grain constituted a staple food. This can be seen in the countless mentions of beer and its production in the memoir – it is almost omnipresent. The municipality had a brewery and malthouse, and a beer brewer was appointed. Stüeler was one of the licensed brewers and recorded when he brewed beer together with whom, and how much. He also noted down carefully when he first spotted blossoms in the vines, how they developed through the year and when mildew hit.[135] Wine and beer were not only a vital part of the diet and local economy, but also important for communal consumption and frequent items of gift exchange.[136] Drinks appeared in 44 instances of gift giving, and these were

---

[131] Kilián, *Michela Stüelera*, 490 (11.12.1642).

[132] Heide Wunder, "'Der süße Brei.' Vom Sattwerden und Überleben in der Frühen Neuzeit," in *Dinge und Menschen. Geschichte, Sachkultur, Museologie. Beiträge des Kolloquiums zum 65. Geburtstag von Helmut Ottenjann*, ed. Uwe Meiners and Karl-Heinz Ziessow (Cloppenburg: Museumsdorf Cloppenburg 2000), 45–57.

[133] Muldrew, *Food*, 65–83. See on public drinking and taverns also the work by Beat Kümin, *Drinking Matters. Public Houses and Social Exchange in Early Modern Central Europe* (Basingstoke: Palgrave Macmillan 2007).

[134] See on wine and excise tax also Groebner, *Liquid Assets*, 23.

[135] In June 1642, e.g., he recorded that he saw the vine flowering. Kilián, *Michela Stüelera*, 474 (21.6.1642); on eligibility to brew beer see 838. See Hallwich, *Graupen*, 143 on winegrowing in this region; 133 on the privileges to brew wheat and barley beer.

[136] Davis correspondingly found wine as a frequent gift between city neighbours, Davis, *The Gift*, 35.

consumed communally on many occasions. Drinks were therefore not only a source of carbohydrates, but also a communal favourite.

Wine appears in 25 instances between 1630 and 1648. Its use could range from alms to political negotiation gifts, for Christmas, New Year or as a reward for Stüeler's services as a cantor. However, in almost half of the instances (12) it was part of the conclusion of a task such as the measurement of a piece of land, the collection of donations, the finalising of the guild's accounts or the fishing of the municipal fish ponds. Afterwards, wine would be drunk together to mark the successful conclusion of the task.[137] But drinking together could also cause trouble: In 1638, for example, the church administrator Georg Janich was drinking in the house of his predecessor, Nickel Wagner. He got very drunk and was overheard insulting his host. Afterwards he was asked by Stüeler and two other neighbours whether this was true. He denied it, of course, but later came to Wagner's house, shook his hand and promised to give him 12 *Seidel* [c. 5.76 litres] of wine. Wagner in turn treated them all with 4 *Seidel* [c. 1.92 litres] of wine and the case was closed. Wine could act both as the source of trouble and as a reconciliation gift.[138] Wine could also be a useful gift when negotiating with the troops. In 1643, the municipality went to the quartered troops and tried to persuade them to stay until other troops had finished marching through. The town needed security guards against more looting. Only when they were promised more wine could the troops be persuaded.[139]

Beer appears in only nine instances of gift giving between 1632 and 1647. There are occasions of communal beer drinking in settings very similar to those we have seen for wine, and the function could be the same. In 1632, for example, the aristocrat Kinsky's forest warden asked permission to do some alterations on the neighbouring lands, and after a municipal inspection and successful negotiations the schoolmaster contributed a small barrel of beer which they all drank together. Afterwards they parted as good neighbours.[140]

The annual production of beer had to be adjusted due to the volatility of the grain yields or lootings by the troops. And when Stüeler lacked the money to buy

---

137 Kilián, *Michela Stüelera*, 154 (18.10.1631): "Mittelteich gefischt. Haben 22 R. Thlr. Gemarckt, jedem Rathsperson 4 Karben und 2 Hechte geben und Eltesten. Auch haben 3 SS im Wain vortruncken. Gott gesegne es uns. Amen." (Fished the middle pond. Have made 22 Reichstaler on the market, each member of the *Rat* received 4 carps and 2 pikes and for the elders. Also have drunk wine for 3 Schilling. God bless it for us. Amen.)

138 Kilián, *Michela Stüelera*, 370 (14.12.1638): "[…] und haben sich miteinander vortragen. Hat ihm die Hand geboten und 12 seidel Wein, das Seidel pro 3 Kr geben, Wagner aber 4 seidel geben zum besten. Ist also beigelegt worden." For conversion of historic units see Johann Friedrich Krüger, *Vollständiges Handbuch der Münzen, Maße und Gewichte aller Länder der Erde* (Quedlinburg and Leipzig: Gottfried Basse, 1830).

139 Kilián, *Michela Stüelera*, 502 (3.3.1643): "Entlich haben wir ihm Wein vorheischen, daß er ist blieben." (Finally we promised him wine, so he stayed.)

140 Kilián, *Michela Stüelera*, 198–200 (15.7.1632).

additional beer he expressed how he felt the lack of it. When Caspar Rach refused to 'lend' him a *Kanne* [c. one litre] of beer in 1642, Stüeler added angrily in his memoir that he would remember this in his will.[141] At Easter of the same year, he noted down that he didn't have the money to buy a jug of beer. He was, however, helped out by his friends and neighbours, who gave him meat and bread for the holiday.[142]

The gift of a communal drink, as we have seen, could also be given as a reward for a special kindness. Stüeler and his friend, for example, helped at the funeral of the son of a common friend and magistrate of the town, Bernhard Kraft. Kraft donated 14 *Seidel* [= 6.72 litre] of wine which they consumed together.[143] Stüeler was open about the personal consequences of excessive drinking and that it could lead to domestic violence. In one occasion, for example, he recorded how he came home drunk and slapped his wife in the face. He also mentioned that she did not spend the night with him.[144] Wine appeared to be a more important and frequent gift than beer, and this is also reflected in Stüeler's end-of-year résumés. Here he reported the yield for grain, fruit, nuts and wine – but he did not summarise the beer production.

Communal drinking had several meanings: it constituted sociability and especially male bondage within the social sphere of municipal office-holders and artisans. It was used as a gift in thanks for a favour or to celebrate the successful conclusion of an official event. It carried strong meaning for the municipality, especially when it was rebelling against the landlord and cohesion was important. For example, in 1636 the council called for a committee meeting and asked if it would support the council in defending their privileges against the landlord, to which they unanimously agreed. But Stüeler's restraint in this indicates that there was not always unanimity and that it had to be garnered.[145] Groebner identified gifts of wine in Basel as political gifts, used for demonstrating political legitimacy and drunk at formal occasions. He also stressed the foremost economic role of wine and that the excise tax was a very important source of income for the

[141] Kilián, *Michela Stüelera*, 460 (3.3.1642): "hat Caspar Rach mir sollen eine 1/2 Binte Bier borgen, hat es nicht gethan und mein Weib lassen ledig gehen, sol in Testament gedacht werden."

[142] Kilián, *Michela Stüelera*, 466 (Easter 1642): "Der Ostertag ist schon und helle gewesen, und habe kein Geld gehabt, daß ich mir hette können eine Kanne Bier kauffen."

[143] Kilián, *Michela Stüelera*, 576 (29.9.1644): "Und haben beim Michel Pazelt 14 Seidel Wein getruncken, welchen uns Bernhard Krafft vorehret, daß wir sein Sohn begraben haben."

[144] Kilián, *Michela Stüelera*, 376 (9.1.1639): "meiner Elisabet 2 Maulschellen aufn Abent, bin truncken gewesen, in der Kammer. Ist die Nacht nicht bei mir gewesen."

[145] Kilián, *Michela Stüelera*, 298 (11.9.1636): "Den 11. dito ein Rath ein Ausschos aufs Rathaus erfordern laßen, sie befraget, ob sie bei ein Rath stehen wollen wegen Ihrer Gn., unserer Freiheiten halben. Sind sie einhellig vorblieben, daß sie es fechten wollen und vor ein Mann stehen. Ich habe nichts darzu gesaget." See also Hallwich, *Graupen*, 189, where he describes how the municipality vowed to stand together in defending their wine and beer dues against the landlord in 1648.

municipality.[146] This is to some extent true for Graupen as well – although on a much smaller scale. The burghers of Graupen had to defend the income from dues against the demands of the landlord, and while some of the wine gifts had the character of political gifts, the entries by Stüeler also show their personal meaning: he cherished good wine, monitored its growth carefully and valued a gift of wine highly. Also, wine and beer gifts were mostly drunk communally and taking all these aspects into account, such gifts represented a plethora of complex meanings: social, political, economic, and dietary. In many cases, they were gifts reciprocated. A direct comparison with Groebner's findings is therefore not applicable. Beer and wine gifts were liquid, but not "dangerous".

Conclusion

The memoir revealed that gifts were an important part of the local economy and for maintaining and creating social bonds. Gifts were very much involved in social and economic life and existed alongside commercial transactions, exchanges and credit relationships. Stüeler, for example, recorded all his land transactions, purchases of household goods, the prices for grain, debts and their repayment or due date, and gifts given and received. While commercial transactions were legally binding, gift-giving was not. However, both needed the public sphere to be legitimate. But gift-giving had a moral obligation, as emphasized by Marcel Mauss and highlighted by Felicity Heal in her work as a "moral economy of the gift". From the memoir it becomes clear that Stüeler understood gift-giving as a result of a God-given capability to give or share with others which carried an obligation to do so. However, God was involved in all transactions, whether harvests, purchases, exchanges or gifts, and thus they all carried a moral dimension.[147] With this came the expectation of reciprocity. This study shows how reciprocity resembled more a payment rather than a gift reciprocated: the fact that the author of the chronicle kept records on the gift-giving cycle and that he was furious when such a cycle was broken, points not only to a fluid boundary between payment and gift giving, but to the gift-giving cycle being understood as a marketplace. The difference was that gifts were not dependent on price formation and in addition their reciprocation was delayed.. Nevertheless, gifts required payment in the form of a reciprocated gift and like market transactions, their accomplishment was based on trust in human obligations, as Muldrew has shown.[148]

Gifts, therefore, cannot be separated from the local economy. In fact, in some cases Stüeler's mode of recording a gift, a purchase or the repayment of a debt

[146] Groebner, *Liquid Assets*, 23–24.

[147] See also Davis, *The Gift*, 100; Heal, "Food Gifts," 47.

[148] Muldrew, *Economy of Obligation*.

remained fluid when he set a value on some items.[149] Similarly, the line between borrowing and gift giving seems blurred, although this could be explained by Stüeler's understanding of gift-giving where he expected the recipient to return the gift sometime in the future. In his case, he even explicitly stated that he hoped to be able to give again to poor people as well. The favour therefore did not necessarily have to be returned to the same person but to a person in need within his social sphere. Stüeler's meticulous recording of market transactions, debts, exchanges and gifts could appear as an attempt to keep an account book or list of obligations. This is reminiscent of the late medieval bookkeeping of gifts as discussed by Groebner but also of Muldrew's results for early modern English diaries as a transition between memory and account books.[150] However, Stüeler not only listed gifts to or from himself but also to others, and these entries constitute just one part of his memoirs, which otherwise also contain personal, demographic, political and religious material.

The description of a mixed economy which emerges from his memoir has an important implication for food history: not all foodstuffs were either home produced or bought on the market. Considerable amounts were given and received as gifts within Stüeler's own social sphere, and thus local produce was part of a more complex network of exchange. This means that, when looking at non-elite populations and their diet, it is necessary to look at everyday foodstuffs and the meaning of food production, its intention for home consumption, market production or use as a gift. Using local produce also reflects the fact that people gave as gifts what they could afford, what they could part with, and that carried meaning for them. In this context the aspect of durability of foodstuff and their properties as gifts should be considered as well. Some of the mentioned foodstuffs such as fresh meat and fish, dairy products, and fresh fruit were not durable and therefore had to be either consumed quickly or conserved. Thus, fresh products such as game or apples lend themselves as gifts as they have to be used up or are ready to be consumed.

Some gift exchange could also be regarded as informal support to smooth out temporary hardships and crises, as Ilana Krausman Ben-Amos has found for early modern England.[151] Stüeler experienced enormous economic difficulties especially towards the end of the war, when he had to sell some of his land to pay his debts. The food gifts given to him by members of his own social sphere supported him and his family and added to his quality of life. The memoir thus shows how the coexistence of different modes of exchange within this economy could help to overcome a time of crisis. But it also shows that increasing hardship could threaten access to this realm of gift-giving by causing social decline. Retaining his social and

---

[149] For instance, in 1629 he gives the regent a gift of a pewter crucifix which he values at 5 ½ Schilling. Kilián, *Michela Stüelera*,71–72 (29.7.1629).

[150] Groebner, *Liquid Assets*, 15–18; Muldrew, "The culture of reconciliation," 923.

[151] Krausman Ben-Amos, *Culture of Giving*, 315–21.

moral status within a certain sphere and thus participation in a social gift-giving culture was important. The gifts signified a favour or honour – to stay close to the expression *verehren*. If people within this sphere needed help, then they could rely on their neighbours to support them; but this also involved an expectation of reciprocity. In this context, Stüeler's prayer for the capability to give to poor people again might have another meaning: he prayed to be able to reciprocate again, but also to be able to maintain those social bonds which offered inclusion in a neighbourly support system.

Food gifts comprised the whole range of diet and nutrition: carbohydrates in bread and alcoholic drinks, protein and fat in meat and fish, some cheese and butter, and micronutrients and dietary fibre in fruits, nuts and some vegetables. Most food gifts consisted of meat, alcohol, bread and fruit. In particular, an examination of meat gifts could shed light on changes in meat consumption, which must have been still quite high in this region in the first half of the seventeenth century. Stüeler felt the lack of meat, as he expected to have meat at certain times, and appreciated the occasional gift of meat. Food gifts can therefore reveal the preferences and meanings that certain foodstuffs had in a specific region and economy.

For food history, it is not only the coexistence of different modes of exchange that is enriching; it is also informative when we look at what is missing: there are no cakes or sweet pastries recorded, for example. For Württemberg, Sheilagh Ogilvie, Markus Küpker and I found that baking utensils for cakes and pastries constituted an important part of the inventories in early seventeenth century Wildberg.[152] But they seem to be absent in Graupen, at least in the memoir. Honey is only mentioned as a gift once; fruit seems to have been the main source of sweetness. Many gifts were from home production, which is a valuable indication for food history as it points to the importance of by-employment and gardens in rural towns. Consequently, there were no gifts of spices, exotic fruits, or lemons; there is no tobacco, and of course no sugar, tea, or coffee; the first coffee house in Prague was only founded in 1714. None of the luxury goods which have dominated some of recent food historiography can be found either as gifts or in other parts of the memoir. They are missing in spite of the proximity to Prague and opportunities for Graupen's delegations to buy them on its markets. Instead, the memoir points to the need to put commensurability at the centre of food history, to look at regional specifics and social differences, at the contexts in which food and drink was consumed, and its access and distribution within a community. Looking at gift exchange can add to the history of consumption, and although it is not quantitatively measurable, it should be regarded as a factor and part of a local economy. By shedding some light on everyday practice, this approach also confirmed the importance of incorporating multiple perspectives in food history.

[152] Ogilvie, Küpker and Maegraith, "Frauen und die materielle Kultur des Essens."

Index

Addresses of the Contributors

Ottó Gescer, Faculty of Social Sciences, Eötvös Loránd University, Egyetem tér 1-3, 1053 Budapest, Hungary
gecsero@caesar.elte.hu

Hans Peter Hahn, Institut für Ethnologie, Goethe-Universität Frankfurt, Grüneburgplatz 1, 60323 Frankfurt am Main, Germany
hans.hahn@em.uni-frankfurt.de

Gerhard Jaritz, Department of Medieval Studies, Central European University, Nádor utca 9, 1051 Budapest, Hungary
jaritzg@ceu.edu

Janine Maegraith, History, Newnham College, University of Cambridge, Sidgwick Avenue, Cambridge CB3 9DF, United Kingdom
cjm80@cam.ac.uk

Ingrid Matschinegg, Institut für Realienkunde des Mittelalters und der frühen Neuzeit, Universität Salzburg, Körnermarkt 13, 3500 Krems, Austria
ingrid.matschinegg@sbg.ac.at

Asa S. Mittman, Department of Art and Art History, 400 W. First St., California State University, Chico, CA 95929–0820, U.S.A.
asmittman@csuchico.edu

Keith Moxey, Department of Art History and Archaeology, Columbia University, 826 Schermerhorn Hall, 1190 Amsterdam Ave., New York, NY 10027, U.S.A.
pm154@columbia.edu

Gabriela Signori, Fachbereich Geschichte und Soziologie, Fach 2, Universität Konstanz, 78457 Konstanz, Germany
gabriela.signori@uni-konstanz.de

John Styles, Social Sciences, Arts&Humanities Research Institute, University of Hertfordshire, Hatfield, Hertfordshire AL 10 9AB, United Kingdom
j.a.styles@herts.ac.uk

* * *

Uwe Israel; Christian Jaser (Hg.)
Agon und Distinktion
Soziale Räume des Zweikampfs zwischen Mittelalter und Neuzeit
Geschichte: Forschung und Wissenschaft, Bd. 47, 2016, 318 S., 34,90 €, br., ISBN 978-3-643-12878-2

Gerhard Jaritz (Ed.)
Ritual, Images, and Daily Life
The Medieval Perspective
Geschichte: Forschung und Wissenschaft, vol. 39, 2012, 264 pp., 24,90 €, pb., ISBN 978-3-643-90113-2

Georg Hinterleitner
Die militärische Kultur der geistlichen Ritterorden
Geschichte, Bd. 134, 2016, 138 S., 29,90 €, br., ISBN 978-3-643-50747-1

Hans Krawarik
Siedlungstypen und Lebensformen im Mittelalter
Austria: Forschung und Wissenschaft – Geschichte, Bd. 15, 2016, 222 S., 29,90 €, br., ISBN 978-3-643-50746-4

Martin Knoll; Reinhold Reith (Eds.)
An Environmental History of the Early Modern Period
Experiments and Perspectives
Austria: Forschung und Wissenschaft – Geschichte, vol. 10, 2014, 104 pp., 29,90 €, br., ISBN 978-3-643-90463-8

Vita regularis

Ordnungen und Deutungen religiosen Lebens im Mittelalter – Abhandlungen
hrsg. von Prof. Dr. Gert Melville (Technische Universität Dresden)

Steven Vanderputten (Ed.)
Abbots and Abbesses as a Human Resource in the Ninth- to Twelfth-Century West
vol. 74, 2018, 184 pp., 29,90 €, pb., ISBN 978-3-643-91070-7

Wolf Zöller
Regularkanoniker im Heiligen Land
Studien zur Kirchen-, Ordens- und Frömmigkeitsgeschichte der Kreuzfahrerstaaten
Bd. 73, 2018, 572 S., 69,90 €, br., ISBN 978-3-643-14159-0

Simon Falch
Das Predigtoeuvre des Rebdorfer Augustiner-Chorherren Balthasar Boehm (†1530)
Zugänge zur Machart von Musterpredigtsammlungen des Spätmittelalters
Bd. 72, 2018, 388 S., 59,90 €, br., ISBN 978-3-643-14045-6

Florian M. Lim
Die Brüder vom Gemeinsamen Leben im 15. Jahrhundert in Deutschland
Vom Münsterschen Kolloquium zum Oberdeutschen Generalkapitel: Eine kirchenrechtsgeschichtliche Untersuchung über Eingliederung und Gemeinschaftsform der süddeutschen Kanoniker
Bd. 71, 2017, 224 S., 34,90 €, br., ISBN 978-3-643-13802-6

Stefanie Neidhardt
Autonomie im Gehorsam
Die dominikanische Observanz in Selbstzeugnissen geistlicher Frauen des Spätmittelalters
Bd. 70, 2017, 486 S., 54,90 €, br., ISBN 978-3-643-13583-4